Islamic Perspectives
on Management and Organization

NEW HORIZONS IN MANAGEMENT

Series Editor: Cary L. Cooper, *CBE, Professor of Organizational Psychology and Health, Lancaster University Management School, Lancaster University, UK*

This important series makes a significant contribution to the development of management thought. This field has expanded dramatically in recent years and the series provides an invaluable forum for the publication of high quality work in management science, human resource management, organisational behaviour, marketing, management information systems, operations management, business ethics, strategic management and international management.

The main emphasis of the series is on the development and application of new original ideas. International in its approach, it will include some of the best theoretical and empirical work from both well-established researchers and the new generation of scholars.

Islamic Perspectives on Management and Organization

Abbas J. Ali
Indiana University of Pennsylvania

NEW HORIZONS IN MANAGEMENT

Edward Elgar
Cheltenham, UK • Northampton, MA, USA

Published by
Edward Elgar Publishing Limited
Glensanda House
Montpellier Parade
Cheltenham
Glos GL50 1UA
UK

Edward Elgar Publishing, Inc.
136 West Street
Suite 202
Northampton
Massachusetts 01060
USA

A catalogue record for this book
is available from the British Library

Library of Congress Cataloguing in Publication Data

Ali, Abbas.
    Islamic perspectives on management and organization / Abbas J. Ali.
        p. cm. — (New horizons in management)
    Includes bibliographical references and index.
        1. Management—Islamic countries. 2. Organization—Islamic countries. I.
    Title. II. Series.

HD70.174A45 2005
658'.00917'67—dc22

                                                                    2004063491

ISBN 1 84376 766 X

Printed and bound in Great Britain by MPG Books Ltd, Bodmin, Cornwall

Contents

v

Figures

Tables

Preface

In writing *Islamic Perspectives on Management and Organization*, I have sought to capture the essence of Islamic thinking and the intellectual spirit of early Muslim thinkers and writers. During the first five centuries of Islam Muslim thinkers approached societal and business problems with creativity and flexibility. Their approaches were guided by a strong moral conviction that diversity, justice and kindness are the foundations for success. Despite the rapid expansion of the Muslim State, within a short period of time, the spirit of openness and inclusiveness did not fail them. It enabled the Muslims to not only overcome formidable problems, but to adapt to an ever-changing environment and to absorb foreign innovations with ease, confidence and enthusiasm.

Most of the current research on Islam and business organization is in a state of infancy. That is, most writings have been general in nature, lack depth, and do not profoundly reflect on the rich resources and ideas that existed in the early centuries after the inception of Islam. This book is undertaken to fill a gap in the intellectual discourse. Furthermore, due to complex relationships that have been recently exposed and that have intensified between Western and Muslim civilizations, the need for a serious and an in-depth treatment of cultural underpinnings of business organizations in the Muslim World has become more urgent then ever. In fact, practicing managers and researchers, along with global policy makers, may find it fruitful to have a reference that adequately covers business aspects and environment in Muslim societies.

In undertaking the challenge of this project, I have had to rely on historical records and original sources. The information is scattered and references are not easily available. In particular, there are challenges pertaining to primary sources, and to the confusion among contemporary scholars in covering the subject of management and organization. The first element stems from the fact that the Quran and the Prophet Mohamed's sayings have been used in the book to clarify certain messages and to understand their business implications. There are various translations of the Quran, but I have relied on three versions (*The Presidency of Islamic Researches, Ifta, Call and Guidance in Saudi Arabia*; translation by

Muhammed Sarwar; and translation by Ahmed Ali). These versions were used for reference. In situations where there are ambiguities in capturing the meaning of the original Arabic statements, these three translations were contrasted and the version that best reflects the meaning was adopted. The sayings of the Prophet Mohamed are mostly known to me. I have had, however, to check several sources (e.g., A *Manual of Hadith*; *Management in Islamic Culture*; *Al-Agid Al-Fared*; *The Directory of Inquirers*; *The Garden of the Righteousness from the Saying of the Prophet Mohamed*) for verification and accuracy. Those sayings that I am not familiar with are quoted, and references are made to their sources in the text.

The second challenge arises primarily from the fact that most of the research, on management and organization in the context of an Islamic perspective, is characterized by conspicuous ambiguity, emphasis on normative aspects, a focus on economic and religious implications and a tendency to ignore circumstances that have led to the rise of an economic and political phenomena. It is my understanding that management and organizational issues belong to the human domain. As such, events and developments have to be examined in the context of these existing conditions. Measuring and comparing these events with agreed on principles facilitates the development of sound management thinking. More importantly, it motivates management scholars in Muslim countries to navigate new avenues for theory development. Almost all chapters in the book address issues that are vital for theory development and effective business conduct. In particular, Chapters 2, 5, 6 and 8 are written with this objective in mind. These chapters offer a brief outline of several stages in the history of the Muslim civilization and demonstrate how perspectives on subjects like power and authority, leadership and group functions have evolved and departed from the early period. The obvious regression in thinking on these matters should be a motivational factor in rethinking current management assumptions and practices.

I am aware that there is a variation among Muslims in different parts of the world of their understanding of Islam. These variations, coupled with differences in experiences and circumstances, influence management outlook and orientation. Throughout the book, this reality is observed. The book is not intended to cover the entire aspects of the subject. Nevertheless, the most essential issues for understanding management and organization in the context of Muslim countries are highlighted. Specifically, the book is a serious attempt to fill a notable gap in management thinking from the perspectives of Islam. It is a platform for understanding management in a non-Western context and for thoughtful discourse.

I am indebted to many people for helping me to complete this project. Professors Helen Bailie, Prashanth Nagendra Bharadwaj and Krish Krishnan helped with editing and proofreading and provided me with very useful feedback. Other scholars, Paul Swiercz of George Washington University, Daniel Twomey of Fairleigh Dickinson University and William Acar of Kent State University, helped in improving the manuscript by commenting on portions of it and provided insightful input. Dr. Musallam A. Musallam, President and Chief Executive Officer of Skab Corporation in Saudi Arabia supplied me with very important books that were used in writing this text. His practical insight and views have been a good source of motivation and reflection. Similarly, Drs. Amin Mohamed from Egypt, and Abdulaziz Taqi, Ali Alkazemi and Abdulah Alowaihan from Kuwait took the initiative and sent me several books that cover historical and economic aspects of Muslim countries. I am thankful for their generosity. Dr. Robert C. Camp, my Dean at Indiana University of Pennsylvania, has provided valuable resources. His thoughtful comments and feedback and our long friendship have tremendously influenced my thinking. I should also thank my student assistants, Richard Yong and Samantha Maley, for formatting the manuscript and Kathy Baker for her useful suggestion for designing some figures. Special thanks to Alan M. Sturmer, the Acquisitions Editor, and Kate Emmins, editorial assistant, at Elgar Publishing for their cooperation, support and understanding.

My wife Huda, and my children Fadil, Aziz and Yasmin have been the source of my joy and enthusiastic involvement in scholarly activities. I am thankful to all of them.

1. Business and Trade in Islamic Thought

Economic integration and interdependence, along with the ease with which communication is carried out across the globe, has initiated an unprecedented interaction among societies and groups. This interaction has increased the awareness of the subtle differences in the thinking, aspirations, and behavior between peoples. These differences manifest cultural, political, and economic complexities, and distinctive cultural and national formations. Religion has played a significant role in shaping these differences and ensuring their continuity. In addition, religion has been an important factor in enhancing cooperation and integration at the national and global levels. Familiarity with major religions, therefore, is a starting point in understanding the nature and scope of the current and future state of the world.

One of the major religions is Islam. Islam has evolved to be a powerful force in today's political and business arena. Its spiritual message has a profound impact on its adherents. As in its early years, the Islamic spiritual message has tremendously influenced the economic and socio-political involvement of those who subscribe to it. Depending on the circumstances and the intensity of interaction with people from other civilizations, certain Islamic aspects and ideas have emerged. These have resulted in a diversity in perspectives and outlooks among Muslims, even though they all are founded on Islamic principles outlined in the Quran, and the sayings and practices of the Prophet Mohamed.

According to Islamic belief and tradition, God first revealed Islam to the Prophet Mohamed in Arabia in a cave on Mount Hira near Mecca around 610. The message was in Arabic but it was universal in its scope, intent, and implication. The relationship, however, between Islam as a religion and Arabs as a nation was strengthened, as Arabs were the first to carry and spread the message. The influence of Islam profoundly affected how the state of Islamic administration and organization evolved in the first six centuries of Islam. In addition, even with the adoption of Islam, certain pre-

Islamic Arab traditions persisted for a long time and shaped the outlook and orientations of non-Arab Muslims for many centuries. Indeed, in their interactions with other nations, the early generation of Arabs showed an exceptional flexibility in adapting their culture to that of Muslims from other cultures (e.g., Persian, Indian) without sacrificing what was essential and cherished. This openness, flexibility, and tolerance of other peoples' cultures facilitated societal and economic achievements and set the stage for establishing a magnificent empire. It was during these years of cultural receptivity and sensitivity that trade and business organizations flourished and grew.

This chapter provides a brief discussion of the environment in Arabia just before the rise of Islam. The discussion is not comprehensive. Nevertheless, it will enable readers to understand the nature of the competing forces that existed in Arabia and its direct and indirect impact on Islamic teaching and the evolution of its thoughts. The chapter presents, too, a description of the centrality of trade and business in Islam. Furthermore, a summary of certain organizational elements and their implications are covered.

1.   POLITICAL AND SOCIO-ECONOMIC ENVIRONMENT

The state of affairs in Arabia was ripe for radical change. Socially, economically, and politically there was a dramatic maneuvering among various rivals. Tribal wars, rivalry to control trade routes, and conflicts among existing empires and their respective satellite states were intense. Indeed, the Arabs were under the mercy of the Persians and the Byzantines and were victims of their internal rivalry. This, combined with the oppression by their own elites and limited economic opportunities, forced Arabs to consider a means to overcome their weaknesses and capitalize on the opportunities presented by the receding power of the existing empires.

Social Conditions

The social structure of old Arabia was complex. It was characterized by an intense rivalry between dominant tribes, city and desert dwellers, merchant classes, and poor and rich groups. Even though there were various tribes in Arabia, rivalry centered around the two major tribes: Khatanes and Adnani. The first were descendants of Khatan, the chief of a Semitic people that were the offspring of Noah. They lived in Yemen and moved eastward to

Iraq. They established a kingdom in Yemen that existed for more than three thousand years. The Adnani claimed to be descendants of Ismail (Ishmael), a son of Ibrahim. Ismail settled near Mecca and erected the Kaba. Quraesh was the main tribe of Adnani stock that lived in and around Mecca. The Quraeshis considered themselves to be the most noble of the Arabs. Their chief rivals lived in Yathreb or Medina and were from the Khatane tribe. The quarrels between both rival factions shaped the events in Arabia and the region. It should be mentioned that the rivalry centered not only on the claim of ancestor prestige and nobility, but also around the control of trade and of political events.

Conflicts between the city and desert dwellers were common. The Desert dwellers or Bedouins prided themselves on being the true Arabs. As a people the Bedouins appreciated courage, pride, and generosity. They valued their freedom, individuality, and eloquence in speech and poetry. The Bedouins were victims of a continuous rivalry between each other. Not only did tribes compete with each other to control grassland and water, but also subtribes engaged in conflicts related to various matters (e.g., nobility of ancestors, protecting trade routes, raids). Being mostly poor and unsophisticated, the Bedouins often rendered their services to advance the sedentary adventures. The urban dwellers, on the other hand, more easily submitted to rulers. Among the qualities they valued were endurance and cunning, especially in trade.

The majority of Arabs in Arabia worshiped idols, angels and the stars. There were hundreds of Gods that were worshiped by both the urban and tribal people. Kaaba was the holy place that housed most of these idols and where they were displayed in designated places. These idols were highly regarded and were the source of pride for their respective tribes and cities; Christians, Jews, Zoroastrians, Unitarians (Ihnaf) and those who believed in the creation, but denied the existence of prophets and messengers of God, also lived in Arabia. In fact, diversity in religious beliefs was common. At that time the Arabs designated a month for worship and festivities. During that month, Arabs from all parts could travel safely and join celebrations in Mecca and other cities. To facilitate the gathering, there was a common understanding that war was not permitted in the holy month and people were supposed to enjoy trade, poetry and other more general pleasures.

There were various trade centers such as Mecca, Yathreb, Aden, and Akhaz that were scattered in and around Arabia. The first two centers, Mecca and Yathreb, were more prominent than the others, mainly because people from major tribes and from various cultural backgrounds and religious beliefs populated them. In Mecca, the trade was controlled by members of the Quraeshi ("merchant" in old Arabic) tribe, especially the Ommeyades. In Yathreb, the trade was primarily in the hands of the Jews.

Since there was no central government and the nearby empires never managed to control the heart of Arabia, trade routes were subject to continuing raids by various tribal groups. Powerful social classes had to provide protection to all trade centers. These classes allied themselves with the military and political forces in and around Arabia to secure trade routes and ensure their profitability. In an environment that was harsh, not hospitable to law and order, and where commodities had to be brought to isolated communities and cities, trade was a risky profession. Consequently, merchants were held in high esteem for their courage and bravery, as they were the primary instruments for maintaining survival and prosperity for the communities.

The economic division between the poor and rich was common. The majority of Arabs, especially the Bedouins, were poor. In contrast, merchants, warlords, moneylenders, and chiefs of tribes were conspicuously wealthy. The slave market was an active and dynamic one. Slaves, who were mostly prisoners of war, were instrumental in accumulating wealth for their masters. Some slaves were from Ethiopia, while others were either Arabs who were captured in local wars or prisoners of wars between the existing empires, the Roman (Byzantine) and Sasanians (Persian). Both empires sold prisoners of war in Arabia, or sent them as gifts to noble Arabs and chiefs of tribes (Delo, 1985).

Wealth played a significant role in determining the social and political power in Arab. For example, in Mecca, the residential areas around the holy places were designated to families according to their relative wealth. Those who were very rich were given lots close to Kaaba (Delo, 1985). Indeed, the classification of people in Mecca was strictly based on wealth and nobility (attributes were characterized by hospitality and generosity toward others). Therefore, the Quraeshi aristocracy was restricted to few families. Those with low incomes were divided into several categories: those whose trade was not looked upon favorably (Saaluek), the poor, slaves, and those who were landless. Generally, rich people mistreated and subjected these groups to hardship. Furthermore, the rich "amused themselves with gambling, wine, women and song, and cared all too little for the sufferings of their unfortunate neighbors. No higher aims in life set limits to their pursuit of pleasure" (Hurgronje, 1957, p. 7).

Political Situation

Around the year 600, the state of power and influence in Arabia was in flux. The existing Roman and Sasanians empires were in decline. The Arab kingdoms to the north in Syria (Ghassanids) and to the west in Hira, Iraq (Lakhmids) were allied with the Roman and Sasanians, respectively. The

Bedouins had no loyalty except to their tribal chiefs, who often resided near an Oasis. The importance of the Oasis, then and now, stemmed from the availability of scarce resources, water, and grassland. The allegiance of tribal chiefs was determined by circumstances and by their immediate interests. Like the situation of most tribal societies, blood relations played a significant role in securing allegiances. Tribal raids and conflicts were common. In addition, the two empires competed to gain influence in the regions via trade and the extension of protection to some tribes, cities, and groups.

Among the most notable conflicts was that between Mecca and Yathreb. The Quraeshi tribe of Mecca had a long-standing enmity between the tribes of Awos and Khazerag of Yathreb. The conflicts led to major wars in the region. Furthermore, there was a deep-seated rivalry between two major families in Mecca: the Hashimis and Ommeyades. The conflict between these two families has shaped Islamic history and outlook, and the repercussions of these conflicts have affected political events up to the present time. The first family, the Hashimis, inherited the guardianship of the Kaaba and the administration of water supply to Mecca. The second was responsible for the *Majlis Al-Nadwa* (the Seminar Board) and the military standard. Both families were engaged in trade. Nevertheless, the Ommeyades gradually came to control most of the trade and accumulated a large sum of wealth that enabled them to forge alliances with various tribes and powerful groups and to recruit military guards and guides to protect and lead trade caravans.

Economic Environment

Generally speaking, before Islam, Arabia was economically depressed. The Bedouins roamed the desert searching for water and grassland. The urban people were mostly farmers and merchants. Arabic oases were scattered across a vast desert land. Among the relatively populated areas were Yethreb and Taaif. Both had fertile land. In contrast, the surrounding land of Yemen, Oman, Syria, and Iraq was endowed with rivers and rich farmlands. The Arabs of Arabia traded with these neighbors but envied them. Arabians pursued trade with particular enthusiasm and energy. Merchants were respected and yielded a disproportional amount of power in society. This allowed them to play significant social and political roles. Quraeshi merchants, for example, entered alliances with existing political powers and tribes to ensure the safety of their trade caravans and routes. In Mecca, they established two councils to sustain their power and influence. The first was Al-Mal'a (Arab Aristocracy), which represented the most important families that were responsible for trade and war. The second was

Majlis Al-Nadwa (the Seminar Board). The Seminar Board decided, after consultation and debate, social and military affairs and represented the senior members of the Aristocracy.

Originally, the Quraeshi merchants made four trade trips a year. Each trip was destined to a specific region: Yemen, Persia (Iran), Sham (Syria), and Ethiopia. Later on, only two major trips were taken during the summers and winters, to Yemen and Sham. There were eight major trade shows: Dowma Al-Gedal, Hajer, Oman, Musgaer, Shajer, Aden, Sana, and Akhaz. These trade shows took place in different months to give people from other regions the opportunity to attend them. Money (gold and silver) and bartering were the means for exchange. Trade gatherings were also used as occasions for poetry recitations, demonstration of rhetorical abilities, and to engage in sporting activities, such as horse-racing and "mubaraza" (fencing). The Akhaz Show was the largest and the most prestigious, as Arabs from all tribes, regions, and faiths attended it. It was, also, the place where each tribe displayed or communicated its achievements and the Arab famous seven (Al Malaqat) "suspended poems" were placed. Al Malaqat represented not only poetic beauty and eloquence but they also recorded special historical events and achievements and highlighted the prestige of their respective tribes.

Moneylenders also assumed an important social and economic role. They facilitated the operations of merchants, farmers, and chiefs of tribes. Due to economic uncertainty, war, and changing allegiances, moneylenders tended to charge usury well above the principal. This practice while accelerating the accumulation of wealth for moneylenders enlarged the gulf between the rich and poor and increased jealousy and resentment between the classes. Agriculture and craftsmanship were other important sectors in the Arabian economy. Both sustained trade and ensured the continuity of the sedentary life. Nevertheless, their members never played a prominent role in Arabian life, as did merchants.

2.   ORGANIZATIONAL ELEMENTS IN ISLAM

Islam emerged in Arabia as the community in Mecca was thriving commercially and intellectually, and when the Arab elite of the city of Mecca had accumulated wealth by controlling trade and trade centers. The birth of Islam in Arabia about the year ad 610, however, should not be seen as a sudden and isolated event. Rather, it was a creative evolution of existing religions (e.g., Judaism, Christianity, and Zoroastrian) and an indispensable solution to persistent political, social, and economic crises that prevailed in

Arabia and the surrounding regions. As indicated in the following chapters, Islam provided the Arabs with a moral outlook and framework to deal with chronic social and political problems (e.g., social injustice, political fragmentation). It enabled them, despite some obstacles, to move ahead with confidence and in a clear and coherent direction for many decades. Indeed, Islam motivated the Arabs to be forward-thinking and to espouse tolerance and risk. These qualities enabled them to unite, within a short period, the surrounding Arab areas and to expand swiftly into new regions in Africa and Asia with considerable ease.

Today, one of the most influential forces in the Islamic world that forms and regulates individual and group behavior is Islam. Religion is an influential force in the Muslim-Arab world as (1) most Islamic societies are still traditional in the sense that commitments to honor, honesty, respect for parents and older persons, loyalty to the primary group, hospitality, and generosity remain deeply held beliefs by a majority of the population; (2) family and other social institutions still command the respect of almost all individuals, regardless of their social backgrounds. These institutions carefully and creatively employ Islam to sustain their endurance and influence; (3) most people recite/listen to Quranic verses more than once a day; and (4) Islam is a comprehensive religion that regulates not only asceticism, but also worldliness. Almost all social, political, and military precepts are addressed in the Quran.

In Islam there are certain tenets and guidelines that regulate worship and behavioral affairs. In this section the organizational implications, not the literal spiritual meaning, of the tenets and selected guidelines are specified. There are five pillars in Islam: Unity of God (Tawheed), Fasting (Saum), Prayers (Salat), Pilgrimage (Haj), and Alms (Zakat). These pillars, along with other guidelines, have several implications for business organizations. Below is a brief reflection on each:

Unity of God

It represents a submission to the almighty God. In the organizational setting, it means a deep consciousness of the unity of direction, clarity of purpose, avoidance of wrongdoing, and of equality among people.

Fasting

Fasting conveys a sense of self-control and a community that is united in sharing pleasure and suffering. It also implies that humbleness and some hardship can sustain and enrich civic and organizational responsibility.

Prayers

The prayers five times a day indicates an obligation toward the Almighty, an undivided commitment to principles, and a time to reflect on spirituality.

Pilgrimage

This is a reaffirmation of responsibility and the strengthening of a commitment to supreme principles. It conveys a simultaneous celebration of unity, equality, and diversity of the community.

Alms

The giving of alms represents an obligation toward the needy and those in hardship. It conveys a commitment to social and economic justice. Most importantly, it indicates that those who are capable and who are in a position of responsibility have a moral and social duty to narrow the gap between the haves and have-nots. Mohamed declared, "No Muslim plants a plant, or sows a field, and birds, men, and beasts eat there from, but it is his alms-giving."

Several general guidelines pertaining to organizational aspects exist. These guidelines are examined in detail in related chapters. Here, attention is focused on the ones that Prophet Mohamed articulated in the formative years of his administration. Originally, Mohamed faced several urgent social problems: prejudice and discrimination against non-Arab; abuse of power by the elite; poverty; discrimination against females; rivalry among tribes; and brutal collective punishment. Mohamed showed a firmness and creativity in eliminating or minimizing these problems. He tackled each issue forcefully and by example.

Prejudice and Discrimination

Prejudice and discrimination was a serious problem that could have potentially crippled Mohamed's infant administration. Mohamed's message was universal and challenged existing beliefs and practices. The Arabs of that time discriminated against others based on tribal origin and ethnicity. Mohamed prohibited discrimination and declared that people were equal. He appointed an Ethiopian, Blal, to lead the "Call" for prayer and held the hand of Sulyman Al-Farsi, a Persian, saying "Sulyman is a member of my family," adding, "there is no preference of an Arab over a non-Arab" and that "a white has no superiority over black nor a black has any superiority over white except by piety and good action." Furthermore, the Prophet denounced slavery and encouraged Muslims to abandon its practice. He said, "The worst of men are those who buy and sell man."

Abuse of Power

In terms of the abuse of power, Mohamed gave access to trade to non-Quraeshis, appointed leaders from various groups, and announced that problems must be solved through consultation. "Those who oppress will soon know with what kind of welcome from God they will face."

Poverty

Widespread poverty in Arabia was a source of instability and serious social problems. Mohamed considered poverty to be a manifestation of injustice, and morally wrong. He made alms obligatory to help the poor. In addition, he specified the rights of the poor people, as citizens, on the state (Department of Treasury). He gave the poor and oppressed a special place in his administration and alleviated them to the status of the "friends of the prophet." Furthermore, he declared that equality was one of the guiding principles of Islam and that society, individually and collectively, had a responsibility toward the poor. It was declared, "Those who hoard gold and silver and do not spend for the causes of God, should know that their recompense will be a painful torment on the day of Judgment and that their treasures will be treated by the fire of Hell and pressed against their foreheads, sides and back with this remark, 'These are your own treasures which you hoarded for yourselves. See for yourselves what they feel like.' "

Tolerance

Mohamed had a relatively extensive interaction with members of other religious communities, especially Christians and Jews. Some of his interactions took place during his trade trips to Syria. This fact, combined with his universal message, allowed him to preach tolerance and receptivity. As the Quran commands, "There is no compulsion in religion" (2:256) and "To you be your religion and to me, mine" (109:6).

Diversity

The issue of diversity was considered a natural and a source for the exchange of ideas and creative input. The Quran (49:13) reminds people of this fact: "O mankind! We created you from a single (pair) of a male and female, and made you into nations and tribes, that you might know each other" and (5:48), "If God had so willed, He would have made you a single nation." Both the Prophet and his immediate Caliphs did not discriminate among people based on race, or faith. In addition, it was reported that Mohamed stated that, "Difference in opinion is a virtue."

Gender Prejudice

At that time it was common in Arabia to kill newborn girls. Poverty, hardships and economic deprivation prevented people from taking care of their families. Fearing that they might not be able to provide adequately for members of their families, some people sacrificed their newborn babies. Mohamed prohibited the killings and women were given rights to inheritance, education, and ownership of property.

Rivalry

The rivalry among tribes and groups was the source of conflicts and division in Arabian society. The Prophet Mohamed declared that there should be no allegiance except to Islam, and tribalism or loyalty to one's tribe was sinful; a legacy of an era of ignorance.

Collective Punishment

Mohamed prohibited collective punishment. It was customary at that time that families or clans were held responsible for the misdeed of their members. This was outlawed. The Quran (17:15) declares, "No bearer of burdens can bear the burden of another."

The pre-Islam Arabs were highly individualistic. They showed extreme self-assertion, pride and self interest, and valued their independence in pursuing their pleasures. They resented authority and strict orders. These qualities obstructed national formation, unity, and the possibility of establishing a unified governing institution. Imam Ali (1989, died 661, p. 167) succinctly described the Arabs before Islam: "Arabs were practicing the worst of all religions, in the worst of all places. [They] inhibited houses made of rough stone, together with venomous snakes. [Their] food and drink were impure. [They] shed [their] own blood and severed . . . family relations. [They] worshipped idols and were immersed in sins." In short, the pre-Islam Arabs were not inclined toward law and order and their loyalty was almost exclusively toward their primary groups. Their extreme pride, selfishness, and perceived righteousness were serious obstacles to building unified institutions. The Prophet Mohamed recognized these traits and the need for law and order and combined firmness with fairness in promoting the above principles. More importantly, he made it clear to Arabs that it was almighty God, not himself, who set out these principles. This facilitated acceptance and a commitment to new guidelines from the various tribes.

3. CENTRALITY OF COMMERCE IN ISLAMIC THINKING

The Quranic principles and the Prophet's prescriptions serve as a guide for Muslims in conducting both their business and their family affairs. The Quran instructs Muslims to persistently work whenever and wherever it is available, "disperse through the land and seek of the bounty of God" (Quran, 62:10) and "God hath permitted trade and forbidden usury" (2:275). The Prophet Mohammed preached that merchants should perform tasks that were not only morally required, but that were essential for the survival and flourishing of a society. He declared, "I commend the merchants to you, for they are the couriers of the horizons and God's trusted servants on earth" and "the honest, truthful Muslim merchant will stand with the martyrs on the Day of Judgment."

During the first six centuries of Islam's Golden Age (since the sixth century), knowledge, trade, industry, agriculture, and construction of complex organizations flourished. Work and creativity were honored in all their forms. Quranic principles and prophetic prescriptions served as guides for Muslims in conducting their business and family affairs. Izzeddin (1953) examined the contributions of the Arab/Muslim people, during the golden age, to organized works, noting that:

> The industries and trades were organized in corporations or guilds. These corporations were of great social importance. They maintained the standard of craftsmanship and prevented underhand competition, thereby insuring a friendly society. Based on religious and moral foundations, they impressed upon their members a sense of duty toward one's craft and toward one another. Honesty and sobriety were characteristic qualities of Moslem artisans. A tradition of mutual aid prevailed (pp. 30-31).

It was during this Golden Age that highly esteemed organizations emerged. The status of merchants and trade in Arab-Islamic thinking was reflected in the Prophet Mohammed's saying: "He who brings supplies to our market is like a warrior in the war for God" and "the truthful, honest merchant is with the prophets, and the truthful ones, and the martyrs" (quoted in M. Ali, 1977, p. 294). Likewise, Imam Ali (1989, ad 598-661), in his letter to the Governor of Egypt, demonstrated his esteem for merchants as he urged the Governor to:

> Take good care of the merchants and artisans, and ensure their well-being whether they are settled or traveling, or working on their own. Those are the providers of benefits and goods, which they bring from far away by sea or by land through mountains and valleys, securing them for people who are unable to reach them. Those are the people who will assure you a durable peace and respected allegiance. Give them due care in your vicinity and in other areas of your land (pp. 329-330).

This view concerning the merchant classes was in direct contrast to the beliefs that prevailed among other civilizations that prospered before or after the Islamic empire. For example, Dessler (1986, p. 15) pointed out that in ancient Greece "Business in general, and money-lending in particular, were. . . carried out by slaves and less-than-respected citizens; manual workers and merchants, in fact, were not permitted citizenship in the Greek democracy." Likewise, the European peoples regarded business as a degrading occupation. Adam Smith, in the *Wealth of the Nations* (published in 1776), indicated that businessmen are "an order of men, whose interest is never the same with that of the public, who have generally an interest to deceive and even to oppress the public and who accordingly have, upon many occasions, both deceived and oppressed it" (quoted in Koontz, O'Donnell and Weihrich, 1980, p. 31).

4.   RATIONALES FOR ENGAGING IN TRADE

Islam positioned itself to be the leading force for promoting economic growth and development by its emphasis, in the early stage of its inception, on trade. The centrality and necessity of trade in early Islamic thinking and practice was grounded in a deep understanding of the social and economic conditions and was crucial in strengthening the foundation of the new state.   That is, Mohamed not only recognized the need for preparing the ground work for eventual victory against his immediate rivals, the elite of Mecca, but also the necessity of trade in spreading his spiritual message to other regions. Trade was viewed, in early Islamic thinking, as an instrument for realizing religious, political, social, and economic goals.

In pre-Islam, the elite of Mecca assumed the leading roles in trade. It is mostly this elite class that organized a campaign against Mohamed and his message, despite the fact that Mohamed was a merchant, married to a merchant whose name was Khadija, and who was from a noble family that engaged in trade. The Meccans' elite saw the new message as a threat to their established roles and domination of other tribes and trade routes. Fearing their reprisal, Mohamed originally sent some of his followers to Ethiopia for safety. In addition, he chose a nearby city, Taaif, to be his stage for promoting his message, but met with little success as the residents of Taaif forcefully rejected him. Mohamed had to return to Mecca and transmitted his message to people during the pilgrimage session, and to travelers and merchants from other cities. When visitors from Yethreb met him, they accepted his message and invited him to settle there. In ad 622, Mohamed emigrated from Mecca to Yethreb. The year was called Hijra (emigration) and the name of the capital was changed to Medina Al-Rasool (city of the Prophet). In this city-state, Mohamed assumed religious and political responsibilities along with the role of social arbitrator and, initially, the regulator of the market.

In Medina, the Prophet gave considerable attention to trade and was determined to weaken the Meccans' elite stronghold on trade. Several battles took place between the Muslims and the Meccans. By ad 632, the Muslims defeated the Meccans and entered Mecca. That event assured the control of Muslims over Arabic trade and trade routes and Mohamed became the undisputed leader. As usual, members of the commercial class assumed political positions and leadership roles in the new Muslim administration. The Merchants were granted unlimited support during the reign of Prophet Mohamed and his four successors, the wise Caliphs. All viewed trade as a noble and essential profession for the survival and revival of the faith and for the prosperity and the growth of the state. Lewis (1993, p. 97) reviewing the book *On Earning* written by Muhammad al-Shaybani (died 804) pointed out that the writer showed that "earning a livelihood is not merely permitted but incumbent on Muslims. Man's primary duty is to serve God, but to do this properly he must be adequately fed, housed, and clothed. This can only be achieved by working and earning. Nor need his earnings be limited to providing for the bare necessities of life, since the acquisition and use of luxuries is also permitted." Al-Shaybani asserted that money earned through trade or crafts is preferred by God over money received from government for civil or military service.

After the death of the fourth Caliph, Imam Ali, in 661, the Ommeyade dynasty (661-750) ascended to political power. The Ommeyade family had been the leading merchant group before the establishment of Islam and had, initially, led the opposition to Islam. Its patriarch, Abu Sufian, had personally led the campaigns and wars against the Muslims. He and his immediate family converted to Islam only after the Muslims were successful in defeating them and entered their strong hold, Mecca. After converting to Islam, members of the Ommeyade dynasty managed to position themselves in strategically political places. Muawiyah, the son of Abu Safian, was a shrewd person. He relied on creative maneuvering and war to attain the highest position, the

Caliph of Muslims. The ascendance of Muawiyah to the throne transformed the Arab social and economic environment and gave it new energy. It enabled the senior merchants to be the "merchant–rulers." The "merchant–rulers" lured Arabs into the army and extended their tribal loyalty to national loyalty in an attempt to capture new regions (e.g., Africa, Spain, South Asia). They used material rewards and ideology (Arab solidarity) in service of their economic and military expansion goals (Abdel-Rahman, 1989).

The Ommeyade dynasty was remarkably successful in utilizing its newfound political and military power to advance its trade interest. Leading members of the dynasty had accumulated wealth that had to be invested. Since Arabia's environment was not conducive to industrialization and agriculture, the Ommeyade dynasty had to rely on commerce to expand and invest the available capital. In addition, they moved the capital from Medina to Damascus. The latter became the thriving commercial center for a vast empire. Gradually, a form of partnership evolved between the state and the merchants. Consistent with its tribalistic outlook and its sense of Arab superiority, the dynasty created a "merchant-warriors" class strictly from Arabs to expand its trade and accumulate wealth. It is this class of "merchant-warriors" who were able to integrate the Arab world and transform it into a center for international trade between Asia, Europe and Africa. Non-Arab merchants and craftsmen were given access to the ruling elites. Nevertheless, their role was subordinate to that of the "merchant-warriors" class.

It should be noticed that trade, agriculture, and construction of a sophisticated system of government were developed during the Ommeyade era. Work and creativity were honored in all their forms. A case in point is the capitalist sector. It was the most extensive and highly developed in history before the establishment of the world market which later was created by Western European businessmen (Rodinson, 1974).

After the defeat of the Ommeyade dynasty, the Abbasid dynasty (a major family of Hashimis) assumed power. It moved the capital to a newly established city, Baghdad. The dynasty strengthened the already existing partnership between the state and merchants. The Abbasid dynasty learned from the Ommeyade dynasty's mistakes. It used religion to legitimize its hold on power. It adopted an inclusive policy that intended to promote further engagement and participation of all; that is the Abbasid dynasty did not exclude non-Arabs from any role. Indeed, it relied heavily on other ethnic groups, especially Persians and Turks, to sustain power. Second, unlike the Ommeyade dynasty, the Abbasid dynasty viewed trade as an instrument to expand its political power, not vice-versa. The rulers and their representatives warmly received merchants and craftsmen from all regions and ethnicities. In both cases, the dynasty projected itself as the trustworthy guardians of the faith and community.

During the era of the two dynasties, Ommeyade and Abbasid, great cities were built and became trade and manufacturing centers. These centers served not only the market of a vast empire but also foreign cities and markets in Europe, Asia, and Africa. Credits were available and agents of major traders were found in various cities. Hourani (1991, p. 112) noted that two trade arrangements evolved during that time. The first was partnership. This was often "between members of the same family" where two or more partners shared risks and profits in proportion to their investment. The second was the commenda (mudaraba). In this case, the investor "entrusted goods or capital to someone who used them for trade, and then returned to the investors his capital together with an agreed share of the profits." Lewis (1993, p. 98) noted that an eleventh-century Muslim writer, Abu'l Fadl Ali al-Dimashqi classified merchants into three categories: Wholesaler (*khazzan*), exporter (*mujahhiz*), and traveling merchant (*rakkad*). The author provided detailed commentary on the dangers of fraud and waste; and on various market and trade issues such as "the appointment of agents, the obtaining of information about market prices, the fixing of prices, the delivery of goods, and financial and commercial administration."

The *Ikhwan-us-Safa* (Brothers of Purity) who rose in the tenth century indicates that engagement in trade and manufacturing served physical, psychological, social, and spiritual purposes. Specifically (Vol. 1, p. 286), they identified the following for pursuing business activities: alleviating of poverty; motivating people to be persistent and engaged creatively in an appropriate profession; complementing human soul with verified knowledge, good manners, useful ideas, and responsible deeds; and reaching salvation. Similarly, Ibn Khaldun (p. 273), the medieval Arab sociologist, specified that engaging in business serves four objectives: facilitating cooperation and mutual understanding among people, satisfying the needs of people, increasing wealth and influence, and spurning the growth of cities.

Just before the collapse of the Abbasid dynasty, the Muslim world experienced fragmentation, political disintegration, and infighting. These escalated the demise of the dynasty. More importantly, they facilitated foreign occupation and economic stagnation. There were, however, few examples of emerging states in some parts of what had been called the Islamic empire that went through a moderate era of prosperity, openness, and engagement in international trade (e.g., Safavid dynasty in Iran and Azerbaijan, 1502-1737; the Akbar of India, 1556-1605). The influence of these states, however, was meager, not immediate, and lacked the enthusiasm, energy, and invigoration that characterized the early decades of the Ommeyade and Abbasid empires. Likewise, the other states that emerged during that time did not appreciate trade and were suspicious of merchants. For example, some of the rulers during the Mamluk era (1250-1517) in both Egypt and Syria were not friendly to merchants. Goitein (1968, p. 351) states that the "rapacious Mamluks, always watchful not to let any one become too prosperous and mighty, destroyed systematically the great merchant houses by imposing on them exorbitant contributions or by wholesale confiscation of the remaining estates."

5. CONCLUSION

There are certain factors that facilitated the birth and phenomenal growth of Islam. In this chapter certain social, political, and economic factors were identified. Their influence was tremendous and shaped the progress of subsequent Islamic states. During the first few centuries of Islam, trade and other economic activities were encouraged and promoted. During that time, rulers displayed an enthusiasm and commitment to trade. They played a significant role in providing protection to merchants and trade. As such, merchants and commerce were held in high regard. Consequently, Muslim merchants reached foreign lands and operated in different countries. As inflexible attitudes, rigid beliefs, and foreign domination swept across the Muslim lands, trade, creative thinking, and scientific discoveries experienced serious stagnations and setbacks. Since that time, economic and organizational activities have not progressed adequately. Consequently, management and organization studies and research have not been invigorated and have lagged behind development in other parts of the world.

What is certain, in terms of business and management, is that Islamic principles and the original thinking of the early Muslim generations are conducive for building business institutions and for a market economy that is founded on justice and responsible competition. Moral principles, hard work, and commitment to the community helped to strengthen commerce in the vast land of the early Islamic empires. They were and are vital for independent thinking, genuine creativity and dynamic commerce. Many of these factors and principles are, unfortunately, overlooked by most Muslims and researchers in organizational studies. In the following chapters these factors, perspectives, and orientations are discussed. Their relevance and implications to today's business will be highlighted.

2. Human Nature and Motivation

The nature of human beings is difficult to analyze in static terms, to quantify, or to mold to predetermined models. Nevertheless, scholars and practitioners alike have shown an increasing interest in understanding human nature and behavior. What makes people react or act in certain ways, what stimulates them to select specific jobs and careers, and how their expectations originate and evolve have fascinated researchers in different fields and regions.

Scientists and social scientists have developed their own conceptualization of and approaches to human nature. As such, our knowledge of human beings has been substantially improved. This has been evident in the business world where organizations and managers have embarked on various motivational and human resource programs to improve productivity and sustain growth. Since the Hawthrone studies in the late 1920s, the subject of human nature and work environment has been the focus of organizational studies and analysis. Several motivational approaches have been developed and applied worldwide, especially in the Western world. Indeed, in the Western world the philosophies of human nature have developed around three traditions of thought: the tradition of reason and nature, the tradition of will and artifice, and the tradition of the rational will (Wrightsman, 1992). Under the tradition of reason and nature, people are part of the natural order of things. They have the faculty of reason through which they can discover the natural laws that govern the universe. Human behavior is subject to these natural laws. The tradition of will and artifice assumes that human beings are ruled by passions and appetites rather than by reason. The third school of thought advances that history belongs to persons of action rather than to persons of contemplation. Consequently, ideas and passions are realized and articulated only in practice, and "only through action do the mind and will make themselves public and visible" (Wrightsman, 1992). These general schools of thought have had a tremendous influence on Western assumptions about human nature in academia and business.

1.   ASSUMPTIONS ABOUT HUMAN NATURE

There are various sets of assumptions concerning the nature of human beings. These assumptions vary in their implications and organizational strategies. Three general classifications of human nature that are commonly discussed in literature are: modified trait approach, integrated human economics, and human complexity and differences. These classifications are debated in the business and organization literature in the West. They seem to cover a wide range of perspectives and offer a deep insight into the reality and complexity of human nature. Their popularity in the literature reflects an interest in understanding human motives and psyche in the business world. Following is a brief description of each:

Modified Trait Approach

This approach has been developed by Wrightsman (1992). Wrightsman measures six dimensions of what he calls "philosophies of human nature." They include:

1.   Trustworthiness versus untrustworthiness, or the degree to which an individual believes that people are basically trustworthy, moral, and responsible, or vice versa.
2.   Strength of will and rationality versus external control and irrationality, or whether or not one believes that people have control over their own lives and understand the motives behind their behavior.
3.   Altruism versus selfishness, or the degree to which an individual believes that people are basically unselfish and show interest in other people, or are selfish and unconcerned about others.
4.   Independence versus conformity to group pressures, or whether or not an individual maintains his convictions under pressures from a group, society in general, or some authority figure.
5.   Complexity versus simplicity, or the degree to which an individual believes that people are basically easy to understand and simple rather than complicated and hard to understand.
6.   Similarity versus variability, or the degree to which one believes that people differ in their basic natures.

Several empirical studies have been conducted to test the scale of the philosophies of human nature (see Wrightsman, 1992, for detail). It has been found, for example, that women hold a more favorable belief about human nature than men, and college students have less favorable beliefs about human nature than do older adults. In addition, the scale is also found to be related to locus of control, interpersonal trust, attitudes toward desegregation, and interpretations of the motives behind government policies.

Integrated Human Economics

John Tomer (2001) attempts to provide a comprehensive view of the concept of human nature as it is viewed by economists. He examines the economic man in the context of the stages of human development and the heterodox man. His comprehensive review provides a broad picture of human nature. A summary of each concept is listed below.

Economic man

This is a person who is selfish, rational, unchanging, and does not stop to consider the rightness of his choices. That is, the economic man is mainly preoccupied with material gain and limits his/her options to those that supposedly maximize his/her interests.

Institutional economic man

This individual behaves according to institutional norms and rules, that is, those of a church, workplace, or government. His/her behavior has evolved based on institutional reinforcements and his/her capacity to acquire new skills and concepts. Therefore, this person is not separated from his/her human and physical environment.

Social economic man

This is a person who has a conscience and acts out of concern for justice. A person in this category strives simultaneously to improve his/her economic conditions and social belonging.

Humanistic economic man

Individuals in this category show the capacity for altruism, self-reflection, creativity, spontaneity, and are non-power-seeking. In terms of human development, this stage represents the more complete view of human nature.

Socio-economic man

Individuals subscribing to this category are motivated by simultaneous consideration of self-interest and a deep regard for group or community norms and values.

Tomer argues that the economic man concept, the one most commonly used by business academics, has many deficiencies and is unrealistic. He suggests that institutional economics, social economics, humanistic economics, and socio-economics are closer to true human nature than economic man. Furthermore he suggests that using a fully human concept of man requires that economic development be viewed not as an entirely material process, but also as a partially a human process.

Human Complexity and Differences

Schein (1980) examines human nature in the context of psychological and organizational perspectives. He is interested in developing an understanding of the human nature concept in order to provide managers with clues on how to recruit, select, develop and manage people. Schein believes that familiarity with human nature allows managers to improve productivity and satisfy employees. He asserts that assumptions about human nature are products of past experience, cultural norms, and education. He articulates four sets of assumptions that are relevant to organization and management studies: rational-economic, social actor, self-actualization, and complex assumptions. Since the first one is similar to institutional economic man, the focus will be on the following remaining classifications.

Social actor

Under this category the assumptions are that people are primarily motivated by social needs and belonging would like to be members of teams (hopefully a winning one), are more responsive to social forces of the peer group than to material incentives, because the mechanized work is not that interesting. Meaning for life is mostly found in social relationships at work.

Self-actualization

The self-actualized individual is assumed to be self-motivated and self-controlled and seeks to use his/her potential and capacity to grow professionally. That is, these people are independent and have a confidence in their ability to grow and meet goals. Furthermore, they have no difficulty in reconciling their goals with those of the organization.

Complex nature

People have multiple needs and various potentials. The pattern of those needs differs across age, stage of development, roles and relations with others. Therefore, the needs and motives will have varying degrees of importance to each individual and a given person may exhibit different needs in different organizations. These individuals are constantly changing and learning, and acquiring new needs and learning new skills through organizational experience.

Schein documented evidence for each assumption. In his overview of the literature on human nature, Schein concludes that human nature and motivation are highly complex and not yet fully understood. In addition, he asserts that personal assumptions and biases can operate as powerful filters to make the world look simpler than it actually is.

2. ISLAMIC ASSUMPTION ABOUT HUMAN NATURE

Scholars in their search for understanding humans normally rely on varying sources and perspectives in developing their conceptions. Of course, religion to some degree influences researchers' assumptions and outlooks. Perhaps, this is true in almost all scholarly endeavors. For example, Wrightsman (1992) suggests that Freud focused on the "evil" and "deficient aspects of human nature." These aspects are highlighted in the Talmud, Judaism, and Christian tradition (Lowry, 1998). It is likely that Freud was influenced by religious studies. This may reflect his assertion that "in the depth of my heart, I can't help being convinced that my dear fellowmen, with few exceptions, are worthless" (quoted in Wrightsman, 1992, p. 57). More likely, however, upbringing, past experience, education, career choices, and aspiration are shaped by many factors including religion. In terms of human nature, however, religion plays a significant role. The concepts of duality, creation, soul, transformation, consciousness, among others, are covered in all major religions, especially in Judaism, Christianity, and Islam. These concepts relate to both worldly and spiritual affairs. They come to shape our perceptions of and our assumptions about the world. Consequently, they influence individual perceptions of others in and outside the work environment.

The monotheistic religions (Christianity, Judaism, and Islam), generally, and without reflecting on specific sectarian perspectives, share a number of similarities, in rituals and principles. One of the areas in which these religions seem to exhibit both definitive similarities and dissimilarities relates to the concept of human nature. All agree that human nature is characterized by duality, among other things. Nevertheless, they disagree on other aspects. In Christianity the belief is that all human beings are born with a sinful nature. Judaism and Islam do not share this belief and maintain that individual is born free from any sin. Both Christianity and Judaism, however, strongly believe that the human "capacity for evil is not only a fact, but a shocking fact" (Lowry, 1998, p. 2). The Judaism and Christian belief system, therefore, is based on a doctrine that man is created in the "image of God," but every human being is inclined to evil. The propensity to evil perhaps "not ultimately the stronger, is by far the more clamorous. It is like a mighty king who lays siege to a city, says the Talmud, and the good inclination is like a meek man inside the besieged city" (Lowry, 1998, p. 3). Rabbi Harold Kushner (2001, p. 55) advocates, "God has planted in each of us something called the *yetzer ha-ra*", or "the evil impulse." That is, the evil impulse is essential for the existence of human beings because any attempt to "amputate the part of a person that leads him or her to be selfish and aggressive . . . would be a disaster. What we'd be left with would be less than a whole human being." Previously, Rabbi Levi Olan (1964, p. 173) reaffirmed that "The temptation to sin is real, and the desire on man's part to follow it stronger than his desire to choose good. Indeed, evil is part of God's creation and is therefore endowed with purpose . . . . There is strong indication that the *yetzer ra*, the inclination toward sin, is a necessary ingredient in life."

The Christian tradition "affirms that the perfection of human beings is unattainable in history and that it is sinful to even try to attain it" (Hanson, 1999). Likewise, Hanson suggests that in the Christian tradition a human being has his/her limits and "is unaware of the limits of . . . possibilities." In Christianity and in the Protestant perspective in particular, "all aspects of human existence," in a certain aspect, are defective. Any treatment or technique to improve human abilities and motivate people is viewed "with suspicion" (Hanson, 1999, p. 127). Similarly, in Judaism much of "man's life is predestined; it is decreed at birth whether he will be strong or weak, wise or foolish, rich or poor. But in the matter of morality he is master and must choose and take the consequences" (Olan, 1964, pp. 174-5).

The Islamic view of human nature is described in the holy Quran and is distinguishable from that of Judaism and Christianity (see Table 2.1) in that the view is clearly articulated and situates man in the highest possible position. It is based on at least four foundations. First, a human being is

God's vicegerent on earth: "Behold, thy Lord said to the angels: 'I will create a vicegerent on earth'" (2:30). Furthermore, man is God's trustee in the universe. The Quran (33:72) manifestly states: "We offered the trust to the heavens, the earth, and the mountains; but they refused to undertake it, being afraid thereof. But man undertook it." Second, human beings are endowed with a free will to determine what is good or bad for them. The Quran states (17:15) "Whoever receives guidance receives it for his own benefit: who goes astray does so to his own loss" and (17:84) "Everyone does as he wants. Your Lord knows who has the right guidance." Indeed, the Quran clearly articulates the belief that that each individual is responsible for his/her action; (6:164) "Every soul draws the need of its acts on none but itself; no bearer of burdens can bear the burden of another." Third, each individual is endowed with various needs and has multiple goals (92:4): "Verily, (the ends) ye strive for are divers" and (53:39): "Man can have only what he strives for." Fourth, a human being is a creature with two dimensions: the spirit of God and putrid clay (15:29): "When your Lord said to the angels, 'I will create man out of pure mud-molded clay. When it is properly shaped and I have blown My Spirit into it, you should then bow down and prostrate before him.'" This not only placed humans in a superior rank relative to angels, but situates man between two extreme possibilities: perfection (God Spirit) and lowliness (clay). Therefore, according to Islamic tradition, human beings have infinite choices to make in life. Shariati (1979, p. 92) argues that as a human being is in an "infinite direction," either toward clay or toward God, man is "compelled to be always in motion. His own self is the stage for a battle between two forces that results in a continuous evolution toward perfection." Consequently, attaining perfection in Islam is not a sin. Rather, it is desirable and a virtuous goal.

In terms of needs, the nature of human beings in Islam dictates that human needs are complex and not necessarily hierarchical. That is, based on the assumption that God created man from clay (physical) and spirit (spirituality) and subsequently God bestowed man with trust (free will) and knowledge (taught man the names- aptitude for understanding and comprehending the complexity of the universe). These factors shape and influence the formation of human needs. Scholars in Islamic studies, therefore, conclude that there are five general categories of needs: physiological, material, psychological, spiritual and mental, or intellectual (Al-Jasmani, 1996; Glaachi, 2000; Nusair, 1983; Shariati, 1979). The first two categories are mostly related to the clay or physical part of human nature. The last three categories are more likely derived from the spiritual part and the knowledge and independent thinking that God granted specifically to human beings. Physiological needs include food and shelter. It is important to indicate that in the early Islamic State (the era during Prophet Mohamed and his four successors), a minimum level of physiological needs was guaranteed for citizens by the state. The material concerns the need to achieve acceptable levels of wealth and economic enjoyment. Psychological needs concern aspects such as emotion, love, belonging, fear, and internal struggle.   Spiritual needs focus on faith, harmony, and confidence. The spiritual need represents a cushion that helps to absorb frustration, crisis, failure, and so on. Theoretically, it is supposed to provide a balance among existing needs. The intellectual revolves around capitalization on potential, maximizing contributions, and continuing learning and development.

Table 2.1   Human nature in Christianity, Judaism, and Islam

Factor	Christianity	Judaism	Islam
Human Status	Image of God	Image of God	Vicegerent on earth
Sin	Sinful	Sinful until reaching 13 and more inclined to sin afterward	Not sinful
Free will	Limited	Free will in the matter of morality only	Unrestricted
Capabilities	Limited	Determined at birth	Determined by one's will and environmental conditions
Possibilities in life	Very limited	Predestined	Unlimited
Enhancement techniques to improve	Should be viewed with suspicion	Viewed positively	Viewed positively
Nature perfection	A sinful tendency	Possibility for gradual perfection	Desirable and sought

Source: Hanson 1999, Lowry 1998, Niebuhr 1964, Olan 1964; Shariati 1979, 1980.

The underlying assumption of human needs in Islam is that human beings are complex and dynamic creatures. That is, they are born to strive, ponder vice and virtue, and seek and reach perfection. They have various choices and options in life. These choices have consequences beyond immediate self-interest. Therefore, Muslims are reminded to view their actions in a broad context. The Prophet Mohamed once said, "One has an obligation toward God, self, and family; give a due attention to each" (quoted in Glaachi, 2000, p. 59). As indicated above, physiological, economic, and spiritual needs are not hierarchically arranged. Rather, they are considered simultaneously. The consideration, however, is influenced by intellectual insight, aspirations and emotion. A reasonable balance in satisfying these needs is a virtue. The Quran

(28:77) instructs Muslims, "seek through your wealth the gains of the hereafter without ignoring your share of this life." Nevertheless, Islam situates intellectual and spiritual needs in a unique place. In the Quran (58:11) people are told, "God will exalt those of you who believe and those who are given knowledge to high degree." The spiritual need functions as a cushion that helps in sustaining self-confidence and security in adversity and hardship. The intellectual need makes it possible to clear vision and insight, reduce doubts, and ponder alternatives.

In the context of organizational perspectives, the humanistic economic man and complex perspectives contain many elements that are integral parts of the Islamic view of human nature. The multiplicity of needs, free will, infinite potential, and the desire for perfection, among others, is highly regarded by the three perspectives. As such, religious beliefs offer promising avenues for understanding human nature and motivation. Indeed, the recent growing interest in spirituality in the workplace attests to this potentiality.

3. PSYCHOLOGICAL LEVELS OF EXISTENCE

Psychological perspectives on human existence and development have produced fascinating yet conflicting assumptions. Most of these studies attempt to probe the motives beyond human behavior and actions. Their findings enable students of organizations and practicing managers to devise techniques to improve human relations, interaction, gain satisfaction, and productivity at the workplace and reduce conflict among groups and nations. Sigmund Freud (1856-1939), one of the pioneers in studying human psychology, suggested that people, due to their differences in personality, deal with their fundamental drives differently. He postulated that there is a battle between two parts of the soul, the "It" or id (unconscious part) and the "I" proper or the "ego" (an individual's picture of physical and social reality) and the "superego" (storehouse of an individual's values). Freud views "It" as the hidden or essence of the soul and the "I" is the open, and apparent part of the soul. The "It" and "I" parts are destined to remain continuously at war and that only "compromise, but never harmony, [can] be achieved between them" (Wilber, 1999, p. 583). Freud asserted that "It was stronger than I" and "It" represents an "'urge which the weak "I" would like to resist, because it feels that . . . this urge may involve danger, may result in a traumatic situation, a collision with the outer world'" (quoted in Wilber, 1999, pp. 583-4).

Erikson (1964) describing the fundamental human developmental stages suggested that people mature and grow as a result of their handling various problems and crises. He identified seven stages: infancy, young childhood, childhood and adolescence, adolescence, young adulthood, adulthood and middle age, middle and old age. At each stage, a person faces different problems and difficulties. For example, at the young childhood stage, an individual struggles with autonomy versus shame, and initiative versus guilt. As people mature they face the problem of maintaining effort and interest. In the later stage (middle and old age), individuals attempt to maintain a sense of self-worth and integrity.

Graves (1970) speculates that people progress through consecutive levels of "psychological existence." This progression is determined by their ability to acquire and assimilate knowledge and to exercise and to develop talents. Depending on the person's cultural conditioning and perception of the opportunities and constraints in the environment, his/her level of psychological existence can become arrested at a given level or it can move upward or downward. The level of existence of the mature human being is an unfolding process marked by the progressive subordination of the older lower level of existence to newer, higher-level value systems. Graves identifies six levels for a mature person or groups of mature human beings. These are: tribalistic (a submissiveness to authority and/or tradition), egocentric (aggressive, selfish, restless, impulsive, and, in general, not inclined to live within the limits and constraints of society's norms), conformist (sacrificial, has a low tolerance for ambiguity and needs structure and rules to follow), manipulative (materialistic, expressive, and self-calculating to achieve an end), sociocentric (a high need for affiliation and little concern for wealth), and existential (a high tolerance for ambiguity and for those who have different values, usually expresses self but not at the expense of others). Unlike, Erikson and Freud, Graves places great emphasis on values as the major determinant of human attitude, behavior, and action. Feelings, motivations, preferences, thoughts, and acts reflect the value system at that particular level of existence.

In the context of Islam, there are four levels of existence. These levels are in a state of flux and dynamism. This is because people are endowed with mental faculties and a free will to decide what is good for them. Choices and priorities are shaped by upbringing, social and economic constraints, knowledge, and perceived and actual opportunities. The Quran specifies and details the levels of existence (e.g., 12:53; 75:2; 89:27-30). The Quran, too, clarifies not only the circumstances that shape the evolution and existence of each level, but also the conditions that induce changes and progress. These levels are briefly discussed below.

Sawala (a passion for temptations)

At this level, a person's soul prompts him to follow only his/her desires, and to shy away from enlightenment. In the stories of Moses and Jacob and the difficulties they encountered, this psyche was explained well. The propensity to evil made the Samiri lead Moses' people astray in his absence. Moses asked the Samiri what he had done. "'The Samiri told Moses, "I had the skill (of carving), which they did not have. I followed some of the messenger's (Moses) tradition but I then ignored it. Thus, my soul promoted me (to carve a golden calf with an artificial hollow sound)"' (20:96). Similarly, in the Quran there is a story of how Joseph was betrayed by his brothers and left him to die. The brothers told their father, Jacob, that Joseph was killed by a wolf ("'Jacob said [to his sons], 'your souls have tempted you in this matter [providing false proof], (for me) patience is most appropriate against that which ye assert, it is God whose help can be sought"' (12:18). In both cases, these individuals, Samiri and Joseph's brothers, acted in a way that eventually inhibited their optimal future organizational engagement. It can be inferred that the primary preoccupation of a person at this level is to pursue self-interest. That is, people may possess the mental capacities for differentiating between good and bad, but they lack the capacity to integrate their needs with the rest of their surroundings. Their obsession with self-interest inhibits them from rationally capitalizing on opportunities and engaging in effective organizational behavior.

Ammara (the prone-to-evil psyche)

This is a stage where a person is aware that his soul induces him/her to do bad things and yet shows no resistance. A person at this stage admits that his/her soul is the source of evil or wrongdoing. The human soul is a burden with its desires and temptations. According to the Quran, too, Joseph was put in Pharaoh's jail and then brought to the Pharaoh to interpret the latter's dream. Joseph was put in jail because he was accused by the wife of his master of trying to seduce her. She had invited noble society women and motivated them to seduce Joseph. When Joseph stood firm and refused temptations, he was sent to jail. When the King asked his servants to bring Joseph before him, Joseph requested that the King first ask the ladies who had induced them to prosecute him. The King asked the women about their encounters with Joseph and demanded the whole truth. All women except one acknowledged the truth of Joseph's innocence. When the rest finished, the one who kept silent decided to admit her guilt. She testified that it was her own soul which was prone to evil. She admitted that because he was attractive and handsome, she wanted against his will to make love to him. The Quran states (12:53), "Yet, I do not absolve myself (of blame): the human soul certainly incites evil, unless my Lord bestow His mercy." In this context, a person is inclined intentionally and, perhaps contrary to self-interest, to engage in wrongdoing. Nevertheless, a person at this stage is willing to confess mistakes under pressure or when they understand that conditions are no longer conducive to serving his/her interest. Perhaps this manifests a lack of internalization of the spiritual beliefs. But there is hope that a person may learn from his/her mistakes and can engage in behavior that leads to satisfactory involvement.

Lawama (self-reproaching)

At this stage, Man is conscious of evil. There is a struggle between good and evil and Man seeks to repent to achieve salvation. In sections 75:2 and 75:14-15, the Quran specifies this stage of human development: "And I swear by the self-reproaching soul" and "Nay, man will be evidence against himself, even though he were to put up his excuses." Thus, the Lawama soul either drives a person toward good and perfection or toward evil action and aggression. In the latter, the person experiences anxiety and fear (Al-Jasmani, 1996). People at this level are sensitive to moral and ethical standards, aware of their weak tendencies, resist selfish pursuits, are troubled when things go wrong, and consider what happens to them a consequence of their own choices.

Mutamainna (the righteous)

This is the ultimate point in human development. At this level, the mind is perfectly in tune with good deeds and a person realizes complete satisfaction and self-actualization. The Quran (89:27-28), says, "To the righteous soul will be said 'oh soul come back thou to thy Lord, well pleased (thyself), and well-pleasing unto Him.'" Muslim scholars describe this soul as one that is content and satisfied with what it has regardless of "abundance or scarcity, prosperity or shortages, prohibitions or permissiveness, content without any doubt, and does not change heart or deviate from the straight path, and is not fearful during terrifying events" (Al-Jasmani, 1996, p. 16). Shariati (1979, p. 121) argues that an individual at this stage of development has traversed the difficult path of servitude, and carried the burden of trust. According to Shariati, people who reach the Mutamainna stage "fend the earth . . . with the power of their industry . . . create a life overflowing with abundance, enjoyment and prosperity" without suspending feeling and all sense of value. They are those in whom the peculiarly human capacity "to perceive the spirit of the world, the profundity of life, the creation of beauty, and the belief in something higher than nature and history has been weakened or paralyzed."

The above four levels of psyche are descriptive of personal values and life-styles. The domination by a particular psyche determines the intensity and priority of human needs and behavior. At each level, a person is conscious of his/her actions. This is significantly different from Freud's model. In Islam, a person is free to choose his/her direction in life depending on the psyche at a particular stage. The constant struggle or war within oneself, as Freud suggests, is found in the second (Ammara) and third (Lawama) levels. Even at these levels the inclination to progress toward "goodness" and "perfection" is always an aim. That is contrary to Freud's assumption; the urge to do things right is not considerably weaker relative to the urge to do evil. At the last level (Mutamainna), people, more likely, appear to display no uncertainty or doubt in their choices in life. The Quran (49:15) explicitly refers to this state by stating that believers are the sincere ones who "never since doubted." Furthermore, contrary to Freud's thinking human beings in Islam are not unworthy and are considered the best creatures on earth. The Quran (17:70) declares, "We have honored the children of Adam, carried them on the land and the sea, given them pure sustenance and exalted them above most of My creatures." That is, human beings are vicegerents and are endowed with knowledge, trust, and discretion to pursue multiple interests and activities. This is in contrast to Freudian ethic which asserts that "man is by nature (or at least by virtue of the inevitable conflict between man's nature and society) a weak and irresolute creature without the stamina to endure the stresses and strains of living, and who cannot therefore hope to enjoy life on this earth" (LaPiere, 1959, p. 60).

The Islamic levels of development differ, too, from that of Graves' model. Graves assumes that the value system determines human motive, aspiration, and action. Certainly, values influence individuals' feeling, attitude, and behavior. Nevertheless, in the Islamic perspective, values are a reflection of the human level of existence. At each level, individuals acquire certain tendencies and dispositions. These are the result of the nature of human "duality." Human beings are in a constant struggle toward perfection and realization of infinite possibilities, at least according to secular and Islamic models. In Islamic thinking, God has inspired in people both good and evil. It is their knowledge and faith that guards them from going astray. The knowledge illuminates their path and faith helps to sustain hope and absorbs frustration, crisis, and difficulties. The Quran (91:7-10) illustrates this state, "By the soul and the proportion and order given to it; and its inspiration as to its wrong and its right. Truly he succeeds that purifies it, and he fails that corrupt it."

4. IKHWAN-US-SAFA AND ISLAMIC PSYCHE

Some liberal Muslim thinkers divide human existence into five levels. For example, *Ikhwan-us-Safa* (Brothers of Puritytenth-century thinkers) developed the following categories (1999a p. 311): Plantlike, animal-like, human, *molakia* (wisdom and intellect), and kudsia (prophetic) level. Their study of the levels of existence is a blend of Islamic perspectives and ancient Greek philosophies. This group of thinkers studied philosophies, mathematics, astrology, biology, chemistry, psychology, and theology, among other subjects, and attempted to provide a comprehensive view of the existence and evolution of the world.

Plantlike level

This is the level where human beings desire and long for food and refreshment. People insist on obtaining them at any expense even if this leads to suffering, hardship and humiliation. Their presence gives people pleasure and happiness, and induces a state of relaxation, and good feeling. But once they get satisfaction, people feel bored. Normally, people at this stage seek these needs without forethought and caution (Ikhwan-us-Safa, 1999a, p. 313).

Animal-like

In addition to the above needs, people display a desire for belonging, revenge, and authority. At this stage people recognize what does and does not serve their interests. Therefore, they resort to domination, cunning, cheating, manipulation, suspicion, and the establishment of policies to sustain interest (Ikhwan-us-Safa, 1999a, p. 314).

Human

In addition to the above needs and qualities, people at this level are concerned with science, knowledge, discoveries, acquiring skills and crafts, prestige, self-esteem, and professional progress. People at this level long for and persist in satisfying these needs. They get pleasure and happiness, relaxation and enjoyment in satisfying them. The lack of them fills them with sadness and sorrow (Ikhwan-us-Safa, 1999a, p. 315).

Molakia

At this level, people are primarily concerned with knowledge and science. They have specific qualities that ease their accomplishment in science and discoveries such as: a clear mind, good understanding, intelligence, purity and firmness of heart, good common sense, imagination, sharp recognition, insight, caution and reflection, consideration, investigation and conclusion, retention and remembrance, knowledge of history and events, setting measures and figuring outcomes, prediction and sound judgment, acceptance of God's revelations, and a familiarity with the creation of creatures and astrology (Ikhwan-us-Safa , 1999a, p. 316).

Kudsia

The dominant need at this stage is to be close to God and have complete faith in His power, an acceptance of God's bounty and sharing what it is bestowed on them with the rest of the people at other stages (Ikhwan-us-Safa, 1999a, p. 316). Ikhwan-us-Safa asserted that individuals at any stage share in common the desire to live up to their potential and the willingness to reach perfection. Their classification, however, was not accepted by the traditional Islamic scholars even though they were said to be based on the Quran. This might be attributed to the fact that Ikhwan-us-Safa in the development of their typology of levels of existence relied on implicit references to Quranic verse. Furthermore, Ikhwan-us-Safa existed in an era that had just experienced the downfall of the Arab and Islamic civilization and the domination of foreign powers over most of the Arab and, subsequently, the Islamic world. Since then, pessimism, rigidity and a lack of flexibility and creativity have dominated the Islamic view of world affairs.

5. IMPLICATIONS FOR MANAGEMENT

Managerial perceptions of human nature and the complexity of employees' demands determine management strategies and its understanding of the nature and scope of the relationships between employees and organization. This means that managers develop various strategies to effectively deal with employees at different levels of existence. Table 2.2 presents organizational implications at each level of human development. At the first level (Sawala), a person is motivated by the urge to engage in temptation for the sake of personal enjoyment. Consequences are not thought about and the aim is to maximize personal pleasure. Individuals at this stage see the world from a very narrow angle and believe that their pleasure and enjoyment bring them recognition and status. Neither spiritual nor intellectual needs are motivators. Physiological and material needs are the primary motivator (see Table 2.3). Managerial strategies should be designed to enhance performance through incentives that satisfy employees' needs for pleasure, including monetary ones. The managers, however, have to be tough and make it clear that he/she is in charge. This is because employees at this stage appreciate firmness and this is precisely what keep them performing within established parameters. Their preoccupation with their self-interests prevents them from identifying with the needs and expectations of others. Furthermore, they have difficulties in grasping the logic of organizational goals if these goals are perceived as obstacles to maximizing their pleasures.

Table 2.2   Human levels of development and organizational implications

Area	Sawala	Amara	Lawama	Mutamainne
Leadership Styles	Tough and aggressive and should clearly and firmly identify and enforce rules	Rely on authority but clearly relate rewards and incentive to one's career	Clarify benefits and rewards for performance and gain personal acceptance through active consultation and involvement with subordinates	Catalyst and facilitator
Control Systems	Emphasis on accountability, individual incentives, and clearly identify and strictly enforce rules	Link rewards to personal performance and highlight boundaries of acceptable conduct	Allow subordinates to participate in setting standards and goals and the necessity of meeting organizational standards	Flexible and is left for individual control
Communication Systems	Formal system and manager is closely involved	Formal system but manager actively seeks subordinate's feedback	A mix of formal and informal system that allows subordinates to clarify expectations	Open and informal

Area	Sawala	Amara	Lawama	Mutamainne
Reward Systems	Economic rewards and personal incentives; emphasis on punishments	Economic rewards that are based on personal achievement and meeting organizational goals	Tangible and intangible rewards are emphasized and good performance is publicly acknowledged and appreciated	Reward comes from personal control over their work and personal fulfillment of mission
Growth Opportun-ities	Promotion and personal advancement is strictly based on performance and following organization-al guidelines	Promotion and personal advancement are possible when organizational goals and objectives are observed	Allows exposure to groups and working with others to advance self and serve organization and show concerns for development of employees	Communicate existing and possible opportunities that strengthen involvement with group, society and organization
Planning	Must be stated in economic terms and objectives are clearly measurable	Stated in economic terms and specifies unacceptable deviations	Essential as a road map that identifies goals and possible rewards	General and seek to ensure involvement and participation in company affairs
Conflict	Is inevitable. Management must be involved in preventing and solving it, and those who engage in dysfunctional conflict must be punished	Management must keep close eye on conflict and be firmly involved in reducing dysfunctional ones	Management explains the consequence of conflict in the context of organizational performance and goals	Is a rarity and is not the result of competing self interest, rather it is organizationally based; seeks to move forward in optimizing contributions to community and society

At the second level (Ammara), a person is motivated by the urge to take action, even though there might be unpleasant consequences or harm might be inflicted on others. Unlike the previous stage, individuals at this level are aware that they are not separate from others. Therefore, they recognize that maximizing self-interests may dictate a manipulation of situations and events to achieve goals. Psychological, physiological, and material needs are given priority. The managerial strategies should focus on the personal benefits of career development and opportunities. Managers should highlight rewards and incentives in the context of individual's career goals.

At the third level (Lawama), a person is clear about the advantages of change, but is influenced by selfish desire. Thus, people at this level are aware of their actions and consequences. Nevertheless, spiritual needs are not yet completely internalized and the mental pondering is left without a strong censor to temper selfish desire. A person at this stage, therefore, does not give considerable attention to spiritual needs. Management strategies should clarify and highlight the desired approach and outcome. Techniques such as job enrichment and management by objectives help employees at this level to focus on doing the right things and realizing their potential. Management should reinforce desired behavior by making work and the work environment more meaningful and challenging. Both extrinsic and intrinsic rewards should be used; the intrinsic rewards may prove to be a powerful motivator.

Table 2.3   Level of existence and human needs

Level of Existence	Needs Emphasis
Sawala	Physiological and materials
Amara	Physiological, material, and psychological
Lawama	Physiological, material, psychological, intellectual in addition to some spiritual needs
Mutamainne	All needs with considerable emphasis on spiritual ones

The fourth level (Mutamainna) represents perfection and happiness in doing one's job and realizing one's goals. Spiritual and mental needs strengthen the quest for perfection and actualization of one's potential in serving the community and organization, while pursuing his/her activities. Mutamainna people are non-power seekers and receive comfort and pride from self-reflection, involvement, and creativity. This is a unique, but certainly a very challenging opportunity for managers. Traditionally, managers have dealt with employees who have been driven, to various degrees, by self-interest, especially material gain. Therefore, most managerial strategies focus almost exclusively on motivating employees to do their best to improve performance. Employees at the Mutamainna stage exhibit an ideal situation where there is a state of harmony between rights and obligations, self and others, nature and material needs. Employees believe that there is no inconsistency between personal growth, doing things right and serving society. Their intrinsic feeling rather than extrinsic factors induce them to engage, participate, and excel. This deepest and most genuine feeling ensures a striving for excellence and is the foundation for the truest joy that stems from serving a noble cause. The managers' task, therefore, is to make sure that organizational goals are designed to optimally serve society and employees. In addition, managers should align organizational culture with the prevalent societal norms and values.

6. CONCLUSION

In this chapter we have examined human nature and levels of existence. The examination has sought to highlight the fact that there is a wide spectrum of views regarding human nature. Both religious (Christianity and Judaism) and organizational perspectives were presented. These were contrasted with the Islamic view. It was documented that Islamic perspectives provide insights that are consistent with humanistic and complex organization perspectives. More importantly, the Islamic view offers a unique perspective on a level of human existence (Mutamainna). The quality and characteristics of this type are qualitatively different from existing typologies in the organization literature and, therefore, challenges most of the prevailing management assumptions on human beings. Indeed, this type provides a challenge to existing human resource strategies and necessitates profound changes in organizational approach.

3. Islamic Schools of Thought

The pursuit of knowledge has acquired a special place in the teaching of Islam. That is, the Islamic tradition emphasizes that acquiring knowledge is a virtue that sustains not only personal faith, but also the continuity and evolution of the community. Having knowledge is perceived as a desired quality that is highly appreciated and rewarded. Therefore, during the first six centuries of the golden era of Islam, individuals were encouraged and obliged to pursue intellectual endeavors and share their knowledge with others in all parts of the world. The Prophet Mohamed was quoted as saying, "Seek knowledge even it is in China," "The learned are the heirs of the prophets," and "The benefit of knowledge is better than the benefit of worship." Seeking knowledge is recommended in the Quran (20:114): "And say, O my Lord! Increase me in knowledge."

Differences in opinion and approaches to urgent and new developments, religious and otherwise, are encouraged in Islam. Prophet Mohamed considered innovation and fruitful discourse a blessing. He declared, "The differences [of opinion] among the thinkers of my community are a blessing" and stated that even if they make a mistake in exercising their right to think in a matter of religious law, they are rewarded. "He who arrives at the right opinion receives two rewards and he who errs receives one." Consequently, differences in religious interpretations, outlook, and civility in discourse are valued highly and sanctioned. The latter is illustrated in the Quran (16:125): "And argue with them in ways that are best and most gracious."

During the life of the Prophet, the Prophet was the authority and people consulted him regularly on issues that were not clear to them. Furthermore, people considered his instructions and behavior as their guiding principle. This, however, does not mean that there was no division among the Muslim community at that time. Rather it means that differences did exist in terms of economic achievement, social structure, and seniority in allegiance to Islam. Nevertheless, commitment to religious principles and the presence of the Prophet considerably minimized these issues. In fact, during the Prophet's era, loyalty and allegiance to the new faith transcended Arab tribal division and rivalry and transformed the Arab into an unprecedented coherent group.   The Arabian society, at that time, became vibrant intellectually, socially, politically, and economically.

The unity that the Muslim community exhibited almost collapsed after the death of the Prophet. Various groups aspired to fill the leadership vacuum and others renounced Islam. Omar bin Al-Kattab, the second Caliph, brilliantly and in a timely fashion handled the crisis. He recognized the nature of the threat that faced the new State and sought to capitalize on the event by building his power base and cultivating an image of an undisputed statesman. Having learned that the Supporters' Camp (the residents of Medina who invited the Prophet and his followers to leave Mecca and join them) organized a meeting to select a successor to the Prophet, he immediately took Abu Baker, an elderly and pious follower to the meeting. Omar, diplomatically yet forcefully nominated Abu Baker, to be the successor (Caliph).   Thereby, Omar prevented the Supporters' Camp and the family of the Prophet from endorsing their own representative to be a successor. After Omar and Abu Baker gave speeches, the Supporters' Camp, publicly showed allegiance to Abu Baker, as did the majority of the Muhajirin (migrants or followers who accompanied the Prophet in his migration to Medina).

1.   FOUNDATIONS OF INTELLECTUAL DISCOURSE

During the tenure of the four "Rightly Guided" Caliphs, competing schools of thought had not yet formally evolved. The poor, the intellectuals, and most of the urban people allied themselves with the Prophet's son-in-law and first cousin, Ali. They considered him their defender, an enlightened believer, and the most knowledgeable on Islamic matters. The rest of Arab aristocracy showed a primary interest in receiving their share from the public treasury without neglecting their duties in promulgating the faith. Religious issues were judged according to the Quran and the Sunnah (sayings and actions of the Prophet). Challenging developments and new and urgent state and religious matters were examined and decided by a special council that aided the Caliph.   This practice and the geographic expansion of the State profoundly changed how things should be addressed and implemented, especially during the rule of the first two Caliphs.

After the death of the second Caliph, Omar bin Al-Kattab, Othman bin Affan was selected as Caliph. During his era, a group of Muslims began to hold weekly lectures at the main Mosque in Medina. The lectures focused on philosophy and logic, history, rhetoric, and law (Ali, 1961). This, however, was not transformed into a school of thought with clearly a articulated philosophy, outlook, and framework for analysis. Nonetheless, immediately after Othman's selection, a division within the Muslim community, especially among the senior followers of Prophet Mohamed, took place. His selection triggered a fresh discourse among Muslims on issues related to eligibility, principled conduct, and the nature of the Republic. Muslims saw the first two Caliphs as true followers of the prophets. In their practice and decrees, they closely observed Islamic principles and instructions. They did not differentiate themselves from the rest of Muslims and lived literally simple and austere lives. The situation changed after Caliph Othman's ascendance to power. Ashmawy (1992, p. 112) indicates that Othman was an empathetic and gentle ruler, but loved spending: for example, immediately doubling the state allowances for Muslims. He was wealthy and very attached to his relatives. Unlike the first two Caliphs, Othman allowed senior Muslims to live in other cities, accumulate wealth and influence, and gave access to his relatives and members of his clan to the public treasury. Therefore, he "initiated what is contemporarily called government or management corruption." Most importantly, Ashmawy argued that Othman coined the term "Caliph of God": a term that was not used by his predecessors, but used commonly in the Roman Empire.

Al-Masudi (died 968, pp. 341-357) reported in his second volume of *Muroj Al-thahib* [Prairies of Gold] that Othman was both generous and conspicuous in his spending habits. Once he became a Caliph he built huge castles and owned vast estates. Likewise, he showed nepotism and preferences to his relatives from the Ommeyade clan, especially those who had fought against the Prophet and those who violated Islamic teaching. He positioned them in high places and rewarded them lavishly. In the meantime he isolated, exiled, or punished some of the close followers of the Prophet. Taha Hussein (1999) in *The Great Discontent* argues that on five accounts, Othman clearly violated the precepts instigated by the first two Caliphs: treating the position of Caliph not as a successor of the Prophet but as a God given right, considering the public treasury not as the Muslim treasury, but as God's treasury so he would be responsible not to the people but to God, establishing a new aristocracy in Islam, spending public revenues on his relatives and appointing corrupt officers to run government affairs.

The above accusations incited a hot debate in various parts of the State. Eventually, the debate was transformed into a popular revolt in Iraq, Egypt, and other provinces. The rebels dispatched their representatives to the Capital to negotiate with the Caliph. When the negotiation failed, the rebels killed Caliph Othman. Ali, the first cousin of the Prophet, was elected as

Caliph. His era was characterized by unrest. The newly established Arab aristocracy saw his principled conduct as a threat to their power. In addition, the Ommeyade clan viewed his election as a return of its rival group, the Prophet Mohamed's family, to power. Therefore, both groups initiated revolts against the Caliph under the disguise of avenging Othman's blood. This upheaval and Ali's determination to enforce what he considered people-oriented Islamic principles gave birth to a genuine discourse on what it means to be a Muslim and what denotes the foundation of good government. Unfortunately, this new dynamic was short-lived. Within a few years, Ali was murdered and the chief of the Ommeyade clan, Muawiyah, assumed the power.

The ascendancy of Muawiyah to power inaugurated a new era in Islamic history. Muawiyah was an heir to the legacy of an Arab clan, the Ommeyade, which dominated the political and economic scene in Arabia for many decades. The fortunes of the clan after the birth of Islam were unsettled. Senior members of the clan led by Muawiyah's father Abu Sufian were the major enemy of Islam and led the Quraeshis of Mecca against the Prophet Mohamed. After many attempts, the Muslims, led by the Prophet, defeated them and captured Mecca, Abu Sufian and members of his family, including Muawiyah, pronounced allegiance to Islam. As a brilliant strategist Abu Sufian established an alliance with influential individuals and determined to reacquire, sooner or later, the lost power of his clan. Muawiyah was an experienced politician and a wealthy person. Once he assumed the Caliph's position, he displayed a fierce loyalty to his clan and a strong preference for Arabs over other ethnic Muslim groups. Furthermore, he was a shrewd diplomat and a good listener. In maintaining power, he relied on material rewards to sustain loyalty and submission, but used force and brutality when the first did not work.

Al-Masudi reported in his third volume of *Muroj Al-thahib* that the Ommeyade clan knew that there was no religious or moral justification for their power base. Their interests revolved around power to gain fame and accumulate wealth. They pursued expeditions and traded constantly and energetically and did not invoke religion in asserting their authority. Consequently, they did not encourage religious and intellectual discovery and research, and generally avoided philosophy, logic, and history. They reinstituted pre-Islamic rituals, customs, and beliefs, especially those that ensured submission, loyalty, and tribal rivalry. Mohamed Amara (1988, p. 31) argues that Muawiyah was the first during the Islamic era to promote predestination and compulsion thinking. In fact, the Ommeyade rulers commanded that the people "should not pass judgment on the beliefs of the rulers, governors, and the Empire's employees; discuss their eligibility and qualifications for positions; apply Islamic measures in judging them; debate rulers' oppression and justice; and to delay all that to the hereafter." The decline of Ommeyade, however, facilitated the rise of new thoughts that challenged the official thinking and highlighted the Ommeyade's deficiencies, especially their abuse of Islam and their oppression of the public in general and non-Arabs in particular. This led to public revolt that eventually ended the Ommeyade power (661-750) and brought the Abbasid dynasty to power.

The debate and uproar that contributed to the demise of the Ommeyade dynasty formed the nucleus of the intellectual movement during the Abbasid era. Indeed, the Ommeyade rulers, in their attempt to stifle the intellectual Islamic life, failed to recognize that in a young State, faith and ideology is not easily suppressed. Their actions were strongly resented by the followers of the Prophet and even by the second generation of Muslims. Indeed, the practices of Ommeyade awakened old fears and suspicions in the minds of the faithful concerning the true qualities of those who resisted Islam until the last minute. For example, the saying of Muawiyah that "Land belongs to God and I am the Caliph of God. What I take is mine and what I leave is for the people and it is because of my generosity" (quoted in Ashmawy,1992, p. 132) and that of the fifth Ommeyade Caliph, Abdul Malik, " If any one asks me to obey God, I will cut his neck" and "I do not treat this Muslim nation except by sword, until it submits to me" (quoted in Ashmawy, p. 134) generated a discourse in various parts of the States on the legitimacy of the Caliph, the qualities of leaders, the responsibilities toward God or people, human fate and will, and principled conduct.

Once the Abbasid dynasty was in power, they encouraged discourse on the above matters and viewed intellectual endeavors as essential for building their empire. There were several factors that contributed to the flourishing of intellectual discourse. First, the Abbasid dynasty justified its power on religious grounds and on their blood relation to Prophet Mohamed, just as their rival, Beni Talib, the direct descendant of Caliph Ali and Prophet Mohamed, also based his claim to power on religious grounds. They were intellectually active, established teaching centers in various parts of the State and formulated a clear vision of what a Muslim state should be. So, the Abbasids were obliged to counter their claims theologically and intellectually. They espoused and supported new thoughts and established schools to disseminate information and built foundations ensuring an educated government and religious cadres. The first nine Abbasid Caliphs took pride in hosting philosophers and thinkers and generously rewarded them.

Second, the Empire had expanded, since about 661, to vast new lands in Asia, Africa, and Europe. People in these lands had different experiences and educational legacies. They brought with them their cultural heritages and contrasted them with that of Islam. This made cross-cultural interaction and intellectual dialogue, after the demise of the Ommeyade dynasty, a normal aspect of the government. In fact, various Caliphs supported translations of Greek and other nations' literatures.

Third, the Abbasids relied mostly on non-Arabs to defeat the Ommeyade dynasty. Therefore, they were inclusive in their outlook and promoted non-Arabs to senior positions in managing the empire. Fourth, the Abbasids showed exceptional openness and religious tolerance for non-Muslims in the early decades. This encouraged dialogue and philosophical discourse and broadened the Muslims' perspectives on religious, social, and administrative matters. Fifth, during the Abbasid era, rivals who claimed to be descendants of the Prophet and Imam Ali, the Fatimide (969-1171), gained power in North Africa and established Cairo as their Capital. They displayed a genuine interest in intellectual and philosophical discourse and opened their court to learned people. The Abbasid had to compete with them and counter their message theologically and politically.

2. THE SCHOOLS OF THOUGHT

Consequently, various schools of thought evolved during the Abbasid and Fatimide era. These schools addressed a wide range of issues such as philosophy, politics, religion, economics, psychology, literature, and cultural affairs. That is, these schools debated issues that were of concern to a society that was characterized by diversity, multi-cultural, openness, tolerance, and dynamism. In addition, the early Abbasid era was known for its widespread prosperity and dynamic trade activities across vast regions. Therefore intellectual discourse and intellectuals were highly respected. Intellectuals were generously rewarded, were a privileged class, and held in reverence.

Syed Ameer Ali (1964), in an effort to bring order to this vast body of experience, divides Islamic thought into six schools. Since differing rulers espoused and supported a particular school instead of others, at different times, some of these schools had a profound influence on various political and economic structures in the Islamic and Arab states.

Jabria

This school emphasized compulsion or predestination. The school asserts that man is not responsible for his actions, and that tradition must take precedence over the power of choice. It relies on clearly defined rules and commands obedience to authority. According to this school of thought, a man does not need to use rational arguments, but only needs to follow and accept the leader's instructions. Followers of this school maintain that God creates the conduct of people, good or bad. An extreme version of this school, called *Sifatias* (Attributes), asserts that man has no power, knowledge, or free will. It adheres strictly to the doctrine of predestination in all its pessimism and intensity. The role of the absolute leader who has answers to everything and provides rewards or punishment is glorified. Organization and organizational work-group roles are subordinate to the role of the authority figure.

The Jabria school originated before Islam. Some pre-Islam Arabs were influenced by existing religions (e.g., Judaism, Zoroastrian) and found their unsophisticated *Jabria* principles attractive, appealing, and easy to understand. Therefore, once the four "Rightly Guided" Caliphs' era ended, some Arabs regressed back to the Jabria principles. This was done despite the fact that Prophet Mohamed and his immediate Caliphs preached against predestination. The Prophet was reported to indicate that no one's conduct is the result of fatality: "Every moral agent is furthered to his own conduct." The first Caliph, Abu Baker, when asked to pass judgment on a specific issue stated, "I judge it according to my knowledge. If I am right, it is guidance from God. But if my judgment is wrong; it is because of my mistake and the influence of the devil" (quoted in Amara, 1988, p. 22). Furthermore, Abu Baker strongly advocated that God neither compels nor induces people to do wrong. The fourth successor warned of predestination when he affirmed that God does not compel people to evil or good: "Verily, if you will not guide and warn yourself, none other can direct you," and that if things are predetermined then "there is no need for reward and punishment, the righteous will not be preferred over bad people. This [predestination] is the doctrine of those who worship idols, devil followers, and false witnesses. They are the compulsives of this nation and its Zoroastrians."

The Jabria school ascribes certain attributes to God. Its members reject all doctrines that claim that knowledge comes through reason and that reason enables people to distinguish between what is good and bad or obligatory. The school asserts that people are predestined and that their prosperity, illness and health, death and life are the doings of God. Individuals, however, are responsible for moral good and evil.

Tafwiz

This school emphasizes free will and unqualified discretion in the choice of wrong and right, because rules and regulations constrain human and organizational life. The Tafwiz school advocates that individuals should have absolute freedom in choosing things they consider to be good or bad. The school apparently grew during the Ommeyade Empire and continued through the Abbasid era. The school was an outlet for those who were highly discontented with the affairs of the Muslim nation and the intense conflict among rival groups competing for power. Many intellectuals who were originally members of the fourth school, the *Mutazilas,* espoused this school.

In the organizational context, the school appears to promote a type of arrangement that allows maximum freedom for interaction, networking, and involvement. In this context, there is no clear set of responsibilities and duties. Employees assume different tasks and duties, and collective responsibility is preferred.

Ikhtiar

This school shares the Tafwiz emphasis on free choice, but differs in the beliefs about man's capacity to turn evil into good. Unlike the Tafwiz School, it stresses that Man is at liberty to commit a good or bad deed, to experience pain or joy, and that he is solely responsible for his actions. Man is believed to be a responsible social actor striving to work with the group and to achieve the group goals in a harmonious and cooperative environment. In terms of leadership, this school asserts that a leader must have certain moral and mental qualities and must be elected directly by the community. Imam Ali (598-661), who was brought up by Prophet Mohamed stated (1989, p. 240): "If the presence of the entire people is necessary for the validity of the selection of Caliph, then I swear by my life, there is no way to command such gathering. But those who are eligible should represent those who are absent." Al-Masudi (vol. 2, p.425) reported that just before his death, people approached Imam Ali for approval to vote for his son (Hassan) as Caliph. He informed them, "I neither command nor forbid you what to do. You are capable of making your own decisions." Ali strongly believed that no one's conduct is the result of fatality. In advocating his view, he relied heavily on the Quran and the practices and teachings of the Prophet.

The followers of the *Ikhtiar* school suffered tremendously during the Ommeyade era and during most of the Abbasid's rule. As calamity and misfortune grew, followers of this school, in the later years of the Abbasid era, discarded an important assumption upon which it was founded - the leader ought to be elected by a popular vote (Osborn, 1876). Nevertheless, the school's primary assumptions regarding free will, social and economic justice, and responsibility of the people to change an oppressing ruler have been vehemently sanctioned.

Mutazilas

This is commonly referred to as the rationalistic school. The *Mutazilas* believe that all knowledge must be attained through reason. This school holds that nothing is known to be wrong or right until reason has enlightened us to the distinction and, further, that everything is liable to change or annihilation. As in the Ikhtiar school, the Mutazilas believe that performance is the criterion for reward and punishment. The fundamental principles for Mutazilas are five: divine unity; justice; promis;, position between the two (positions); and propagation of virtue and forbiddance of vice. Unity means God is the creator of everything, He has no human attributes, and He is everywhere and without a beginning or an end. As for justice, it centers on the belief that God does not like corruption and does not create nor induce people to do what they do; it is their own actions. God does not burden human beings, but expects them to do no evil and does not compel any one to engage in any deed. In term of promise, God does not change his instructions and forgives those who have committed sins if they repent. The position between the two indicates that a person who commits a grave fault cannot be called an infidel or a believer, but something in between the two. Avoiding vice and promoting virtue is seen as a duty that each should engage in to ensure justice and minimize corruption.

The Mutazilas suggest that Man is capable of distinguishing between right and wrong. They believe that there is no eternal law pertaining to human actions, that people are the creative efficient of their actions and gain reward and punishment in the hereafter by merit of what they do. The Mutazilas maintain that reason alone tells us what is good or bad and that all knowledge comes through reason. The Mutazilas assert that human desires, inclination, and free will, along with capability, are the foundation for freedom. The school maintains that free will and democracy are prerequisites to action and the prosperity of society. Denial of ability and free will stifles creativity and destroys the soul. The primary measure of right and wrong in any organizational setting is the promotion of welfare and the happiness of its members. In terms of leadership, the Mutazilas assert that any person is qualified to be a leader regardless of race or ethnicity. The leaders, however, should be elected by the community and should have the reputation of being just and faithful.

Ibn-Rushd

The fifth school of thought, advocated by *Ibn-Rushd* (or Averroes, c. ad 1126), holds that actions depend partly on free will and partly on external environmental forces that serve to restrain and/or determine individual and collective actions. The participative democratic process is thought to be the ideal organizational form, and autocracy is believed to open the door to human misery. Ibn-Rushd and his followers recognized that free will and spirited debate lead to productive and creative work, stimulate imagination and makes philosophy and scholarly work accessible to people. More importantly, it teaches truths in a manner that is comprehensible to all people. They considered the ascendancy of the Ommeyade to power to be a setback in the development of a free-thinking and ideal Islamic state. This school believes that perfection can only be attained by study and speculation, not by mere sterile meditation. In addition, women were considered equal in every capacity to men. Ibn-Rushd asserted that there is no contradiction between rationalism and spirituality.

Ikhwan-us-Safa

The sixth and the final school, the *Ikhwan-us-Safa* (Brothers of Purity) arose in the tenth century in response to the oppressive practices of the Jabria school. During the tenth century, liberal-minded thinkers and philosophers were tortured and prosecuted. Nevertheless, a small body of thinkers formed themselves into a brotherhood to hinder the downward course of the Muslims toward ignorance and narrow-mindedness. They established secret organizations across the Islamic nation and used letters as a way to disseminate thought. The school advocated rationalism, self-discipline, and self-control. Ikhwan-us-Safa suggested that because of the dual nature of human beings (material and spirit), the desires and needs are destined to be material (e.g., wealth and related necessities for life) and spiritual (e.g., knowledge and religion). Wealth allows humans to have ample access to enjoyment, food, and drink. Knowledge enlightens and cures the soul, while faith enables humans to meet the aims of the hereafter. The School divided people's behaviors into seven general categories (*Ikhwan-us-Safa*, 1999a, p. 321): craftsmen and professionals; merchants and bankers; landlords, kings, sultans, policy makers, and soldiers; employees, servants and transients; the unemployed, leisure lovers, the permanently ill; and learned people including philosophers and religious jurists. These people all have various qualities, values, behavior, and desires that are shaped by their work, profession, and experience. In terms of ethics, Ikhwan-us-Safa asserts that while some may be innate, the majority is the result of psychological free choices, deep and rationalistic thinking, or spiritual quest. Consequently, they argue that behavior is determined by experience, knowledge, exposure to different people and cultures, profession, and environment.

Ikhwan-us-Safa advocates that human beings are not forced or directed by God to engage in any activity, work, or business. They believe that faith without work and knowledge without practice is futile. They display a strong faith in Man's ability to make progress and control the environment. Furthermore, they insist that human beings can know everything in this world and that ultimately there is an end to everything. It is interesting to note that Ikhwan-us-Safa asserts that people with clear goals normally get results faster than others. Their underlying assumption is that people with goals are more likely to follow the straight path (the shortest), and avoid mistakes and obstacles. To effectively achieve objectives, people should have "vision, a right yardstick, and clear indicators." Although this school contributed to setting high moral standards in commerce and politics, its main contribution was the belief that liberty of intellect is an essential precondition for a creative and healthy society. They believed that corruption and disorder are symptomatic of tyranny.

3.   INFLUENCE AND PROSPECTS

The above schools had a tremendous influence on the way in which states were organized and on the way business and personal transactions were conducted in various parts of the Arab world. For example, the Ommeyade Empire (661-750) subscribed generally to the Jabria school, whereby centralization of government affairs and strict adherence to specified rules were the norm.

The rationalistic view, and the Ikhtiar or Mutazilas forms, prevailed during the reign of the enlightened Abbasid's Caliphs Mamun and Mutasim, and in the Fatimide state. During the Fatimide era (969-1171), the power of the mind, the concept of liberty, and the role of knowledge were promulgated. The increasing influence of non-Arab elements in the Muslim world contributed to the gradual disappearance of this participative approach and to the solidification of traditional or authoritarian forms of government. The defeat of the Arab Caliph and the ascendancy of the non-Arab Ottoman Empire (1412-1918) helped to institutionalize autocracy and furthered the demise of trade association and freely organized business activities in Arab lands. The Turks, historically, have looked upon their chiefs as the direct descendants of God; conversion to Islam did not erase this belief (Ali, 1964). Their adherence to the Jabria school and its associated fanaticism influenced the theological perspective of the Muslims during the Ottoman Empire.

Just after the Muslims gained their independence in the twentieth century, they established similar authoritarian regimes in the new nation-state (e.g., Algeria, Iraq, Morocco, Pakistan, Saudi Arabia, Syria, Tunisia). Independent thinking, concepts of liberty, and power of mind were condemned, and Jabria principles were sanctioned in every aspect of life.

The above schools, except the Jabria and Ikhtiar, have become part of history. Some of the newly established nation-states have discouraged innovation and creativity and fear freedom of information. Single-minded thought is advanced to serve the goals of each regime. Muslim and Arab governments, both the conservative and self-proclaimed progressives, exploit the influence of Islam on the life of population. Religious figures (e.g., sheikhs or mullahs) have been recruited and appointed as mosques functionaries, teachers, and judges. They are given titles and lucrative salaries, and many have become paid employees of the state bureaucracy. They exist to legitimize and justify the power of unjust rulers. Their roles vary slightly from one state to another, but their function remains the same. In Saudi Arabia, they play very vital roles and have been integrated in daily functions of government (e.g., approving new laws, advising, and participating in official ceremonies). On the other hand, in Egypt and Iraq, their roles are highly regulated and the government makes sure they do not exceed their prescribed limits. In Iran, the Ikhtiar and rationalistic schools gained tremendous influence after the Iranian Revolution in 1979. The Iraqi invasion of Iran in 1980 and credible foreign threats to national security have since created a political and social environment that distrusts openness and progressive views. Consequently, new measures have been established under the disguise of risks to national security. These measures have constituted constraints to individual liberty and have helped to strengthen political and social views that may not be consistent with the principles that were cherished by the Founding Fathers of the Ikhtiar school.

The close of the twentieth century was full of setbacks and tragedies that distracted the attention of the learned and ordinary Muslims and that kept them from tackling issues that were vital for economic and organizational development. Indeed, in the last century, Muslim countries witnessed a decline in human growth and prosperity relative to the rest of the world. Revivalism movements in many parts of the Islamic world have been in retreat and the voices of Jabria are on the rise. For example, the *UN Arab Human Development Report 2002* indicates that the Arab countries, relative to other countries, have experienced a restriction of basic freedoms. The

Report states (p. 2), "This freedom deficit undermines human development and is one of the most painful manifestations of the lagging political development. . . . Freedom of expression and association are frequently curtailed. Obsolete norms of legitimacy prevail."

The dawn of the new millennium is not expected to be better under the existing political and economic conditions. The Muslim people face formidable challenges. These cannot be overcome if Muslim people fail to espouse openness, tolerance, and creative approaches in all aspects of life, especially in the area of politics and economics. However, it is still possible to nurture the spirit that guided Muslims during their golden age through genuine commitment to simple principles and views (e.g., social and economic justice, egalitarianism, tolerance) that have been the hallmarks of the Islamic civilization.

4.   CONCLUSION

Six conclusions can be drawn from the proceeding discussion. First, in the early days of the rise of Islam, ideology was highly influential and people expected society to be managed according to agreed upon principles. During the Prophet's era people experienced an enthusiasm and fierce loyalty to the Prophet and his message. As the state evolved and geographically expanded during the era of the Rightly-Guided Caliphs, typical matters were solved directly by the Caliph and his representatives. New and innovative issues were referred to a council that assisted the Caliph.   If the Caliph was perceived not to treat matters according to established standards, the people warned him and if he did not rethink polices and actions, people directly removed him.

Second, economic prosperity is not a substitute for freedom and political inclusion. During the Ommeyade Empire, economic prosperity, trade growth, and wealth accumulation were widespread. The rulers, however, treated the public treasury as their own, gave preference to Arabs over non-Arabs, demanded obedience, promoted rivalry among Arab tribes, and discounted spirited dialogue and the power of mind. Devotion to faith, among rulers, was absent and spiritual endeavors had an intense hold upon the people's minds. People, despite their relative economic prosperity, resented brutality and what they perceived was a deviation from Islamic conduct. The Ommeyade rulers failed to recognize the significance of leader legitimacy and that the use of force could and did ultimately lead to their demise.

Third, the geographic expansion of the state fostered the spread of Islam among many nations. Most of the newcomers were from well-established civilizations (e.g., Iranian, India). Their adoption of Islam stemmed from a deep conviction. They reached a conclusion that Ommeyade rulers were arrogant, corrupt and illegitimate (Ashmawy, 1992). Therefore, they resorted to Islamic reasoning and traditional channels (e.g., official complains, religious sermons, etc.) to convey their message. When these attempts failed, they cooperated and supported openly those with claims against the Ommeyade Empire.

Fourth, the newcomers were active in theological, philosophical, and scientific inquires. These activities stimulated Arabs to participate actively in matters beyond military, aesthetic, and religious matters. Consequently, debate and spirited discourse flourished across the Empire.

Fifth, the Ommeyade's heavy-handed policies and their aversion to knowledge and intellectual inquiries accelerated populist resentments and the Ommeyade's eventual demise. That is, the Ommeyade' experience demonstrated that blind and brutal policies may appear to be effective in the short term and may give the impression of control and confidence, but they have devastating consequences.

Sixth, the rise of the schools of thought was stimulated by ethnic diversity, cross-cultural interaction, social dynamism, the flourishing of trade, and the rulers' need for ideological justification and legitimacy. These schools shaped business, cultural, and political affairs.

4. Islamic Work Ethic and Values

The issue of work ethics and value systems associated with work has captured the attention of scholars for the last seven decades. Most discussions about these topics have been concerned with Judeo-Christian contributions and, to a large extent, have been carried out in Western countries. Despite the fact that many other religious and ethnic groups have achieved prosperity and tremendous economic advancement during part of their history, their contributions have been almost totally ignored in management literature. The Islamic view of work and ethical considerations have either been misunderstood or not widely studied in the field of organization studies. This chapter provides insights into the Islamic Work Ethic and the underlying assumptions for personal value systems. The emphasis will be on the meaning of work and organization in early Islamic teaching.

1. ISLAM AND WORK

The Quranic principles and the Prophet's prescriptions serve as a guide for Muslims when conducting both their business and their family affairs. The Quran instructs Muslims to persistently pursue whatever work is available whenever it is available.   The Quran states, "He [God] has also made subservient to you all that is in the heavens and the earth" (Quran, 45:13). Interestingly, the Quran (2: 68), with foresight, views poverty as the promise of the Devil, and prosperity as the promise of God, "The Devil threatens you with poverty and bids you to conduct unseemly. God promised you His forgiveness and bounties." The Prophet Mohammed not only preached that hard work caused sins to be absolved and that "no one eats better food than that which he eats out of his work" but also asserted that "work is a worship." Similarly Imam Ali, the fourth successor of Prophet Mohammed, (ad 598-661, p. 483) stated, "Persist in your action with a noble end in mind. . . Failure to perfect your work while you are sure of the reward is injustice to yourself" adding, "poverty almost amounts to impiety."

The elevated status of merchants and their trade in Arab-Islamic thinking is reflected in the Prophet Mohammed's saying, "He who brings supplies to our market is like a warrior in the war for God," and "the truthful, honest merchant is with the prophets and the truthful ones and the martyrs" (quoted in M. M. Ali, 1977). Likewise, Imam Ali (1989, ad 598-661) in his letter to the Governor of Egypt highlighted the exceptional role and function that merchants play in sustaining the welfare and prosperity of a nation. He asserted that even though tax collectors, judges, administrators, government agents, and soldiers play a vital role in the state, none of them, however (p.315), "can do without traders and craftsmen who build and maintain facilities and markets, a task which they themselves [state employees] are unable to perform."

This view contrasted with the beliefs that prevailed among other civilizations prospering before or after the Islamic empire. For example, Dessler (1986, p. 15) points out that in ancient Greece "Business in general, and money-lending in particular, were. . . carried out by slaves and less-than-respected citizens; manual workers and merchants, in fact, were not permitted citizenship in the Greek democracy." Likewise, the European peoples regarded business as a degrading occupation. Adam Smith, in the *Wealth of the Nations* (published in 1776), indicated that businessmen are "an order of men, whose interest is never the same with that of the public, who have generally an interest to deceive and even to oppress the public and who accordingly have, upon many occasions, both deceived and oppressed it" (quoted in Koontz, O'Donnell and Weihrich, 1980, p. 31).

Islam emerged in Arabia when the community in Mecca was thriving commercially, socially, and intellectually. Trade was the means that enabled members of the Quraesh tribe to achieve prestige and influence. The Quraesh elite accumulated wealth by controlling trade and trade centers. Since there was no central authority and since Arabia, in general, was not under the control of any of the neighboring empires, the Quraeshi merchants assumed a military role and leadership in accordance with their wealth and economic fortune. The Prophet Mohamed was a member of the Hashimi clan of Quraesh. The clan positioned itself culturally and religiously as the leading entity in Meccan and Arabian affairs. Its members acquired fame as wise and generous people. Their involvement in trade, however, never resembled their rival clan, the Ommeyade, in Mecca. Long before receiving the revelation, the Prophet Mohamed was engaged in trade representing a Quraeshi woman called Khadija whom he later married. The majority of the merchant classes, especially those from the Ommeyade clan, initially rejected the Islamic faith. Primarily, they considered the new faith a threat to their established power and a destabilizing factor. Years later, most of the merchants in Mecca adopted Islam. Many of them participated in early Muslim expeditions to Syria and surrounding regions. Despite their outstanding achievements in war, their favorite craft remained trade. As years went by and Islam took root in Arabia and nearby countries, senior members of the "merchant warrior" class transformed themselves into a new aristocracy. This new aristocracy was outward-looking and, unlike the pre-Islamic Quraeshi aristocracy, was ambitious politically and economically. In general, members of the "merchant warrior" class prided themselves in promoting trade, protecting trade routes and reviving agriculture and industries. In their quest to pursue their trade interest, this class of "merchant warrior" was able, in a short period, to integrate the Arab world and transform it into a center for international trade between Asia, Europe, and Africa. Remarkably, this class managed to blend Persian and Byzantium skills and knowledge and build a comparatively high sophisticated system of trade and finance. In fact, during the first centuries of Islam there was enormous ethical, artistic and industrial inventiveness and expansion. Consequently, the Arab financial and commercial sectors were sophisticated relative to other societies (Rodinson, 1974; Turner, 1981). The ascendancy of the Ommeyade dynasty (661-750) to power witnessed the ultimate transformation, when some members of the "merchant warrior" class became the "merchant rulers." During their era, they supported and encouraged trade. The dynasty aggressively lured Arabs into the army and relatively extended their tribal loyalty to national loyalty in an attempt to capture new regions (e.g., Africa, Spain, South Asia). They used material rewards and ideology (Arab solidarity) in the service of their economic and military expansion goals (Abdel-Rahman, 1989). Gradually, a form of partnership evolved between the state and the merchants. This partnership continued until the late years of the Abbasid Empire.

2.   THE ISLAMIC WORK ETHIC

The Islamic Work Ethic (IWE) is an orientation that has had a tremendous influence on the Islamic people and its organizations. It implies that work is a virtue in light of a person's needs, and is a necessity for establishing equilibrium in one's individual and social life (Nasr, 1984). It stands not for life denial, but for life fulfillment and holds business motives in the highest regard (Ahmad, 1976). IWE views work as a means to further self-interest economically, socially and psychologically, to sustain social prestige, to advance societal welfare, and reaffirm faith. The concept has its origin in the Quran and the sayings and practice of the Prophet Mohammed. The centrality of work and deed in Islamic thinking is succinctly addressed in the Quran (6:132): "To all are ranks according to their deeds." As such it is work and commitment that enable people to realize their goal (Quran 53: 39); "Human being can have nothing but what they strive for." The Quran, specifically and clearly prohibits dishonesty in business dealings (17:35; 27:9; 2:188; 9:34; respectively): "Give a full measure when you measure out and weigh with a fair balance;" "So establish weight with justice and fall not short in the balance;" and "do not swallow up your property among yourselves by wrongful means, neither seek to gain access thereby to the authorities that ye may swallow up a portion of property of people wrongfully while ye know." Furthermore, the Quran clearly promotes commerce and forbids usury and monopoly (2:275; 25:67; respectively): "God hath decreed trade lawful and hath forbidden usury;" "Those who, when spending, are not extravagant and not niggardly, but hold a just (balance) between those (extremes)," and "Those who hoard gold and silver and spend not in the way of God: announce unto them a most grievous chastisement."

The Prophet Mohamed who, both deliberately and extensively, addressed issues related to work and business set out the above instructions. His directives were numerous and innovatively challenged the existing practices. In this chapter, I call attention to sayings that directly address work ethics. These are grouped as follow:

1. *Pursuing legitimate business* Prophet Mohamed explicitly instructed followers that useful work is that which benefits others and society. Subsequently, those who work hard are acknowledged and are rewarded. He stated "Worshiping has seventy avenues; the best of them is the involvement in an honestly earned living." That is, work is the best form of worshiping. He elevated people and their work to the highest rank if their deeds benefited people, "The best work is the one that results in benefit" and "The best of people are those who benefit others."

2. *Wealth must be earned* In Islamic faith, it is acknowledged that people have different capacities. It is these capacities and existing opportunities that enable them to acquire wealth. Pursuing economic activities, however, must be based on moral and legitimate foundations. The Quran states (4:29-32): "Oh ye believers! Devour not each other's property among yourselves unlawfully save that by trading by mutual consent; and kill not your (*own*) selves; Verily, God is Merciful unto you. And whoever shall do this in aggression and injustice, soon shall We cast him into the (*Hell*) fire; for this is (*very*) easy for God. If ye avoid the great sins which ye are forbidden, We will expiate from your (*smaller*) misdeeds, and We will admit you (*to Paradise*) an honorable (*place of*) entry (*it is indeed*). And covet not that by which God hath raised some of you above others; for men shall have of what they earn;

and for women shall have of what they earn; and ask God of His Grace; Verily, God is in the Know of all things."

3.   *Quality of work* The pre-Islam Arabs lacked discipline and their commitment mostly revolved around a primary group. Mohamed understood this fact as a statesman and reformer and he attempted to transform the Arab communities into a functional society. His emphasis on discipline and commitment intended not only to highlight the essence of work, but also to draw a link between faith and work and to eventually steer the Muslim community towards becoming an economically and politically viable entity. In this context, he reiterated, "God blesses a person who perfects his craft (does the job right)" and "God loves a person who learns precisely how to perform his work and does it right."

4.   *Wages* Prophet Mohamed instructed Muslims to be fair and just and prompt in compensating workers. He declared, "One must give a worker his wage before his sweat dries (should be given on time)" and "your wage should be based on your effort and spending." That is, payment for wages should be timely, fair, and adequate. In fact, the Prophet considered denying a worker his/her full wage to be an immoral act. He was quoted saying that he would personally plead against, "He who received work from a laborer and did not pay him in full."

5.   *Reliance on self* One of the most important functions of work is that it sustains confidence and self-reliance. Mohamed stated, "No one eats better food than that which he eats out of the work of his hand" and "No earnings are better than that of one's own effort."

6.   *Monopoly* In Islam, monopoly is considered a great fault that produces pain, unlawful profit, and ensures inequality. Prophet Mohamed, therefore, forbade it stating, "The supplier is blessed and the monopolist is cursed" and "whoever withholds commodities, is a sinner."

7.   *Bribery* Like monopoly and cheating, bribery is strongly condemned in Islam. Mohamed declared, "God cursed the one who gives and the one who receives bribery."

8.   *Deeds and intentions* These constitute significant pillars in the IWE. They clearly differentiate the IWE from the work ethics of other faiths. One of the fundamental assumptions in Islam is that intention rather than result is the criterion upon which work is evaluated in terms of benefit to community. Any activity that is perceived to do harm, even though it results in significant wealth to those who undertake it, is considered unlawful. Prophet Mohamed stated, "God does not look at your matters [shapes or forms] and wealth, rather God examines your intentions and actions."

9. *Transparency* Business and work in general have to rest on ethical and moral foundations. The precondition for propagating and realizing this goal is transparency. It was reported that Prophet Mohamed once inspected a bin for dates and found that those that were not good were hidden underneath the fresh dates. The prophet ordered the merchant to differentiate between the quality of the dates saying, "He who cheated us is not one of us" and if buyers and sellers "conceal and tell lies, the blessing of their transaction shall be obliterated." His saying "Those who declare things frankly, will not lead to each other destruction" underlies the significant of transparency in any business transaction, and the necessity for enhancing trust and reducing problems in the marketplace.

10. *Greed* In Islam, greed is considered a threat to social and economic justice. The Prophet Mohamed in his struggle against the elite of Mecca consistently and tirelessly criticized their greediness. He stated, "Be aware of greediness; it is the living poverty" and "Two qualities are not found in a believer: greediness and immorality."

11. *Generosity* Generosity is a virtue in Islam. The Prophet Mohamed incorporated this pre-Islamic Arab virtue in his teachings and his conduct. He declared, "The generous person is closest to God, heaven, people and far from hell" and "He who removes a distress, God blesses in this world and the hereafter."

3. THE PILLARS OF IWE

Generally, the IWE is built on four primary concepts: effort, competition, transparency, and morally responsible conduct. Collectively, they imply that conducting business with minimum or no restrictions and in a spirited environment will, essentially, result in higher performance and widespread prosperity. Effort is seen as the necessary ingredient for serving self and society. That is, productive involvement minimizes social and economic problems, while allowing a person to obtain reasonable living standards for self and family. What is significantly important is that effort in Islam is held in the highest regard. The Second Caliph, Omar, was quoted saying, "I would prefer dying while struggling for my sustenance and the sustenance of my children, to dying while fighting in the defense of faith (quoted in Abdul-Rauf, 1984, p. 23) and "The strength of any deed, is not to postpone today's work to tomorrow." The Fourth Caliph, Imam Ali (1989, p. 469), stated, "'Do not be one of those who hope for a better world to come without working for it "and" He, who does not perfect his/her work, will bring confusion to self.'" Individuals must compete fairly and honestly and trade with good intentions.

The Quran (4:29) declares, " Do not divide your property among yourselves falsely except that it be trading by mutual consent." Prophet Mohamed was very clear that trade should be conducted without limitations that may obstruct prosperity. He stated, "Why do you restrain your brother from that which will benefit him and is also profitable to you?" Transparency is based on mutual understanding that faulty conduct and acts of deception obstruct justice and limit freedom of action in the marketplace. Morally based conduct is an essential precondition for sustaining a prosperous economy and a vital business community. Nasr (1984) asserts that Islam provides a climate of work within which the ethical is not separated from the economic. He argues (p. 35) that Islam bestows "an ethical dimension on all kinds of work and in extending the ethical to include even the qualitative aspect of the work in question."

The simultaneous presence of the above four concepts ensures a balanced benefit to the individual and the community. This is accentuated in the Quran (62:10): "Disperse abroad in the land and seek of God's bounty." Effort and competition have to be conducted in such a way as not to inflict any intentional damage on others. Those who conduct their business in a morally acceptable manner are held in high esteem. The Quran (49:13) states, "The noblest of you in the sight of God is the best of you in conduct."

This concept of morally responsible business conduct represented at that time a major breakthrough in the world of trade. At that time, merchants and producers had no guidelines and no ethical standards to rely on. Mohamed profoundly altered that culture and insisted on moral conduct not only as a means for profitable business, but also as a foundation for salvation. He stated, "The truthful, honest merchant is with the prophets and the truthful ones and the martyrs." Mohamed seemed to recognize that a business could not flourish in an environment that is characterized by abuse and unethical behavior. This recognition prompted him to declare two essential foundations for fair competitive environment: "Religion is found in the way of dealing with other people" and "He who cheated us is not from us." In the context of these two pillars, he strongly rejected the concept "Buyer bewares." The underlying assumption of this concept implies that deceiving is not only a possibility, but a fact of market condition. It further shifts the responsibility of inspection from the producer/supplier to the buyer or customer. Therefore, the concept entails a hidden cost and creates formidable obstacles to free and fair market practice. In fact, the concept conveys that a competitive environment is subject to corruption and abuse. Consequently, the outcome is a mistrust of market institutions.

The introduction of transparency and honesty in the marketplace highlight two things: the importance of character and credibility of those involved in sustaining market stability and that the prosperity of business people, both as individuals and as a group, is interwoven. That is, the moral stance of business people is the only credible assurance for minimizing or preventing market scandals, abuses, and disruption. Only moral and honest conduct inspires confidence in the market and reinforces social contract, ethical understanding, and motivates market actors to focus on meeting their primary business responsibilities. Hence, partners, clients, competitors, and customers acquire faith in each other's good intentions.

4. THE IWE IN PRACTICE

As was indicated, the IWE flourished during the golden age of Islam. The defeat of the Arab Caliph and the ascendancy of the non-Arab Ottoman Empire (1412-1918), however, helped to institutionalize autocracy and further the demise of trade associations and freely organized business activities in Arab/Islamic lands (Ali, 1990). Turner (1981) argues that Islamic stagnation and the servile imitation of traditions were the inevitable consequences of Turkish military absolutism. In order to maximize their control over the Islamic *umma* [nation], the Turks encouraged a conservative theology of strict obedience to authority. Intellectual pursuits and formal schooling were prohibited and Jabria principles were advanced. With the absence of written communication, the lack of knowledge of general Islamic principles, and the isolation of Muslims in different parts of the world, many Muslim people adopted various foreign rituals and legends as their own. The supremacy of Western colonial powers over the Arab/Islamic lands, especially after the breakdown of the Ottoman Empire, further reinforced cultural discontinuity and alienation. For example, even though the Western powers allowed schools to open in various Muslim countries in the first decades of the twentieth century, they established authoritarian regimes and attempted to replace the Arabic language with French or English in the Arab world and in other non-Arab countries. Attempts were made to replace the Arab alphabet with the Latin one. In fact, in Morocco, Tunisia, and Algeria, the French colonial power forced its language on the indigenous people. After independence, the new governments did not make serious attempts to revise the colonial legacy, and the French language is still used for instruction at university level and in the workplace.

It is important to note that the dominant features of the IWE are contained in all Islamic schools of thought, except in the Jabria school. In its spirit and meaning, the IWE stands in contrast to the teaching of the Jabria school which is currently sanctioned by existing Arab/Islamic governments. Since the Iranian revolution, however, a cultural awakening has spread throughout the Islamic countries, and many groups and associations have been established to advocate cultural revivalism. The IWE, thus, appears to attract many segments of the population, not only for cultural reasons but because the IWE encourages the individual to better him/herself and to strive for economic prosperity. Despite the emphasis on work ethics in Islamic literature, there had been no scholarly attempt to construct a contemporary IWE until Ali (1988) embarked on a mission to develop and scale an IWE. The development of an Islamic Work Ethic scale was achieved in three phases. The first phase included a search of the literature pertaining to the IWE. The IWE has a wide range of components and is viewed differently by scholars belonging to various Islamic schools of thought. Nevertheless, all Islamic schools of thought sanction the necessity of work. The work of Islamic and Arab scholars (e.g., Abdul-Rauf, 1984; Alaki, 1979; Ali, 1986/87; Almaney, 1981; Al-Sadr, 1983; Baali and Wardi, 1981; Boase, 1985; Elkholy, 1984; Faridi, 1985; Hawi, 1982; Nabi, 1982; Nagvi, 1981; Nasr, 1984; Yahfoyfi, 1982) was used to develop the conceptual framework that would structure the IWE scale. Fifty-five statements were assembled. These statements capture unique assumptions and attitudes toward work and interpersonal relationships. They are briefly described below.

Work is an obligatory activity and a virtue in light of the needs of Man and the necessity to establish equilibrium in one's individual and social life. Work enables Man to be independent and is a source of self-respect, satisfaction, and fulfillment. Success and progress on the job depends on hard work and commitment to one's job. Commitment to work also involves a desire to improve the community and societal welfare. Society would have fewer problems if each person were committed to their work and avoided unethical methods of wealth accumulation. Creative work and cooperation are not only a source of happiness, but are considered noble deeds as well.

The second phase was a refinement of the initial statements by selected scholars in Islamic and Arab culture. Six scholars of various backgrounds and national origins in the United States participated in the refinement stage. They were chosen because of their scholarly activities or religious responsibility (e.g., the Imam of a major mosque). They were asked to examine whether all statements were relevant to an IWE and to omit or modify statements as needed. Received comments and suggestions were incorporated, and finally 46 statements were approved by the panel. These were used in the final form of the construct.

In the third phase, about 250 questionnaires were sent to Arab (all Muslims) students attending five major universities in the United States. A covering letter indicated that the purpose of the questionnaire was to identify personal beliefs about work in Islamic/Arab states. Respondents rated the importance of each statement on a five-point scale ranging from *strongly disagree* to *strongly agree*. A total of 150 questionnaires were returned, a response rate of 60 per cent. Among the participants, 86 per cent had worked in their home countries and 28 per cent were working in the United States. Those who had worked in their home countries were on study leave from work.   Table 4.1 shows the mean and item-total correlation for each statement. The data indicates that participants scored high ($M = 4.26$) on the IWE scale. In addition, all items except items 3, 26, and 41 correlate positively with one another and have high mean concentrations, thus indicating that they are appropriate items (Nunnally, 1967).

Table 4.1   Item-total correlations and means of Islamic work ethic

Item	Islamic Work Ethic	*M*	Item-total correlation
1.	Cooperation is a virtue in work	4.83	0.36
2.	Laziness is a vice	4.60	0.35
3.	Dedication to work is a virtue	4.93	0.05
4.	Money earned through gambling, selling intoxicants, manipulative monopoly, bribery, and the like are harmful to society	4.29	0.20
5.	One should take community affairs into consideration in his/her work	4.65	0.37
6.	The state should provide work for everyone willing and able to work	4.37	0.28
7.	One should not be denied his/her full wages	4.44	0.20
8.	One should strive to achieve better results	4.57	0.50
9.	Good work benefits both one's self and others	4.44	0.50
10.	Justice and generosity in the workplace are necessary conditions for society's welfare	4.63	0.44
11.	Cooperation provides satisfaction and benefits society	4.60	0.45
12.	Competition to improve quality should be encouraged and rewarded	4.52	0.41
13.	Constant struggle for the actualization of ideals and adherence to work values guarantees success	4.48	0.63
14.	Our society would have fewer problems if each person was committed to his/her work and avoided its hazards	3.97	0.45
15.	One must participate in economic activities	4.05	0.44
16.	Work should be done with sufficient activities	4.54	0.57
17.	Producing more than enough to meet one's personal needs contributes to the prosperity of society as a whole	4.31	0.44
18.	Work is an obligatory activity for every capable individual	4.66	0.42

Item	Islamic Work Ethic	*M*	Item-total correlation
19.	Gambling is harmful to society	4.28	0.47
20.	He who does not work is not a useful member of society	3.94	0.40
21.	One should carry work out to the best of his/her ability	4.71	0.48
22.	A person can overcome difficulties in life and better him/herself by doing his/her job well	4.45	0.65
23.	Work is not an end in itself, but a means to foster personal growth and social relations	4.26	0.41
24.	Hard work is a virtue in light of the needs of Man and the necessity to establish equilibrium in one's individual and social life	4.35	0.45
25.	Work is not a source of satisfaction or self-fulfillment[a]	4.25	0.46
26.	One should spend most of his/her time working[a]	2.61	-0.33
27.	Life has no meaning without work	4.24	0.48
28.	More leisure time is good for society[a]	3.65	0.45
29.	Work for its own sake stifles an individual's life	3.69	0.34
30.	Human relations in organizations should be emphasized and encouraged	4.12	0.29
31.	Work does not enable Man to control nature[a]	4.03	0.46
32.	Exploitation in work is not praiseworthy	4.44	0.42
33.	Creative work is a source of happiness and accomplishment	4.51	0.45
34.	Any person who works is more likely to get ahead in life	4.21	0.44
35.	Those who do not work hard often fail in life	3.68	0.49
36.	Work gives one the chance to be independent	4.46	0.47
37.	Work is a source of self-respect	4.46	0.45
38.	Carelessness is unhealthy to one's welfare	4.12	0.47
39.	More leisure time is bad for individuals and society	3.86	0.56
40.	A successful person is the one who meets deadlines at work	4.38	0.54
41.	Hard work does not guarantee success	3.04	-0.01
42.	One should constantly work hard to meet responsibilities	4.52	0.40

Item	Islamic Work Ethic	M	Item-total correlation
43.	Progress on the job can be obtained through self-reliance	4.24	0.37
44.	Devotion to quality work is a virtue	4.58	0.46
45.	Consultation allows one to overcome obstacles and avoid mistakes	4.66	0.46
46.	The value of work is derived from the accompanying intention, rather than its results	3.36	0.20

Note: [a.] Scoring reversed.

Source: Based on Ali (1988).

In a survey using a short version of the IWE in several Muslim countries, it was found that managers scored highly as well on the IWE. The overall mean of the IWE in Arabia is 4.16 (five-point scale), the UAE is 4.26, and Kuwait is 4.32; all are relatively high (see Table 4.2).

Table 4.2   Means of Islamic work ethic in Arabia, the UAE, and Kuwait

		Arabia	UAE	Kuwait
		N = 117	N = 163	N = 762
1.	Laziness is a vice	4.66	4.53	4.57
2.	Dedication to work is a virtue	4.62	4.66	4.72
3.	Good work benefits both one's self and others	4.57	4.59	4.74
4.	Justice and generosity in the workplace are necessary conditions for society's welfare	4.59	4.60	4.57
5.	Producing more than enough to meet one's personal needs contributes to the prosperity of society as a whole	3.71	4.23	4.62
6.	One should carry work out to the best of one's ability	4.7	4.68	4.72
7.	Work is not an end in itself but a means to foster personal growth and social relations	3.97	4.01	4.15
8.	Life has no meaning without work	4.47	4.54	4.46
9.	More leisure time is good for society *	3.08	2.76	2.48
10.	Human relations in organizations should be emphasized and encouraged	3.89	4.00	4.64
11.	Work enables Man to control nature	4.06	4.18	4.17

	Arabia	UAE	Kuwait
12. Creative work is a source of happiness and accomplishment	4.60	4.60	4.70
13. Any person who works is more likely to get ahead in life	3.92	4.14	4.01
14. Work gives one the chance to be independent	4.35	4.45	4.48
15. A successful person is the one who meets deadlines at work	4.17	4.43	4.26
16. One should constantly work hard to meet responsibilities	4.25	4.44	4.51
17. The value of work is derived from the accompanying intention rather than its results	3.16	3.65	3.77

Note: [a] scoring revised

Source: Based on Ali (1992), Ali and Azim (1999), and Ali and Al-kazemi (2002).

There are various implications for the strong commitment to the IWE among Muslim managers. First, there is an emphasis on hard work, meeting deadlines and persistence. This means that in introducing change, the establishment of a timetable and clarification of goals and responsibilities are essential in carrying out a successful intervention. Second, work is viewed not as end in itself, but as a means to foster personal growth and social relations. In this context, group interactions and team activities, if designed appropriately, could result in optimal facilitation of intended changes. Third, dedication to work and work creativity are seen as virtuous. Managers and consultants should focus their process design on the new method of change and on producing results that reinforce existing commitment and enthusiasm. Fourth, justice and generosity in the workplace are necessary conditions for society's welfare. This has three implications: (1) managers/consultants must show that they are attentive to and are concerned about human needs; when considering firing employees for example, they may consider factors other than performance before a decision is made; (2) social skills and mastering public relations are essential to effect change in a successful intervention. In a highly personalized society, once a commitment is obtained there will be smooth implementation; and (3) goals for change are directed toward serving the community or the society as a whole; that is the managers should assert the fruits of the results to the organization and society. Fifth, business transparency is not only a good practice, but also a virtue. It inspires confidence in and sustains market proper functions. Finally, unlike the Judeo-Christian ethic, the IWE places more emphasis on intentions than on results. The Prophet Mohammed stated, "Actions are recorded according to intention, and man will be rewarded or punished accordingly." That is, unlawful work that results in accumulation of wealth (e.g., gambling, prostitution, drug trafficking, deceiving, extortion, hoarding, monopoly) is condemned and those who engage in it are looked upon with contempt.

5. VALUES AND ETHICS

Values provide a major key to the understanding of social and personal change. Human values have considerable influence on the way people behave and conduct their affairs. Evidence indicates that values are related to such practical concerns as strategic decision-making and action, innovation, creativity, commitment and loyalty, managerial satisfaction, and organizational effectiveness and competitiveness. These concerns are not only important in an organizational setting, but are also necessary for understanding national differences and cross-cultural interactions. Studying work values is thus not merely an academic diversion it is a practical endeavor.

Traditionally, philosophers have viewed values in terms of desirability. Sociologists, economists, and management scholars, on the other hand, tend to define values as preferences. Guth and Tagiuri (1965, pp. 124-125) define values as:

> . . . a conception, explicit or implicit, of what an individual or a group regards as desirable, and in terms of which he or they select from among alternative available modes, the means and ends of action.

Hofstede (1981, p. 19) states that values are "a broad tendency to prefer certain states of affairs over others." These broad tendencies are ranked hierarchically according to their relative importance. This hierarchy of values is called a value system (Ali, 1982). Value systems and analysis help individuals to establish priorities, to resolve competing interests, and help in making choices.

Values are determinants of virtually all kinds of human behaviors, social actions, attitudes, ideologies, norms and evaluations, and relationships with others (Rokeach, 1973). Often, however, scholars have confused values with other related terms (e.g., attitudes, beliefs, needs, and norms). This point requires a brief discussion. For example, attitudes constitute the cognitive affective motivational structure of an individual formed through interactions with the environment. Attitudes are derived from social values (Sherif, 1979). Rokeach (1979) distinguishes between values and attitudes.

Values differ from attitudes not in quality, but in depth. Values are determinants rather than the components of attitudes and attitudes are biases while values are metabiases. An individual has reason on many occasions to conceal attitudes, but less reason to conceal values. Beliefs are assumptions about the world around us. They differ from values as there are more beliefs than values. Beliefs are related to what is expected and what is possible, but what is expected may not correspond to what is "desirable" (values). In addition, many beliefs can be labeled as "true or false," but it is difficult to talk about values as "true or false" (Rokeach, 1979).

Maslow (1959) equates values with needs. Needs, however, are not synonymous with values. Whether or not values correspond with needs, it is values which regulate actions and determine emotional responses (Kalleberg, 1977). Rokeach (1973) argues that in the long run, values give expression to basic human needs. He emphasizes that values represent societal and institutional demands and that they constitute a representation and transformation of needs. Unlike needs, values do not dominate behavior in a compelling manner, and a wide range of behaviors can satisfy them.

The distinction between norms and values is not always clear. Values are general and explicit, while norms are specific and tacit (Vickers, 1973). Norms specifically spell out the given actions of an individual and include quite specific demands and prescriptions. Values, on the other hand, do not specifically define an individual's course of action, rather they point to the end states of existence. Afanasev (1979) argues that values and norms share some similarities. First, they regulate people's attitudes toward society and one another, as well as social relations. Second, both make it possible to coordinate the behavior of the individual with the functioning of the society.

Values are often used interchangeably with ethics. Ethics, however, are part of moral and religious doctrines; they address issues of right and wrong. Values are not doctrines, but they do have moral aspects (Mindell and Gorden, 1981). Ethics, nevertheless, are the application of values to human actions and behaviors. In business and political conduct, ethics have often been put forward to question the moral dimensions of personal values. That is, ethics are the principles by which human values are ordered and arranged (Cooper, 1979).

Finally, values and knowledge are interrelated. Knowledge provides individuals with a means to behave appropriately. Thus, knowledge is an aspect of value; an appropriate mode of conduct. Both determine individuals' attitudes toward an object. Without some knowledge it would be difficult to formulate opinion and action. Knowledge by itself, however, cannot be a factor that regulates individual behaviors. To play such a role, knowledge must be assimilated and embodied in the goals of individual behavior. Only after an individual recognizes specific truth in knowledge, and it becomes his/her conviction, can knowledge act as a means to regulate activity (Afansev, 1979).

6. ISLAMIC VALUES AND THE WORKPLACE

Scholars who addressed Islamic values present a wide range of normative and desirable values that have been stressed in the Quran and by the Prophet Mohamed. Like other religions, Islam covers spiritual issues and moral and specific injunctions relative to conduct. Unlike most religions, Islam tenets and instructions have been clear on matters of social and economic behavior. Nevertheless, these instructions have not been translated into operational organizational measures. This has left the discourse on Islamic values in the workplace to speculation and generalization.

To gain a better understanding of values for working in Islamic countries and to grasp an approximation of the cultural and social reality in Islamic setting, an overview of values for working is provided. This overview reflects a summary of empirical studies that have been conducted in some Islamic countries utilizing a "Values for Working Questionnaire." Developed by Flowers, Hughes, and Myers (1975), the "Values for Working Questionnaire" (VWQ) is based on a value-systems framework proposed by Graves (1970). Graves suggests that people seems to evolve through consecutive levels of "psychological existence" that are descriptive of personal values and life styles. Depending on the person's cultural conditioning and perception of the opportunities and constraints in the environment, his/her level of psychological existence can become arrested at a given level or it can move upward or downward. The VWQ provides a method of predicting the attitudes and behaviors of people at the workplace and, because of its relative lack of cultural bias, it is well suited for cross-cultural studies (Ali, 1982). Flowers, Hughes, and Myers (1975) study values concerning supervisors, money, loyalty, size of companies, freedom on the job, and profit. Each dimension in the VWQ has six statements, which are arranged in random order. Each statement is designed in such a way as to measure one dimension of a value system. For example, concerning supervisors, the six statements are:

1. Tells me exactly what to do and how to do it, and encourages me by doing it with me.
2. Is tough, but allows me to be tough too.

3. Knows what he/she wants and isn't always changing his/her mind, and sees to it that everyone follows the rules.
4. Doesn't ask questions as long as I get the job done.
5. Gets us working together in close harmony by being a more friendly person than a boss.
6. Gives me access to the information I need and lets me do my job in my own way.

Flowers, Hughes, and Myers (1975) divide human values into two general categories of three values each. The first is the "outer-directed" with tribalistic, conformist, and sociocentric values. The outer-directed manager is adaptive to his/her situation in life, likes structure, and accepts rules, policies, and group norms. The outer-directed manager prefers a stable environment and job and tends not to set goals, but rather lives according to someone else's plan. The second category is "inner-directed" with egocentric, manipulative, and existential values. Managers in this category tend to be assertive and expressive, bending the rules to accomplish what they want. The inner-directed person is always attempting to influence his/her environment and make changes in it. To achieve that, the inner-directed manager sets goals and pursues them energetically (Hughes and Flowers, 1978). The values are briefly defined as follows:

1. Tribalistic: a submissiveness to authority and/or tradition.
2. Conformist: sacrificial, has a low tolerance for ambiguity and needs structure and rules to follow.
3. Sociocentric: a high need for affiliation and little concern for wealth.
4. Egocentric: aggressive, selfish, restless, impulsive, and, in general, not inclined to live within the limits and constraints of society's norms.
5. Manipulative: materialistic, expressive, and self-calculating to achieve an end.
6. Existential: a high tolerance for ambiguity and for those who have different values; usually expresses self but not at the expense of others.

The survey was conducted at various times in Iraq, Iran, Morocco, and Saudi Arabia, among other countries. Each dimension in the VWQ has six responses (statements) which are arranged in random order. Each statement is designed in such a way as to measure one dimension of a value system. Table 4.3 presents the estimated percentage of managers in the selected countries that espoused each value system. The table shows that a high proportion of managers is sociocentric, existential, and conformist. Almost consistently in all countries, the existential value is espoused by a high percentage of managers. This indicates that in Islamic countries, the prevailing cultural values and norms encourage common and humanistic causes, friendship and harmony, and at the same time stimulate openness, tolerance, trust, and confidence in others to perform their duties. These demonstrate that Islamic principles, as in the case of ethics above, appear to shape work values and orientations. It may indicate too that professional people, like managers, are sensitive to their expected social and economic roles and are familiar with major trends in global thinking and organizational changes.

Table 4.3   Managerial value systems in selected Muslim countries

Value system	Morocco %	Iraq %	Iran %	Saudi %
Existential	19	20	17	20
Sociocentric	18	23	18	18
Manipulative	17	16	17	17
Conformist	13	20	19	23
Egocentric	19	5	12	8
Tribalistic	14	16	17	15

Source: Based on Ali (1982), Ali and Al-Shakis (1985), Ali and Wahabi (1995), and Ali and Amirshahi (2002).

In his review of Islamic ethics and philosophy, Hourani (1985) indicates that Muslims during the Abbasid rule elaborately debated the nature of values. In the first century of the Abbasid rule the intellectual atmosphere was vibrant and stimulating. Ethical behavior and one's moral responsibilities toward God and society were debated. The debate focused on values, its sources, evolution, and functions.   There were various approaches to values that were discussed in terms of theology, philosophy, and practicality. Hourani argues that, in general, there were two main theories of values that opposed each other. The first is "objectivism."   It asserts that values such as what is just and what is good have a real existence independent of any one's will.   That is, acts or behaviors have certain qualities.   The existence of such qualities makes an act right, their absence makes it wrong, independent of the opinions or desires of the person who judge whether they are right or wrong. This theory is divided into two.   There are those who adhere to rationalistic views and believe that what is right can be known solely by independent reasoning. On the other hand, there are those who assert that what is right can be known by reason alone or by revelation or by both.

The second approach to value is "subjectivism."   It postulates that right has no objective meaning except what is approved or commanded by God or another in authority.   This is divided into two theoretical approaches.

The first states whatever the believers consider good is good with God, and what they consider to be bad, is bad with God. The second theory is called divine subjectivism. It asserts that all values are determined by the will of God. That is, a "subject" solely determines values existence. The Scripture is the source for the legal and moral rules and standards. It should be mentioned that the *Jabria* school advocates the second approach. This became the prevailing theory in the second century of the Abbasids and gained momentum in the years that experienced rapid decline of the Abbasid rule and the eventual ascendancy of the Turks in Islamic affairs.

Both approaches to values agree on the general Islamic values. For example, they all place tremendous emphasis on kindness, equality, and goodness, universalism and consultation. However, they differ in two aspects in addition to the issue of the sources of values: the role of the people relative to rulers and accountability. The subjectivism theory places people in a subordinate position to rulers and their rulers are not considered to be accountable to people; they are accountable only to God. Advocates of objectivism disagree and insist that rulers must be held responsible to the people, and that the values of hard work, cooperation, persistence, justice, and sincerity will not be widely and deeply held among people in an environment of strict control and autocracy.

The literature on Islamic values, based both on the Quran and the Prophet Mohamed's sayings and practices, stresses values that are applicable both to work and to general conduct and behavior. These are: equality, accountability, consultation, goodness, kindness, trust, honoring promises (commitment), sincerity, justice, hard work, humility, universalism, consensus, self-discipline, persistence, and cooperation. Generally, these values can be divided into the following categories.

Ethical Values

They concern the issues of good and evil in dealing with people and conducting affairs. They include goodness, kindness, compassion, and sincerity.

Social Values

These values encompass a wide range of desirable behavior and qualities that are essential for enhancing social unity, continuity, and stability. They include respect, forgiveness, mercy, charity, generosity, and the avoidance of jealousy, anger, lying, spying on and defaming others, suspicion, cruelty, and arrogance.

Administrative Values

These are values that address the desirable attributes in managing organizations. They encompass such values as accountability, consultation, honoring promises (commitment), justice, trust, hard work, integrity, consensus, avoidance of nepotism and discrimination, and cooperation.

Business Values

These are values that specify the desirable behavior and attitude in business and trade matters. They include values that prohibit usury, cheating, engaging in unlawful business, swearing, monopoly, withholding of commodities to inflate prices, and those that accentuate discipline, truthfulness, dependability, effort, fulfillment of contract conditions, and observing deadlines.

Well-being Related Values

These deal with preferences in serving one's interest. They include hard work, self-discipline, persistence, content, moderation, loyalty, honesty, and sincerity.

Discovery Values

These are values that set out how truth should be known and the necessity of intellectual and knowledge pursuit for creating a just and prosperous society.

Humanistic Values

These values refer to the ultimate means needed for ensuring social, political, and economic justice. They include equality, humility, good intention, and universalism.

7. PERSONALITY AND VALUE SYSTEMS

In Chapter 2, we provided Islamic perspectives on human development and for psychological levels of existence. Four types of personalities were identified: Sawala, Ammara, Lawama, and Mutamainna. Under each level of existence, a person displays a value system that is particular to that stage.

Sawala

At the first level, Sawala, a person has values that are a reflection of his/her aspirations and desires. Since people at this stage are primarily concerned with their personal pleasure, fame and enjoyment, their values express self recklessly and without regards to others. Therefore, they espouse values that aggrandize their power and material wealth, irrespective of humanistic, ethical, and social values. Whatever facilitates their desire for domination and prestige is pursued energetically and enthusiastically. Sawala people view ethics as situational and flexible. There are no obligatory or universal ethics. In life, there are only interests and these interests are changeable. Ethics that maximize their welfare are sanctioned and those that stand in their way are avoided and denounced as obsolete and outdated.

Ammara

At the Ammara level, individuals are aware that they exist as part of a group or community. They recognize that maximizing self-interests may dictate a manipulation of situations and events to achieve goals. They know that pursuing their selfish desires may put them in direct conflict with other people and may jeopardize their interests. Therefore, they are more likely to be selective in expressing some of the values outlined above. They thrive on gamesmanships, politics and maneuvering. Again, humanistic, ethical, and social values are not held in high regard, except when they are seen as necessary for advancing personal interests.

Lawama

People at the Lawama level are clear about what is bad and what is good. Nevertheless, in conducting their activities and pursuing their interest, they may knowingly act upon selfish desires. That is, people at this level are aware of their actions and consequences. While occasionally they may not pay strict attention to ethical, social and humanistic values, this is often followed by a rethinking and acknowledgment of their wrongdoings and a feeling of guilt. They attempt to live within acceptable social and moral standards and control the zone of deviation. Generally, however, they accept most of the values outlined above.

Mutamainna

When people reach the fourth level, Mutamainna, they become completely in tune with all the values outlined; they are content and seek perfection. They do not show any doubt in knowing the zone of righteousness and wrongfulness. This deepest and the most genuine feeling ensures a striving for excellence in serving self and others. Mutamainna people are non-power seekers and receive comfort and pride from self-reflection, involvement, and spirituality. They resist wrongdoing and promote good. Individuals at this stage exhibit an ideal situation where there is a state of harmony between entitlements and responsibilities, self and others, nature and material wealth. Ethical, social, and humanistic values are their guide in conducting their personal and business affairs.

8. CONCLUSION

In this chapter, IWE and Values are highlighted and are discussed in light of the principles outlined in the Quran and the Prophet Mohamed's sayings and practices. These values and ethics represent, as in any other religion, a commitment to promote good, and resist bad conduct. As such, they are general guidelines and standards for conduct. Indeed, the Islamic emphasis on the constant struggle for the actualization of ideals and for justice and generosity in the workplace as necessary conditions for society's welfare, positions Islam as a leading force advocating productive but humanistic approaches to organized work.

In practice, commitment to Islamic values and ethics varies according to circumstances, personal differences, and political reality and interferences. At the personal level, lack of internalization of these standards and discipline, and familiarity often render these principles to mere slogans. In addition, internal societal forces (e.g., feeling of powerlessness and humiliation, absence of freedom, cultural alienations, and high illiteracy rates) and external conditions (colonization, geopolitical and economic interests of dominant foreign powers) influence commitment to and revivalism of these values and ethics.

In the era of openness, genuine diversity, and tolerance during the first six centuries of Islam, Islamic values and work ethics captured the minds of a large segment of the people. Accordingly, trade and organizations flourished, spirited discourse and knowledge were encouraged, learned individuals were sought after and rewarded, and opportunities and prosperity were plentiful. The spread of authoritarianism and the eventual ascendancy of foreign powers in Muslim affairs accelerated the downfall of genuine Islamic values and ethics.

5. The Structure and Functions of Groups

It is impossible to imagine a functional society or organization without groups. Indeed, the progress/regression of humanity is linked directly to the formation, aspiration, and action of groups. Whether in a formal or informal setting, groups play a significant role in the direction of a society or organization. It is the dynamic of the group, the organized collective energy of its members and the spirit that directs it that has been responsible for the changes and development of normal courses of action in yesterday's and today's world. The nature of the group, however, differs across history and culture. The composition of groups, pattern of interaction among members, and the nature and way of relating to each other within the group and to outsiders have not only differentiated groups from each other, but have also influenced their effectiveness and survival and consequently the development of their respective societies. The emergence of the capitalist groups, for example, influenced the shape and direction of the industrial revolution, and enabled European societies to venture into activities completely different from that of the feudal system. These groups had the shared objectives, among others, of accumulating wealth and gaining social and other forms of influence. Similarly, the rapid formation of a professional management class in the United States in the early part of the nineteenth century eased its economic growth and domination through creative utilization of organizational resources. The evolution of liberal-minded and radical political groups, too, produced mixed results (e.g., economic prosperity, conflicting political ideologies, wars, etc.) in the twentieth century.

Like the Roman Empire and the empires before it, the early Muslim state had its unique experience in the emergence and evolution of groups. That experience is still felt in various parts of the Muslim world. Consistent with their fascination with the ideal, Muslims in various parts of the world refer to themselves as part of a larger and inclusive group called *umma* or community. The concept of *umma,* as perceived by the Prophet Mohamed, depicts a community where members are equal regardless of their ethnic background, and where cohesiveness is highly regarded. The only envisioned theoretical difference among members is related to the degree of piety as judged by the Almighty God. People still long for this ideal group, despite its absence in reality. The concept is useful, however, in understanding the evolution, characteristic, and the significance of groups in organizations.

As was discussed in Chapter 1, the evolution of Islam is dialectically linked to the social environment in Arabia at the time and to the necessity of building a viable community under adversarial conditions. There were two main social groups along with other forms that differentiated the early Muslim society from surrounding communities and, indeed, from the existing forms of organizations. The *Al-mahajeerien* (emigrants) and *Ansar* (supporters) constituted the two primary organized groups. The first group had to rely initially on the assistance provided by the second group until they were reasonably able to establish themselves. Mohamed recognized that the new community of umma (which initially included the Al-mahajeerien and residents of Medina) could not survive if it was based on customary blood relations and tribal identity. Therefore, he relied on ideology (faith) rather than tribal identity as the primary motivational factor and the base for social relationship. Consequently, he introduced a new form of social association (*muakhat*- two Muslims were paired together and declared brothers, replacing the traditional blood relationship). This relationship not only transcended color and ethnic background, but also social classes and former social rank. All members were treated equally and were engaged in social and formal relationships that were revolutionary in an era of social prejudices, tribal rivalry, and chronic conflict. Furthermore, Mohamed profoundly changed the concept and the prestige of the individual and the family. In the pre-Islamic era an individual was just an object in the clan system. Mohamed stressed the individual's right and moral responsibility toward family and society. In terms of family, Mohamed redefined it to include "a new concern for women and children, the stability of marriages, individuality, and decency" (Lapidus, 1988, p. 34). In creating a functional community, Mohamed utilized alliances with various groups and an old Arab moral system (*muruwah*-a system that is concerned with taking care of the vulnerable members of the community and common good) to sustain the newly established city-state. Mohamed, thus, created a community where members were treated equally, protected and rewarded for their devotion. The sense of belonging to an *umma* where faith and goodness were the primary measures, and identification enabled its members to maintain a sense of unity that was seldom exhibited by other groups in the region. This experience, however, was short-lived as subtle differences, be they ideological, tribal or ethnic, appeared after the death of Mohamed.

1. NATURE OF GROUPS

The death of the Prophet Mohamed took place a short time after Muslims successfully entered and consequently controlled Mecca - the power base of their arch enemy - the Quraesh. Leaders of the Quraesh, who were until recently the primary enemy of Islam, became Muslims. Chief among them were some members of the most powerful clan; the Ommeyades. Most of the new Quraeshi converts did not internalize the Islamic message and, more likely, the conversion was a matter of convenience. Indeed, many scholars propose that the conversion was a canny method to regain power (see Ali, 1964; Delo, 1985; Lapidus, 1988).

Islam promotes seemingly contradictory qualities in its teachings: asserting individuality and conformity simultaneously. These two qualities play a pivotal role in the formation and development of groups in early Islam and still hold a varying but powerful influence on contemporary Islamic societies and social institutions. In current history, these two qualities have eased and enriched group dynamics, fluidity, fragmentation, alternation, and rapid regrouping. The rituals of pilgrimage, fasting, alms-giving, for example, reinforce group loyalty, sensitivity, and identity. Nevertheless, the absence of a priesthood and the emphasis on personal responsibility, along with the ability to perform prayer duties individually and in any comfortable place, reasserts individualism. It is plausible, however, that these two qualities contributed to the early signs of division among the Muslim *umma* and to the diverse interpretations of the role of individuals and groups in Muslim societies.

Since the early years the Islamic family and the extended family, beside the concept of *umma*, have been instrumental in group formation and its evolution. Unlike the experience of Europe during the medieval era, Muslim societies did not develop an imposing pyramid of highly differentiated and tightly closed ranks and classes (Goitein, 1967). Instead, there was a greater fluidity and ease for class mobility and dissolving and regroupings of groups (Gibb, 1962). What further facilitated the ease of group formation and dynamic was the geographic expansion of the Muslim empire. Two groups that differed culturally from the Arabs eventually came to interact closely with them and left their marks on the social and cultural development of the Arab Muslims: the *Mawali* (non-Arab Muslims) and the non-Arabs *Ahl-Al-Kitab* (people of the book - Jewish, Christian, and

Zoroastrian). Both groups brought with them diverse and rich cultures. Those with specific skills managed to join the elite class and became tax collectors, scribes, administrators, and estate managers. According to Lapidus (1988, p. 51) the process of absorbing other cultural groups "fostered new group and communal structures, intensified the stratification of new mixed Arab and non-Arab communities. . . . The breakdown of lineage structure made possible new forms of social organizations." Furthermore, as Banani (1977) explains, unlike the Arabs, many of these groups, especially those from Persia had a culture with strong ascribed status and ascribed roles. Their conversion to Islam or their close interaction with Arab Muslims was a potent force in encouraging free will and increasing individuality. Consequently, new forms of group emerged that were characterized by mobility, adaptability, an ease in changing memberships, and spontaneity. These aspects are still found in many groups in some parts of the Islamic societies.

2.   TYPES OF GROUPS

Professional occupation alone did not determine social status or membership in groups in medieval Islam (Goitein, 1967, p. 79). This was true before and to some extent is still valid in contemporary Islamic societies. Goitein specified four factors that enhance status in Muslim societies: the origin and reputation of family, religiosity and learnedness, integrity and sound business practice and generosity and readiness to exert oneself for the public welfare or for people seeking help. The last factor, however, along with humbleness, courage, and tolerance are the most admired qualities that elevate one's status in society and induces groups and other organizations to seek his/her affiliation. Goitein identified five social classes: the upper class; the bourgeoisie of businessmen and professionals; the master artisans; the mass of urban craftsmen and laborers; and peasants. Imam Ali (1989, died 661, p. 312), however, elaborated on the social groups by delineating several groups: the soldiers, public and private secretaries, administrators of justice, social workers, tax collectors, merchants and craftsmen, and the poor. Ali, as a Caliph, divided people according to his perspective as an administrator.

In terms of worldly affairs and behavior, *Ikhwan-us-Safa* (Brothers of Purity) in the tenth century identified (p. 320) seven general group categories: craftsmen, professional and business owners (1999a), merchants, bankers, and brokers; landlords; kings and sultans; politicians and soldiers; maids, those with chronic illnesses, and those who are concerned with daily living; and religious and learned groups. Each category was divided into subgroups that differ in their responsibilities and moral commitment and behavior. What is common about these three classifications is the emphasis on profession and role in society. More importantly, the terminology used to describe groups and social classes are similar to today's terms. This demonstrates that social and business problems might be the same. Nevertheless, the technique or the sophistication in addressing or solving them could be different. In today's Muslim societies, these medieval classifications probably exist in various sectors. Nevertheless, there is some emphasis on what differentiates formal and informal groups. Furthermore, groups are classified across political, professional, social, religious, and academic affiliations. In this context, most of the classifications that exist in Western societies are adopted in most Muslim countries. The classifications, however, retain distinct Islamic expressions. In addition, functions and qualities of groups are shaped largely by local cultures and priorities.

3. FUNCTIONS OF GROUPS

In Islamic societies, business and personal relations are interwoven. Indeed, the web of relationships appears to be complex, but interact with remarkable ease and warmth in communication. The web encompasses people from a wide range of backgrounds and orientations and each of them seems to be at the center of the relationship. Even when the matter of the relationship is business, there is no conflict between business and human concerns. That is, business transactions are not dependent on whether a member of a group places more emphasis on business or humanity. Rather, the transition is viewed as part of the continuum within the context of the network of friendship and trading collaboration (Udovitch, 1977). Indeed, the organizational/societal boundaries are soft if not blurred.

Whether they are modern or traditional, Muslim societies exhibit a relatively higher degree of personal and intimate relations than other societies. That is, personal relations are broader than friendship and focus on individuals and their role in a complex web of network. Personal relationships are fundamental and permeate all societal domains. All relations are personal. In Islam, as Rosen (2002, p. 65) observed, the focus on relationships and consequences places an emphasis: "On who people are in relation to others, rather than where they are in a set life structure, and what consequences have befallen others by their acts." This situation may dictate rethinking of our preconception of the emergence of informal and formal groups. For example, Gibson, Ivancevich and Donnelly (1988) assert that informal groups evolve naturally, while formal groups are the result of deliberate design. In many Muslim societies, formal groups as work committees may emerge instantaneously, resulting from a friendly dialogue outside the workplace. Similarly, informal groups might be an extension of a formal group in organizations.

In any case, the emergence of informal and formal groups results from a variety of reasons. In this section, a brief discussion of a wide range of functions fulfilled by groups in the workplace is provided.

Functions of Informal Groups

Informal groups at the workplace in Muslim societies are a common phenomenon. Their proliferation in organizational setting mirrors the nature of the personalized society and the blurred distinctions between what is business and what is personal in any transaction. The multiplicity of informal groups can serve both as an obstacle and a facilitator to the realization of organizational goals. The existence of informal groups fulfills several functions. Chief among them are:

1. Reducing uncertainty for members of groups. In the case of new members of the corporation, joining an existing group helps to minimize fear and familiarizes the newcomers with the norms and expectations of the workplace. Likewise, the group gives a sense of power to the member in the face of changing circumstance in the company.

2. Enhancing socialization, self-esteem, and self-respect. Even though socialization in an Islamic setting takes much time and is a part of daily life, at the workplace it takes on an added value. This is because it strengthens identity and the sense of belonging to a work group.

3. Enabling members to understand the politics within the organization. Since memberships in a group at the workplace are open to members from various ranks and backgrounds, members generate a better understanding of the nature of politics within an organization. This allows members to sharpen their skills and knowledge in dealing with pressing daily issues.

4. Making members aware of job opportunities. That is, groups in this case serve as a mechanism to communicate to its members existing work opportunities and what is needed to move ahead.

5. Strengthening spirituality and commitment to worthy causes. Members of a group usually perform their daily prayers together and discuss religious and social issues. Since these activities are common during

working hours, people tend to develop a sense of cohesiveness, belonging, and spiritual revivalism.

6. Facilitating the integration of organizational and personal needs. The web of personal relationships and avenues of communications offers a continuous feedback and allows reconsideration of priorities.

7. Facilitating the transformation of societal cultural norms and demands into organizational culture. Concerns about societal problems and values are of significant importance in societies where political issues and economic problems are part of the normal discourse, in and outside of the workplace. Group members utilize their networks to bring them to the attention of management and to the rest of the organization membership.

As indicated, the preceding functions are not exhaustive. Nevertheless, they reveal some of the outstanding functions of informal groups at the workplace. From a management point of view, these groups and their functions can present a serious challenge to corporations. This is especially true when members of these groups perceive management policies to be a hindrance to a just society or workplace or to be inconsistent with societal values and norms. Since these groups are characterized by a spontaneous regrouping around social or national concerns, their impact on operations and performance should not be minimized. For this reason, too, these groups can be instrumental in improving performance and cohesiveness at the workplace, especially under adverse national conditions. In particular, these groups are helpful in situations that are highly interdependent and complex.

Functions of Formal Organizational Groups

In organizations, formal groups denote those groups that are established by managers to engage in activities and tasks related to the organization's basic mission. Membership in any of these groups is deliberately assigned based on their position in the organization. These groups can be called permanent (e.g., senior management team, staff groups) or temporary (e.g., groups that are created to perform specific tasks or to provide work-related recommendations); hierarchical (e.g., department head and immediate subordinates) or task groups (e.g., an established group to execute a specific project). In Muslim societies, as shown in Chapter 9, organizations most often utilize committees in their structures. In addition, there are committees that are not depicted in structures. Committees are a form of formal groups. Their usefulness and effectiveness are a matter for debate in most societies. In the Muslim World, however, committees can be just a show. Often, they are used to give the impression that senior managers are participative. Likewise, senior management may rely on committees and other groups to promote their ideas. Like employees, senior managers are greatly influenced by personal values and network. Their utilization of committees is aimed at strengthening their formal and informal roles. The existence of these groups is often contingent upon the will of the senior manager. This should be kept in mind when reflecting on the functions of these groups. Several functions stand out:

1. Performing operational and supporting tasks that cannot be individually carried out. In this case a group of employees is designated to work on these tasks. The division of labor always facilitates this objective. In oil drilling and processing, for example, various groups are assigned to perform their work. Manufacturing on assembly lines and surgical or emergency teams in hospitals are examples.

2. Legitimizing actions taken by senior managers. Committees and other types of groups' managers may resort to groups to legitimize actions or decisions made. Sometimes these decisions have already been made by senior managers, but the manager feels a need to have a committee to approve them. The aim here is to project the image of a consultative in an environment that condones consultative processes.

3. Motivating employees. This is especially true when there are new work procedures or techniques and in situations where employees feel powerless. In both cases, groups can be instrumental in facilitating learning and in shouldering responsibility. Employees react in a personal way and feel that their contributions are valued by the organization.

4. Mobilizing members of groups. This function differs from the above items in that managers seek to mobilize the employees throughout the organization behind a new/important goal or mission. This is especially true when there is a crisis or the organization is at a critical turning point. While in some societies employees react in impersonal ways or are indifferent to appeals by managers, in Muslim societies the appeal is considered personal and often reacted to enthusiastically.

5. Co-opting disgruntled employees. Co-opting powerful elements (e.g., leaders of labor unions) is common in the United States. Top management includes these individuals on the Board of Directors or on prestigious committee to neutralize their stance. In many Muslim organizations, including potential opponents in groups is a widespread practice. There is always personal negotiation and wheeling and dealing in granting or withholding a favor. Normally, groups are the place for intense negotiation and favor granting.

6. Facilitating the implementation of strategic or important decisions. In many situations, a strategic decision requires the support and involvement of individuals across organizations. Groups make this easier by involving influential people and representatives from various departments. Those represented in the group usually engage and encourage their associates and subordinates to implement decisions.

7. Broadening responsibility. In the Muslim world, almost all business activities have immediate social and political implications. Furthermore, managers normally perform the role of social (community leaders) and political actors. Senior managers, therefore, establish committees to make decisions on matters that are closely monitored by local social and political agencies. This allows managers to shift the blame to others, or to broaden responsibility, in case of objections.

8. Institutionalizing certain behavior and policies. In highly personalized societies, people have a tendency to think of everything as changeable and contingent on the persons in charge. Charismatic and prophetic leaders at the workplace usually help to institutionalize policies and directions. In the absence of a prophetic leader's qualities, managers utilize groups to sell policies and directions and hopefully institutionalize them.

9. Enhancing loyalty. Managers use inclusion in groups as a mechanism to strengthen loyalty and build a supporting network. There is a great deal of energy that goes into maintaining networks and loyalties. Since alliances and loyalties are continually shifting, managers have to extend favors and reinforce alliances; otherwise, loyalty will not be sustained. While this situation poses a challenge to senior managers, it sharpens their diplomatic and social skills and alertness to organizational politics.

The above functions have some similarities with the primary functions of formal groups in other societies. Nevertheless, there are specific functions that are culturally bounded and that, to a large extent, reflect the nature of groups and societies in the Muslim world. For example, in the United States, Schein (1980) argues that groups are used as a vehicle of socialization. This is not the case in many Muslim societies as there is an unusually high degree of socialization in the society in general. Because of this lack of socialization deficit, members of the group expect their leaders or the senior managers to have a clear vision of what is needed to be done. Once they perceive a lack of direction or seriousness, dissatisfaction and carelessness will be instantaneous. Furthermore, Western, including the United States managers may use groups purposefully to delay taking action. Managers in Muslim societies may be tempted to use this approach. They, however, risk losing their reputation and the respect from others. In terms of a group leader's approach to members of the group in the United States and many Muslim societies, there is a noticeable difference. In the latter societies, when there are unsettled issues, the leader appeals to the emotions and friendship to move on. In the United States this may not be the case, as personal and business matters are normally kept separate. Furthermore, groups in the Muslim world, be they formal or informal, resort to subtle forms of protest to show their disapproval of individuals in power who do not take heed of popular sentiments. Rosen (2002) provides a telling story of how shopkeepers across Morocco, in a show of disapproval, removed the picture of the King from their stores after his support of the Western allies' action against Iraq in 1991. In a similar case, but with a different implication, a head of the police department in a small town in Iraq, Naser, insulted a respected merchant. The head of the police was approached by a community leader who asked him to apologize to the merchant, but he refused. When each evening the police chief went through the two main coffee houses in the market, the community intellectuals and merchants refused to answer his greeting. This was an indication that the community had no respect for him and his authority. Immediately, he had to apologize to the merchants in hopes of improving his standing in the community. These types of protest are not limited to the community. They also occur in organizations.

4.   FACTORS AFFECTING GROUP EFFECTIVENESS

There are various factors influencing group performance and the achievement of organizational goals. These factors can simultaneously ease or obstruct the functions of groups whether they are formal or informal, consequently accelerating or paralyzing the integration of organization and personal functions. Though the factors are different, they are intertwined and often their impact is immediate. These factors can be divided into the socio-cultural, the nature and composition of groups, the mission and leadership and organization.

Socio-cultural Factors

Under this category, there are a wide range of factors that play significant roles in shaping groups' functions and vitality. The interplay of both organizational and societal cultures constitutes the most important factor for facilitating the integration/disintegration of groups. In terms of organizational culture, in Islamic settings various assumptions about the role of an organization and the nature of employees exist. Three primary assumptions are relevant here: employees are essentially motivated by firmness and clear and strict rules (autocratic); employees have to be treated with *Rehema* (mercy), *ihasan* (kindness) and *adel* (justice) to be effective (traditional group-centered); and organizations exist to further the interest of the community and society at large (spiritually enlightened). If the first assumption is advocated, formal groups are closely controlled by the top managers and informal groups are not encouraged to play any significant role outside what is specified or dictated. In both cases, the groups are marginalized and their functions are primarily subordinated to that of the senior managers/owners. In this environment, informal groups become both the source of self-esteem and identity for its members, and probably an obstacle to effective achievement of organizational goals.

In an organization espousing the second assumption, informal groups are treated as a natural extension of the formal groups and the organization itself. Members are intrinsically committed to the organization and show admiration of senior managers/owners. The main problem here is that if chief executive officers (CEOs) or general managers are not clear about what is supposed to be achieved and do not give specific directions, groups may fall short in meeting organizational goals in an effective way. What is significant here is that in such an environment, employees do not view the CEO and the organization as adversaries, rather, they look at them as the reinforcement of what is good and desirable in the work environment. The integration, therefore, of organizational and personal goals is highly possible. To sustain a group's functionality, there is a need for clear guidelines and direction to channel energy and utilize resources.

Viewing an organization as an instrument for serving the community and furthering the cause of the society is a common phenomena among spiritually driven CEOs or general managers. A spiritually driven executive displays attributes discussed in Chapter 2 under the *Mutamainna* level of existence. Probably, this situation creates a fit between organizational and individuals' goals. Organizations are seen as instruments for serving both society and the individual. The managers' task is to make certain that that there is an alignment among personal, organizational, and societal goals. In addition, it enhances the functions of groups whether they are formal or informal. Indeed, the clarity of goals and the emphasis on the collective objectives facilitate groups' development and ability to thrive.

Because culture in most Muslim societies is strong and since these societies are mostly traditional, societal cultural factors usually exercise more influence on groups than what might be possible in developed countries. There are certain cultural aspects that strengthen and weaken group functions and effectiveness. The emphasis on the nuclear family and the extended family, general primary groups, spirituality and philosophical discourse, for example, creates a conducive environment for the sudden emergence and overlapping of groups across a long spectrum of ethnicity, gender, social and political affiliations, and national borders. That is, members of groups find it natural to join different groups at the same time, even if these groups seem to have contradictory goals. Figure 5.1 depicts a situation where a person joins several groups in and outside the workplace. The person, however, has the freedom, except in formal groups, to switch alliances and memberships and to join and rejoin new and existing groups. While this situation may ease switching sides and alliances, it could complicate planning for growth and the predictions of patterns of relationships. At the same time, it may enable groups and organizations to sharpen their instinct for survival and revivalism.

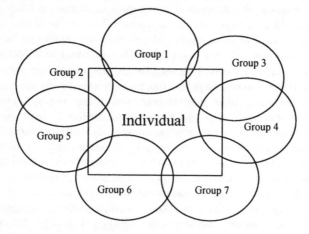

Figure 5.1   Memberships in a group

A typical cultural factor that stands out as the most crucial in understanding group function is that, for Muslims, solutions come only through critical reconsideration of the immediate and undivided (Ali, 1988; Berque, 1978). That is, the first priority in addressing any problem or conflict is developing a framework for understanding its core and its general solution. Once an agreement is reached, then steps are taken to proceed in solving simultaneously the interrelated sub problems. This state of orientation proves to be one of the biggest stumbling blocks in transferring American management techniques, especially organizational development (OD) to Muslim countries. Western managers focus on the mediate and compartmentalization, therefore, they address sub-issues step by step until they reach the whole. For Muslims, this approach is viewed with suspicion and it is perceived to lead to delay and a waste of time and resources, in addition to inflicting injustice on the whole process and matters on hand. This may explain the difficulty that OD consultants face in several parts of the Muslim world. More importantly, it underlies the failure of United States' foreign policy in that part of the world and its subsequent emphasis on using force instead.

Self-censorship is quite troublesome for a group's function and growth. In Muslim societies there is a tendency among group members to not criticize, reveal or inform about others' wrongdoings, regardless of their backgrounds. This tendency may serve to keep group cohesiveness and friendly relationships. Nevertheless, it eventually leads to deterioration of performance and strengthens indifference to the job among the members. In a non-competitive environment, this tendency will be strengthened and may not permit a dynamic and functional integration of formal and informal groups. More likely, however, in a competitive environment, self-censorship will be held to a minimum. Members of the group may realize that self-censorship is an obstacle to their collective interest and advantage.

Along with the above cultural characteristics, the infatuation with the ideal, too, can affect group growth and function. Perceiving the ideal to be identical with practice, rather than merely constituting the criterion by which the latter is judged, may lead to profound conflict in international transactions or diplomacy. The infatuation with the ideal is something ingrained in the psyche of those who follow the Islamic faith. Deviation from the ideal is perceived to lead to injustice, corruptions and decay of morality. This belief can motivate groups to improve performance and inspire enthusiasm. Under adverse conditions, it likely leads to frustrations and disappointment. Thus, there is almost always a fierce struggle to overcome the inconsistency between the ideal and reality. In more pragmatic societies, such as in the United States, this conflict is less apparent, as the main concern is with reality. In these societies, the ideal may be pursued, but it is never an obsession. Furthermore, in these societies, there is a strong tendency to overlook more complex thoughts and to instead focus on easily assimilated information (Witt, 2003). Therefore, conflict is possible, but not necessarily inevitable when individuals or groups from the Muslim world deal with their counterparts from the United States. From the latter point of view, the focus on the ideal and justice may be irrelevant. What is relevant are the current circumstances and the power of equation and reality.

5.　THE NATURE AND COMPOSITION OF GROUPS

Without doubt, the effectiveness of any group is affected by its nature and composition. Whether the group is formal or informal, the nature of memberships and the relations among members significantly determine the vitality and the effectiveness of its functions. Formal groups are influenced by formal status, departmental loyalty, priority of values, members' skills, and so on. In Muslim societies, however, there are additional factors that seem to affect the performance of group tasks. Chief among them are the supervisor's management style and his/her world outlook, age, gender, knowledge and piety. These factors play a decisive role in shaping functions of groups. For example, unlike the Western world, the business and private life of an individual is indivisible. Furthermore, the style and orientation of the group supervisor can either motivate or frustrate the group. If the supervisor is perceived to be either delaying in making a decision or just attempting to create a feeling of consultation, though he has already made up his mind about what decision should be adopted by the group, indifference and fragmentation of the group become a high possibility. In some societies this might be tolerated, but in an Islamic setting, people are sensitive to such a situation and consider it dissembling. In terms of gender, in a situation where the majority is men, there is a tendency to go along with women's suggestions even though they may not agree with them. In a case where there is a serious concern about a woman's suggestion, a member of the group may talk individually to the female member outside the group to persuade her to change her mind. Similarly, people defer to older members of the group, despite their position, and attentively try to please them. It is likely that in both situations, these social considerations compromise groups' functions. On the other hand, the reverence toward learned individuals and piety among the group may be a healthy situation. The respect and attentiveness given to input by such people probably strengthens group confidence, cohesiveness, and direction.

In informal groups in the workplace, the nature and composition of the group is important, too. Most of the aspects that are addressed above are applicable. Nevertheless, informal groups may evolve and cluster along community concerns, neighborhood lines, religious or ideological orientations. Most often these groups are an extension of much larger societal groups. Their evolution and growth are linked closely to these societal groups, even though they function alongside formal groups. The multiplicity of these groups and their interwoven relationships with larger societal groups can be a source of integration and fragmentation at the same time. During national crisis or when a political/religious group shows disapproval of the company, informal groups may be a source for agitation and disturbance. Figure 5.2 shows the complexity of relationships among informal groups, corporations, and societal groups. The figure simplifies the web of relationships that exists among formal and informal groups in a company and with a wide range of societal groups. In reality, the web of the relationship is highly dynamic and complex. Since societal expectations of corporations are not purely business-centered, societal demands on a corporation tend to be immediate and intrusive.

Mission

The mission often differentiates groups from each other. This is especially true for formal groups, but also applicable to informal associations. Formal groups supposedly have specific tasks to perform that aim at meeting corporate goals in an efficient and effective way. The mission of informal groups, however, stems from a complex interplay between societal and formal organizational expectations and demands. Lack of consensus on goals and the absence of congruence between formal and informal groups can lead to fragmentation and inadequate performance. Because of closely-knit societal relations, primacy of personal considerations in Muslim societies and lack of cultural awareness, the clarity of mission becomes an important factor in preventing factions and infighting. This situation makes leadership issues an essential factor in the growth and effectiveness of groups.

Leadership and Organizational Factors

Whether they are formal or informal, most groups in Muslim societies are not effectively organized. That is, groups have low or limited structure and they lack clarity of vision and mission. The vagueness of a mission, ambivalences, lack of clear prioritization of goals and of relationships among members in most groups weakens group functions and effectiveness. The existence of such a state, and the fact that members of groups are generally receptive and attentive initially to leaders' direction, make leadership factors critical in determining a group's success. As indicated in Chapter 8, Muslims, because of their upbringing and teaching, have always longed for a prophetic leader. Under this type of leadership an ideal situation exists for effective and functional groups. In the absence, however, of a prophetic leader, conditions have to be created which encourage informal groups to develop. One of the most important conditions is the sensitivity of the leader to cultural and organizational issues of the group. Neither an autocratic nor a weak leader will be instrumental in enhancing group evolution and growth. A decisive but opened-minded leader can sustain group growth. This leader must display the prerequisite qualities for acceptance (*Rehema, ihasan*, and *adel*) along with adequate knowledge to rally the group behind a specific mission and goal. Decisiveness plays a vital role in focusing on direction and in structuring group functions. This has a far-reaching implication, as most of the Muslims enjoy philosophical and open-ended debate. A decisive leader who acquires the respect of the group can channel this quality into serving the achievement of the planned goals. Likewise, a leader who displays decisiveness that is founded on kindness can give a group a sense of identity and direction, therefore, allowing the group to capitalize on its enthusiasm and loyalty for fostering effective work performance.

6.   ENHANCING GROUP EFFECTIVENESS

Formal and informal groups have certain goals to achieve. The preceding discussion reflected on factors influencing effectiveness. In this section, we identify factors that strengthen group performance. In most Muslim societies there is a deficit of openness in decision-making, sound leadership, clarity of goals and directions, and effective utilization of conditions that lead to cohesiveness. Both religion and tradition offer ample resources and examples to overcome these deficits (e.g., strong commitment to the ideal and to society, widely and deeply held values). The fact that most formal and informal groups have not utilized these adequately in Muslim societies manifest that systematic efforts have not been taken to minimize these deficits. Dynamics training helps to focus attention and sharpen the skills of leaders and group members. Training that is based on recognized cultural qualities and sound knowledge creates conditions that enhance cohesiveness, clarity of goals, sensitivity to group members, and leadership skills. The training should focus on the following:

1.   Appreciating the tendency among group members to engage in philosophical discourse. Group leaders and trainers, while encouraging this tendency, should focus the debate on the core problem and prevent any sidetracking. It is useful to acknowledge spiritual and personal values, while at the same time distinguishing them from the organizational needs.

2.   The process of problem solving and the necessary steps to move from here to there. This is critical as traditional problem techniques rely on

personal relations and behind the scenes' give and take among senior members. Emphasis should focus on problem-solving approaches and the necessary steps needed to reach a conclusion. This requires full participation of group members without completely ignoring the benefits of traditional approaches.

3. The positive aspects of openness and friendly disagreements. In most of the group discussions, the debate normally avoids direct deliberation of the primary causes of problems. It is essential that the leader keeps the group focused on the underlying causes.

4. Capitalizing on the intuitive capability among group members to generate the widest possible range of relevant options. Muslim socialization and spiritual teaching nurture intuition and commonsense tendencies. This asset might prove to be useful in generating alternatives. In most Muslim societies, it is possible to generate possible options. But there is a tendency not to consider seriously the process of evaluation of options. Personal preferences, narrow group or departmental interest and rivalry, along with a disregard for established procedures obstruct objective evaluation. Effective training is needed to underlie the necessity of the evaluation process.

5. Minimizing self-censorship tendencies, while highlighting the significance of the primacy of group goals. Self-censorship is a serious group and organizational problem. Highlighting openness and the benefits to group and the community may gradually erode the foundation of self-censorship.

6. Integrating group goals with that of the larger organization by emphasizing the critical role the group plays in the organization's success.

7. The process for transforming the intense primary group loyalty into organizational loyalty. Successful transformation will minimize rivalry and fragmentation.

8. The advantage of integrating individual or primary group concerns into that of the large group or organization. Probably this reduces dissatisfaction and factions.

9. Using historical precedents and examples to promote a desired change and enhance commitment. Reasonable reference to historical events not only facilitates acceptance and commitment to change, but also enhances the prestige and respect of leaders.

10. Highlighting the advantage of groups and of having common goals. Confidence and consensus-building processes are often ignored or taken for granted. Focusing on them is more likely to lead to improving work group environment.

11. Using storytelling methods to stimulate participation and build trust. This method is a powerful tool for focusing attention on the main problems and generating ideas.
12. Placing the quality of the fascination with the ideal form in the context of reality and changing business conditions. It takes highly skilled trainers and leaders to sensitize and direct the group toward pragmatism and practical solutions.
13. Addressing sub-problems simultaneously and comprehensively. Compartmentalization of group problems eventually leads to mistrust, lack of enthusiasm, and loss of faith in the process.

Leaders and leadership play a significant role not only in preventing group fragmentation, but also in creating conditions for effective group environment and group cohesiveness. As indicated above, in the absence of a charismatic or prophetic leader, a careful consideration must be given to the selection of a group leader. A leader who shows decisiveness and kindness is instrumental in sustaining group cohesiveness and preventing a degeneration of the group into conflicting sub-groups.

7. CRISIS AND GROUP

At best, most Muslim societies are mosaic. In such societies the traditional and modern, the old and the new live side by side producing vibrant relationships and arrangements. In each society and organization there appears intense rivalry and loyalty, enthusiasm and apathy, commitment and indifference, flexibility and rigidity, cooperation and fragmentation, authoritarianism and openness. These qualities tend to be exhibited by individuals and groups depending on circumstances and stimuli. These qualities, with some variations, may appear among individuals and groups in other societies.

In Muslim societies, however, the simultaneous existence of the traditional and modern and the nature of groups and alliances give these societies a unique aspect; acute hindrance to conflict materializing at organizational or societal levels. Various factors have contributed to this state of affairs. First, Muslim individuals hold concurrent memberships in many different social groups. Each group, as Riggs (1969) notes, has its own specific range of activities, goals, and norms. An individual usually spends a great amount of time and effort in making corresponding adaptations in his/her behavior and the symbols with which he/she identifies him/herself. Likewise, these small groups have considerable fluidity and fragmentation and are able to attain common goals readily enough to

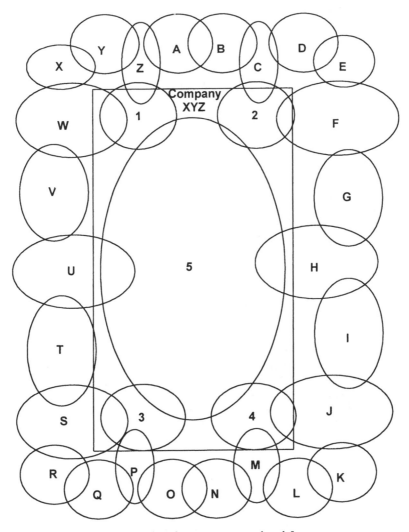

Notes: Company XYZ depicts formal organization; numbers 1-5 represent
informal groups; letters A-Z represent societal groups

*Figure 5.2   The complex relations among formal, informal, and
societal groups*

preclude the need for larger groups (Bill and Leiden, 1984). Second, there is continuing rivalry among sectarian, regional, tribal, and communal groups. Muslims develop an intense loyalty to one of these groups, but they do not seem, at this time, to be able to transcend these groups and develop an affiliation toward any larger entity (Ali, 1988; Issawi, 1970) as they did during the early years of Islam. Third, social groups in most Muslim societies are characterized by alternating fission and fusion. Thus it is possible to divide them and prevent powerful coalitions from forming (Moore, 1970). Fourth, self-censorship and the mindset of fearing God discourage Muslims from publicly revealing the wrongdoings of others. Fifth, the majority of the Muslims espouse the *Jabria* school of thought, which condemns disobeying authority. Sixth, lack of effective agencies and institutions that champion positive change. The examples of Iran and Algeria, where the religious institutions espoused and played an active role in advocating political change during the struggle against the Shah of Iran and the French colonial power in Algeria, were rare. In both countries the message of resistance to abuse and oppression in mosques swiftly spread across the nation. At this time other Muslim societies have not encouraged national or powerful institutions to advocate change. Seventh, the official Islamic message, since the eleventh century, has managed to dominate Islamic thought. This message views conflict as a negative force and contrary to Muslim interests. Eight, the governments that have emerged since the end of colonization have been mostly authoritarian. These governments resort to oppression to quell dissident voices, thereby instilling fear and ensuring submission. Finally, most conflict and tension revolves around personal ties, rather than ideology. This factor, combined with the absence of a charismatic leader to unite the group or masses around a grand vision, works to prevent swift expansion of any conflict across a company or society.

8.   CONCLUSION

In this chapter, the nature and types of groups have been discussed. Several task-centered and psychological functions performed by both formal and informal groups were specified. The focus and the discussion aimed at highlighting those functions that were deemed to be particular to Muslim societies. That is, this chapter has focused on those aspects and functions that are likely to differentiate between groups in Muslim societies from those that exist in other cultures.

Groups, in Muslim cultures, are situated at the center of all societal activities. The nature of relationships among people and the delicate balance of what is personal and what is business uniquely position groups to play a vital role at the workplace and society. It is because of this special aspect that specifying the nature and role of groups has become an imperative in understanding organizational functions and difficulties. Their unique values and behavior, along with their deep historical roots, affect how groups function in Muslim societies. These values enhance group cohesiveness and reduce uncertainty, and enable organizations to optimally serve the individual and society.

Likewise, in this chapter, we discussed the factors that foster/impede group effectiveness. Special attention was given to cultural underpinnings and group dynamics. In the process, reasons that exist in most of Muslim societies that prevent crisis from spreading across corporations or society have been highlighted. Furthermore, the role of training was debated. It is recommended that the use of training should focus on leadership and on problem identification and evaluation.

6.   Power and Authority

Power is an integral part of the daily activities of individuals, groups, and organizations. Indeed, the history of humankind can be viewed as a never-ending quest among competing forces to acquire and use power. It is for this very reason that the examination of power relations has become central to the understanding of organizations and their environments. In organizational studies in Western countries, power and authority are given considerable attention. Their nature, motives, aspects, classifications, and consequences have been thoroughly debated and analyzed. In Islamic societies, there has been an emphasis on the philosophical aspects of power and authority, with little attention given to their antecedents and consequences.

In this chapter the nature and role of power and authority are discussed both in their historical and contemporarily organizational contexts. That is, both the philosophical and organizational dimensions and implications are considered in light of their theoretical and practical aspects. Like the Islamic Work Ethic (IWE), which was discussed in Chapter 4, the meaning and application of power has not progressed in line with the original Islamic thinking as exhibited by the Prophet Mohamed. This observation should be viewed in the context of the internal and external forces that have shaped events in the Muslim world. The evolution of the "Muslim State" and Muslim societies and the stagnation of political and business organizations and institutions have been closely linked to the acquisition and application of power. This relation has not been adequately analyzed, thereby furthering economic and political fragmentation.

In this book, power is viewed as the capacity to induce others to comply with certain instructions or to do things the way one wants them to be done. Of course, actions are not necessarily consistent with the instructions or orders. But the mere willingness to go along or to comply demonstrates that there is a positive response, rather than resistance. People comply with orders or instructions for a variety of reasons, including fear, indifference or merit attached to instructions. Nevertheless, resistance to orders or instructions implies that either the orders do not have merit, or that simply the person who received the orders does not acknowledge the right or authority of the individual giving the order. Practically, the consequences of compliance or resistance are the measure of the existence of power. The history of mankind evidences that resistance to orders or noncompliance almost always leads to conflict and instability.

Authority is a legitimate power. It is based on a formal position in an organization. It conveys the rights to make decisions, to take action and to distribute/withhold resources. Therefore, compliance with authority is relatively common. There are cases, however, in which authority is confronted or resisted. The outcome of this confrontation depends on the situation and the existing power structure. While authority is the most common base of power, other aspects of power exist in and outside an organizational setting. These aspects include reward, coercion, expertise and referent (see French and Raven, 1959). It should be mentioned that with the exception of coercive power, the other aspects might lead to a positive outcome and further the cause of an organization or group. That is, the influence facilitates the implementation of the organizational aim and, therefore, is desirable. In the case of coercive power, the possible use of punishment and seduction (e.g., withholding resources, physical or psychological torture) may induce fear, dysfunctional involvement, or rebellion. These outcomes are not conducive to productive environment and often complicate organizational activities, be they business or political.

The widespread application of coercive power in politics and international relations highlights the negative connotation of power in popular and daily usage. This necessitates the need to differentiate between power and influence. Power conveys dominance and a degree of control exercised over other actors, be they individuals, organizations, or nations. Indeed, power may "seem a heavy-handed technique for achieving desired ends" (Hollander, 1978). Influence, on the other hand, is primarily a persuasion. A report in *Time* (1996) demonstrates that power "gets its way," while influence "makes its way." This distinction underscores a profound difference in orientations between domination and leadership. First, influence is viewed as "a vision" that inspires people or nations to discard their doubts, and "an ability to connect with people" across the globe and to comprehend the way they look at and react to events. Second, abusive use of power (coercive) disregards reality, and those who employ it behave as if others are insignificant.

These two distinctions have several implications for management and business organizations. First, powerful managers who lack vision and resort to coercion in their relations are not influential, as they cannot attract a following and build the confidence and trust necessary for organizational growth. Second, power, if used abusively, creates friction, conflict, and resentment. Third, in today's organizations, managerial decisions must reflect, in general terms, the collective aspirations of the organization's members and incorporate the diverse demands of the rest of the stakeholders. That is, leadership effectiveness is measured, as Chester Barnard argues, solely by "the accomplishment of the recognized objectives of cooperative action" (quoted in Hollander, 1978, p. 111). This means that the chief task of management is to secure the recognized goals with the greatest possible consideration for the community in general. Fourth, coercive power may bring visibility and exposure; it may not, however, ensure influence, because influence requires compassion and a special touch that arouses, inspires, and energizes employees to do their best.

Useem (2002) reported that John Patterson, the chief of National Cash Register, built a company based on fear and intimidation. None of his subordinates felt secure or intrinsically motivated. The recent corporate scandals in the United States, for example, uncovered, too, the fact that many managers who are motivated by self-interest and personal power not only harm employees, but also accelerate the demise of their corporations.

1.   THE NATURE OF POWER IN ISLAM

The concept of power and authority in Islam has evolved over centuries. The evolution has been generally regressive. Despite current revivalism, the acceptance of relatively original Islamic liberal perspectives faces serious social and political barriers. These barriers have deep roots in the collective memory of followers of official Islam and in government practices across the Muslim world. That is, the current perspectives seem to diverge from original Muslim thinking. Indeed, the instructions of the Quran and the Prophet's sayings offer perspectives that generally condemn oppression and abuses, if not totally reject the abusive use of power. The Quran, for example, clearly condemns oppression, dictatorship, and coercive methods. Specifically, the Quran instructs that a leader serves as a model and motivator or a custodian (39:41) but not a tyrant (88:21-22). The justification given in the Quran is that when a person in authority is an oppressor, followers will desert him (3:159). The Quran admonishes that leaders should not be harsh or brutal in the treatment of their followers. The Quran further states (2:217), "Tumult and aggression are worse than slaughter" (4:58), "And when you judge among people, do so with justice," and (16:90), "God commands justice, the doing of good. . . ." In an abrupt departure from the practice of the time and using language that is precise and deliberate, the Quran warns that dictators are a threat to society and to the welfare of the people. It states (27:34), "Kings, when they enter a country, despoil it, and make the noblest of its people its meanest."

The Quran appears to recognize the deep personal psychological aspects of power beyond the general foundations: *rehema* (mercy), *ihasan* (kindness) and *adel* (justice). This personal aspect revolves around the urge to abuse power and to engage in wrongdoing. Thus the Quran states (38:26), "O David! We have made thee a ruler in the land, so judge between people with justice and do not follow (thy) desire." Those in power and authority should not be selected based on wealth or heredity, but on knowledge and physical fitness (2:247). In addition, to knowledge, a person in authority should have wisdom and sound judgment (38:20): "We strengthened his authority, and gave him wisdom and sound judgment in speech and decision." The Quran reminds us that persuasion is considered the means to institutionalize sound vision and profound change (16:125): "Argue with them in the best manner."

The Prophet Mohamed exhibited a keen understanding of his environment. He recognized the Arab aversion to personal power and the nature of power structure in a tribal society. Most importantly, he understood the need for instilling order and a system of management in a disorderly society. His rivals were powerful and well established in Mecca. Confronting them was impossible without establishing a community and a power base. His migration to Medina allowed him to cultivate the necessary conditions for building a city-state. His power was primarily based on legitimacy founded on expertise, referent, and reward. His emphasis on the impersonal aspect of authority and on openness and public participation strengthened his power and allowed him in a short amount of time to expand his authority to surrounding regions. At the time, the newly established Muslim community identified Mohamed with pragmatism and foresight. His vision answered many of their questions and gave them confidence and hope. Therefore, they maintained a level of motivation and cohesiveness that had never been displayed by the Arabs collectively (see Armstrong, 1992).

Understanding the genuine concept of power and authority in Islam is possible by referring to the era of Prophet Mohamed. By relying on reason and the collaboration of highly engaged senior followers, Mohamed set the stage not only for spreading faith, but also for the institutionalization of his power. This was done not only through the designation of roles and positions to manage the affairs of the *umma*, but also in carefully orchestrated events designed to legitimize his actions.

Immediately after immigration to Medina the Awos and Khazerag, the chief social groups, agreed that in any conflict between themselves, Mohamed would be the arbitrator. Furthermore, he entered into a treaty with the tribal and Jewish groups in Medina. Projecting himself as a neutral intermediary, Mohamed specified that those in violation of what had been agreed on would be held responsible for their actions and would not be protected. In both cases, Mohamed situated himself as the leader of the whole *umma*. Of particular importance in the institutionalizing of power were the following steps:

1. Specified procedures, rules and rituals for preferred conduct and behavior. These evolved gradually as new circumstances emerged.
2. Differentiating his message of faith and objectives from existing religions and that of other states.
3. Structuring of jobs and functions. Mohamed appointed governors, advisors, judges, market administrators, and deputies. What is interesting to note here is that most of the selected governors were from highly influential tribes, while judges and market administrators were selected solely based on piety (see Siddiqui, 1987).
4. Organized several groups to disseminate information to members of the city-state and outside world. Jasim (1987) indicates that the Prophet Mohamed had his own subscribers, ambassadors, poets, translators, and special correspondents.
5. Management and distribution of rewards, charity, alms, and bounty from raids. In this context, Mohamed instructed his governors and deputies to distribute wealth to people in a timely manner. The wealth that was brought to Medina was distributed on a daily basis (see Kurd Ali, 1934).
6. Entering into treaties with the head of Arabian tribes and neighboring states. Furthermore, Mohamed sent letters and envoys to heads of other states informing them about the new faith and its objectives.

In differentiating his power base from existing models, Mohamed worked diligently on three important aspects: approach, nature, and source of authority. Mohamed utilized dialogue and persuasion to get his message across and to broaden his power base. Besides relying on close advisors and direct and open communication with followers, Mohamed demonstrated an aversion to conspicuous consumption such as spending on palaces, fancy clothes, and glorified titles. Simply, he called himself the servant and the messenger of God. In terms of the nature of power, he specifically promoted and practiced kindness and avoidance of oppression in his dealings (Armstrong, 1992; Jasim, 1987). He instructed his governors to have mercy in all their conduct and not to force people to do things they otherwise would not do. The Quran instructed Mohamed (10:99), "If it had been the Lord's will, they would all have believed . . . will you then compel mankind against their will to believe?" Furthermore, followers were to obey an authority only in good things. Here Mohamed specified three primary conditions for having and maintaining authority: quality and piety instead of race, "Hear and obey though an African is appointed (to authority);" heeding to authority, as long as the authority is committed to doing good acts and serving the people, "Obedience is due only to that which is appropriate," and followers have the right to change what they consider to be detrimental: "If any one sees a wrongdoing, this must be changed by resisting it, if one could not do this then by voicing concern, if one could not do even this then by denouncing it in his heart and this is the weakest believe."

In terms of the source of power, Mohamed embarked on two distinct but interrelated activities. The first was to delineate the relationship between rulers and followers and the second to differentiate authority in Islam from that in other religions. Both activities sought to broaden the concept of authority and promote it as a moral duty that receives its legitimacy from followers. It was reported that when a companion of the Prophet Mohamed, Abu Zher, who was a gentle and deeply pious man, requested to be put in a position of authority, Mohamed replied, "Abu Zher you are a weak person and authority is a trust, one must be qualified for it and execute it duly, otherwise, in the day of judgment it is a shame and regret." Furthermore, Mohamed stated that, "To any one who swears allegiance to a leader without consulting the Muslim people, there will be no allegiance shown to him or to the one who is nominated."

Four conditions, therefore, are set for legitimate authority and subsequently its power base. First, public authority is granted based on the consent of the people or group; people are the source of authority. Second, direct consultation is the appropriate method for the selection of authority. Jasim (1987) argues that consultation, during the early years of Islam, meant full participation of the members of the community in the selection process. According to Jasim, during that time democratic debate and active collective involvement were the appropriate instruments for deciding who would be the ruler and shape the political system. He argues that the practice was that each individual had the right to voice concern regarding the appointment of a ruler. Third, a person granted the authority must be qualified and perform his/her duties in a way that serves the interests of the people. Fourth, no one had an exclusive right to public authority; rather its custody was in the hands of those who assumed it. Those in authority were viewed as agents of the governed. If those in authority failed to guard the interests of those under their rule, the latter had the right to replace them. These democratic processes, however, did not survive after the death of

Mohamed. Various forces competing for power interpreted them differently or circumvented them according to their political goals.

2. POWER USAGE AND THE EVOLUTION OF THE AUTHORITY CONCEPT

The death of the Prophet Mohamed was one of the most influential factors that adversely left its mark on the evolution of the newly found state and *umma*. During Mohamed's tenure, the jockeying for power was mostly under the surface, as he was the ultimate authority in religious matters and the prophetic leader on worldly affairs. His death instantaneously brought to the surface the old tribal jealousies and animosities, which characterized the Arabian society. The appearance of cohesiveness of the faithful *umma* could not withstand the urge for power. Deep and sharp divisions appeared on the horizon, new alliances and groupings emerged and politics, rather than faith, seemed to be the game of the moment. The death of Mohamed demonstrated, too, that those who aspired to power and acquire political skills could easily overcome difficulties in the early stage of societal growth and evolution. These individuals, therefore, strengthened their position at the expense of other groups.

To understand the usage of power and the changing application of authority across the history of Muslim societies, we divide the latter into six general categories: the Rightly Guided Caliphs era, the Ommeyade era, the Early Abbasid era, the late Abbasid era, the stagnation era, and the contemporary era. Below is a brief discussion of the meaning and application of power and authority during each period:

The Rightly Guided Caliphs era (623–61)

There is a consensus among Muslim historians and experts that this era is the most just and the one that most closely resembles pure Islamic teaching (see Hourani, 1991; Jasim, 1987; Rahman, 1966). Al-Masudi (died 968, volume 3, p. 7) and Abu Talib Al-Makki (died 966, Vol. 2, p. 241) reported that the Prophet Mohamed predicted that: "After my death the Caliphate will be for thirty years [Rightly Guided Caliphs governed for about thirty years] and then it will become a monarchy." Implicitly, the statement acknowledged that the rules of law and order and the consent of the people were not observed under a hereditary system. More importantly, Islamic experts who reported the saying seem to differentiate between the early

Islamic state of the elected Caliphs and the political system that followed, including their own era. The system that followed was not considered legitimate or representative of Islamic thinking. Nevertheless, a careful look at the concept and application of power during the era of the Rightly Guided Caliphs distinctly differed among the four Caliphs. Indeed, the sharp differences manifested the fact that during that time neither power structure nor ideological interpretation and allegiances had taken a clear shape. The state was in the early stage of its existence and the diverse societal groups that were united under the prophetic leader found themselves confronting uncertainties and challenging events. The first Caliph, Abu Baker (623-4), derived his power from the semi-consensuses of the community in Medina in choosing him as Caliph and on the approval of the followers. He stated, "I have been entrusted with a great responsibility and I have no power or ability to turn it down. I would rather the most qualified person among my people be selected instead of me. Obey me as long as I obey God, and if I disobey Him you owe me no obedience. . . . I am not different from you. If you think I do well follow me, and if I do ill, then put me right" (quoted in Al-Denoury, 1997, died 856, p. 19). The authority was primarily based on the consent of the people and their perception that the person in charge should perform according to their expectations.

The second Caliph Omer (634-44) was a statesman. Just after the death of Mohamed, he swiftly orchestrated the ascendancy of Abu Baker to the Caliphate and became his close confidante. During that time, he built alliances to strengthen his power and outmaneuver potential rivals (for details see medieval historians such Al-Denoury or Al-Masudi). Omer understood that power would gradually erode without tangible results to satisfy followers. As such he placed emphasis on institutional power and on competing directly with the existing empires. More importantly, he recognized the seniority and piety of Muslim individuals and families and rewarded them accordingly. These people felt honored and were committed to expanding the Muslim State. Omer based his authority on the acceptance and approval of the community and on his service to *umma*. His tenure in authority was seen as contingent on the consent of the governed: "If you see me doing wrong, then straighten me." His legitimization of authority was strengthened by his personal austerity and accountability (see Al-Denoury, 1997). His direct responsibility for the affairs of his State was exemplified in his saying, "'Even if an animal tumbled on the ground in Iraq, Omer should be asked 'why did you not level the road?'" Omer's instructions to his governors illustrated his deep concern that the ill treatment of followers leads to instability. He stated, "Whether people are relatives or strangers they have to be treated equally. Avoid bribery, judging according to will and sentencing people while in a state of anger."

The third Caliph, Othman (644-56), was selected by a council appointed by Omer and was approved by the people in Medina and representatives of other regions.   The inauguration of Othman to Caliph represented a profound shift in the concept of power and authority.   Othman was a wealthy person and from the most powerful Arab clan, the Ommeyade. Unlike his predecessors, he viewed the position of Caliph as a divine right (Ashmawiy, 1992). It was during his tenure that a popular uprising took place. The rebels demanded that Othman dismiss the corrupt and abusive governors. Othman refused saying, "If I appoint whom you prefer and dismiss those that you do not like, it means then I submit to you and have no role." The rebels replied, "Step down and give back our Caliphate." Othman, however, considered his authority as a divine one saying, "I will not take off a mantle that God placed upon me. It would be better for me to lose my head, than for me to reject the role that God has ordained (quoted in Delo, 1985, pp. 72-3). Unlike the first Caliphs who were accountable to the people, Othman seemed to believe that he had to answer only to God.

The election of Imam Ali (656-61) to be the Caliph was a triumph for intellectuals, the pious, and the poor. Armstrong (1992, p. 258) argues that during his rule, Imam Ali was primarily responsible to the people and that in practice he was a democratic leader and on a par with his followers. For him, justice was the foundation of authority and prosperity, "Justice is the mainstay of a nation." Most importantly, Imam Ali insisted that the Caliph must be elected by the people and that the leader must have reciprocal relationships with his followers. He stated (p. 241), "It would be better that the entire population participated in the selection of the Caliph, but I swear by my life, there is no way to command such a gathering. However, those who are eligible should represent those who are absent." Election of the Caliph was seen as a prerequisite. Imam Ali asserted that sustaining power and authority requires continued approval of the governed, reciprocity between a leader and followers, unwavering commitment to justice, and openness of the leader to input from followers. He asserted that reciprocity between a leader and followers was the basis of legitimacy (p. 245), "God has made it an obligation for his creatures to observe their obligations toward each other. He made them equitable and interdependent.   The greatest of those obligations are the mutual rights of the ruler and the ruled. God has made them reciprocal so that they constitute a basis for their cohesion." In his letter to one of his governors, Imam Ali considered the approval of the followers as the base of authority and he abhorred the abusive use of power. He stated (p. 303), "Good rulers are known by what their subjects say about them. So, the best stock you can build is your good deeds. . . . Do not say. ' I am in charge and I shall be obeyed.' This is a sign of weakness in the heart and of a shaken faith, and an invitation to trouble." In terms of openness, he argued that people in authority must be (p. 283), "modest and benevolent to the people. Receive them cheerfully and treat them equally." He indicated that a legitimate authority is valid as long as it committed to the right path. When the elected person does not perform according to the people's expectations, the people have the right to replace him. He stated (p. 256), "If the elected person rejects or contests their [people] decision, they will bring to his attention the issues that need to be addressed. If he persists in his deviation, they will fight him for not following the consensus of the Muslims."

In general, it seems that during this era those who held the position of Caliphate was understood to be a successor to the Prophet Mohamed and assumed civil responsibility. The position was treated as one of custodial power and its holder had to serve the community and act according to spiritual principles. It was neither a divine right nor a heredity position. This was most vividly expressed by the demands of the rebels to the third Caliph: "Return to us our Caliphate and step down." There were no agreed upon mechanisms for selection except consultation. The consultation was done in an open public meeting in Medina. The killing of Imam Ali was a turning point in Muslim history, as it marked the end of a republic and the beginning of a tribal-based authority (Ashmawiy, 1992; Delo, 1985).

The Ommeyade Era (661-750)

The concept of power and authority changed significantly during this era. The Ommeyade dynasty moved away from an ideology-based authority to a tribal-based authority. As was stated in Chapter 1, this dynasty had accumulated wealth and military strength before Islam. The emergence of Islam weakened its power base for a few years. During the tenure of the third Caliph, Othman, the dynasty regrouped itself and assumed substantial political and economic power. When a senior member of the dynasty, Muawiyah, seized power in 661, he transformed the Caliphate to a monarchy. Muawiyah was a shrewd politician who utilized various methods to sustain his personal power and undermine the foundation of authority in Islam. Instead of resorting to religion to justify his power, Muawiyah relied on his clan's accumulated wealth and political clout, tribal networking, generous rewards, and compensations to loyal supporters and meted out severe punishment to those who did not agree with his polices. He recruited people to his administration from those who were not known for their piousness and who lacked historical, religious, or political knowledge, and infiltrated Islamic thinking with concepts that were borrowed from the Byzantine Empire (see Al-Masudi, Vol. 3, pp 41-43; Delo, 1985).

According to medieval historians, the Ommeyade dynasty was the first to use the term Caliph of God instead of the Caliph of the Prophet. Al-Masudi reported (Vol. 3, p. 52) that Muawiyah stated, "Land belongs to God and I am the Caliph of God. Whatever is taken from God's treasury is mine. Whatever I have left of it is considered mine too." Furthermore, Muawiyah was the first to violate the tradition of previous Caliphs by appointing his son, Yazid, as his successor, thereby making the Caliphate a heredity system.

During this period, the authority, especially the caliphate, acquired divine attributes. For example, Al-Masudi (Vol. 3, p. 151) reported that Al-Hajaj ben Yousef al-Thaqafi, one of the most feared military leaders of the Ommeyade state, advocated that obeying God was not obligatory all the time, it had exceptions. Nevertheless, obedience to the Caliph was a must. Furthermore, the Ommeyade elevated the Caliph to a rank higher than that of angels and prophets. Ibn Abed Raba Al-andelesy (died 985) reported (Vol. 5, p. 43) that Caliph Abd al-Malik (685-705) promoted that the Caliph's position was preferred by God over that of God's messengers and prophets, and that it was the pillar of what is on earth and heaven.

During this era, therefore, absolute power and unquestionable authority were promoted in a society that resented authoritarianism and autocratic rules. Experts on Islamic teaching (see Ali, 1961; Ashmawiy, 1992, Delo, 1985; Naser, 1994) assert that these concepts of power and authority are not Islamic and reflect the influence of Byzantine thinking on the Ommeyade state. The Byzantines, as Christians, believed that the king is a representative of God. As the Bible asserted (Romans 13:1), "Let everyone submit himself to the ruling authorities, for there exists no authority not ordained by God."

The Early Abbasid Era (749-842)

In this era there was significant intellectual discourse on the nature of power and authority. Each Caliph encouraged a particular school to promote his perspectives on matters ranging from law to politics. While the ruling elite was adamant in protecting their personal power and authority, they did not elevate their authority above that of the Prophet. They allowed spirited dialogue and sanctioned diversity in the state apparatus. Nevertheless, their hold on power was given religious justification; blood relationship to the Prophet Mohamed.

Ibn Abed Rab Al-andelesy (Vol. 4, p. 91) reported that Caliph Al-Mansour (754-75) stated in one of his speeches, "I am the sultan of God on His earth; I deal with you according to His guidance, direction, and support. I am the guard of His treasure, I divide it in accordance to His will and order, and give it by

His permission. God has made me the keeper of His treasure. If He wishes, He lets me distribute it among you or hold it. Request God to instill caring in myself and let me be kind in treating you. I say this and ask His forgiveness for me and you." This passage succinctly reveals that authority was considered to be ordained by God, and that power was unquestionable, absolute and beyond the consent of the governed.

The emergence of different schools of thought (see Chapter 3) and intellectual openness promoted conflicting concepts of power and authority. For example, while the first and second Abbasid Caliphs espoused a moderate predestination version of the *Jabria* School, Caliph Al-Mamun (813-33) encouraged such rationalistic schools as the *Mutazila* and *Tafwiz*. Both schools advocated that the choice of a leader was solely the collective responsibility of the community or nation. At any time, the chosen leader must be from people who were known to be just and faithful.

The Late Abbasid Era (842-1258)

It is during this era that two developments, in terms of power and authority, took place. The first was profound; the actual authority of the state was no longer the Caliph. Rather, it was the head of military or powerful non-Arab dynasties that jockeyed for power. Of particular importance were the Persian (Buwaihid, 932-1062) and Turkish (Seljuks, 1038-1194) dynasties that dominated the state. The position of Caliphate was reduced to a mere figurehead and, consequently, the Caliph became a nominal figure without much say in the administration of the state. Therefore, power was based on the existence of a strong invading army and dynasty. Indeed, both the Caliph and religion were utilized as instruments of the invading army in perpetuating their power.

The second development was related to the articulation of theoretical justifications of power and authority. The articulation of power theory was reinforced by several factors. Chief among these factors were intense sectarian divisions and the domination of non-Arab dynasties in managing the caliphate affairs. The first theory that was promoted by the Caliph was in line with the *Jabria* school and advanced by Abu al-Hassan Ali ben Habab (died 1058), known as Al-Mawardi. Al-Mawardi stated that in a time of crisis and chaos law and order disappear. Al-Mawardi asserted that order is more important than justice. Though, justice is essential, order must take precedence to ensure the continuation of the institute of the caliphate. Al-Mawardi articulated further that how the Caliph reached power and used it was less important than how he maintained order. He proposed that the Caliph was not only the protector of the faith, but was also necessary to maintain law and order in society. In his elaboration on the theory of caliphate, he proposed that the caliphate was a divine institution. The functions of the Caliph were "to guard the religion and world affairs", therefore, obedience to the Caliph was a religious obligation. Deviation from obedience to the Caliph was a defiance of religion.

The second theoretical justification for power and authority was espoused by *Ikhwan-us-Safa*. The theory stated that a power should be based primarily on knowledge, generosity, selflessness, and justice. It proposed that a legitimate authority must be based on the consent of the governed. In this context, leaders must be qualified intellectually and display an unwavering commitment to justice. *Ikhwan-us-Safa* believed that kings or rulers were civic leaders and that their position had no religious dimension. Indeed, they insisted that the ethics of kings could not be consistent with the qualities of prophets, because the role of the monarch deals with worldly affairs, while the position of prophet is for the hereafter; as such the hereafter and worldly affairs are antithetical. They further suggested that kings had a tendency to abuse their power and, therefore, must be monitored by the people (for details see *Ikhwan-us-Safa*, 1999b, pp 493-98).

The Stagnation Era (1258-early 1900)

The collapse of the Abbasid state at the hand of the Mongols and their occupation of the Abbasid capital, Baghdad, initiated a new stage of Islamic history that was characterized by fragmentation, powerlessness, infighting, and regression. In the context of power and authority, new forces assumed power and dominance who were not Arabs (e.g., Mongols, Ottomans, Mamliks, Safavids). Their newness to Islam or their complete unfamiliarity with it forced them to seek or appoint religious figures to justify and legitimize their power. In many cases, these rulers found in the *Jabria* school an answer for sanctioning the authoritarian rules and for strict obedience.

Two theoretical justifications for power and authority prevailed during this era. The first was promoted by Ibn Taimiya (1263-1328) and became generally accepted in many parts of the Muslim world. Basically, his theory stated that mankind by nature is oriented for cooperation and grouping to secure and improve its welfare. For this reason, people must render obedience to a commander and restrainer. That is, authority is necessary for the *umma* to maintain justice and keep individuals within accepted societal limits. How the authority is obtained is not as important as how it is used. He argued that any kind of order is much better than anarchy. For Ibn Taimiya, the exercise of formal power is a kind of religious service and obedience to authority takes on a religious duty, as well.

The second theory was advocated by Ibn Khaldun (1332-1406). Ibn Khaldun (p. 112) argued that goodness and inclination for collective or group feeling are a prerequisite for anyone who wishes to sustain power and be a leader. His theory of power has two aspects: political and social. The first deals with a ruler. In it, Ibn Khaldun distinguished between two stages. In the first stage one obtains power by relying on his social group (his people). As such a ruler appoints them in his administration and relies on them in his army. At the second stage, the ruler starts to claims all the glory for himself, alienating his original supporters and relying on stranger groups. These groups may see that obedience to authority is a necessity and an obligation. Obedience, thus, becomes a tradition. When this situation is coupled with injustice, lavish lives for the ruler and his inner circle and supporters and society is burdened by taxes, people will revolt and the ruler will eventually lose power.

In terms of social power, Ibn Khaldun associated power with social classes; members of higher social class have more power than those in the middle class, and so on. Furthermore, he believed that power is associated with rank in society. Those who have rank and prestige acquire more power than others with lower rank or no rank at all. He differentiated between two types of rank: influential and restricted. Those who acquire influential rank (membership in a higher social class and recognized status) normally have great power. Those who have restricted rank (not important) exhibit less power. Consequently, those who bestow rank on others become the benefactor. That is, bestowal of rank implies power and influence. Ibn Khaldun proposed that those who bestow rank expect the beneficiary to show submission and obedience.

The Contemporary Era (1914-present)

This era represents the rise of colonization in most Muslim countries and the widespread establishment of nation-states during or after foreign domination. Politically, most of the rulers were directly or indirectly approved by the colonial powers. After official independence, rulers espoused authoritarian rule. Since most of these rulers have depended on superpowers for security, they have practiced coercive power and disregarded public opinion. In projecting their power, they have creatively relied on force and religious justification. Authority stems solely from position and legitimacy is secured through complete submission to foreign protectors. Global politics, manipulation of public opinion, maintaining social division and switching or reviving alliances with domestic political groups and creative utilization of religious sayings have hindered political openness and democratic transformation in many Muslim countries.

Consequently, governments have encouraged the teaching and principles of the *Jabria* school. In fact, rulers have found in this school an ally in prompting the necessity of absolute authority, obedience, and the risk of public participation in decision-making. The difference between the use of authoritarian power in this era and the practice since the Ommeyade state is that in previous periods, rulers took note of social demands and gave the impression that they pursued justice within the boundaries of the religious dictate. Furthermore, the religious establishment at that time attempted, in public, to maintain some distance from rulers (Hourani, 1991). Therefore, they often instructed rulers to govern according to the rule of religious law. Today's rulers understand that rights acquired by force or granted by a foreign power have their own legitimacy and that the religious establishment must play a subordinate role to the government.

3. POWER AND AUTHORITY IN BUSINESS ORGANIZATIONS

In traditional societies, power and authority are in line with the prevailing norms and values. Before their contact with the colonial powers, business organizations in Muslim societies were either family-owned or partnerships. In a family-owned business the patriarch of the family or the senior member normally held the power even though he/she was not responsible for supervising daily business. The authority stemmed from seniority in the family and management of the business. In the context of partnership, power was largely determined by verbal agreement in establishing the business and skills of partners, along with the reputation of a partner in the society. Those who were respected in society and connected to powerful individuals in the community or government usually yielded more influence. Since reputation in the community and/or connection to powerful individuals was in flux, individual power in an organization changed accordingly.

Since the periods of colonization and independence, large and medium-sized organizations have been organized, along with typical small family or partnership businesses. Furthermore, large state organizations have been established. In both cases, there has been a dramatic adaptation of *Sheikocray* as a form of management (see Chapter 9). This form of organization sanctions personal relations and an open-door policy. It has relied on hierarchical authority, personal relations, and personal connections, and takes a generally patriarchal approach.

Executives under *Sheikocray* consider the organization as their fiefdom; an extension of the office. They might be authoritarians, but their behavior is always tempered by consideration of what is acceptable or not acceptable by the community and the rule of religious law. While managers are motivated by personal or institutional power, they carefully project the image of someone who observes traditional norms and values. Those who are institutional power builders resort to traditional norms, paternalistic approaches, and openness. These approaches allow them to strengthen the organization's position and its prestige in the community. Executives that are motivated by personal power care more about image and may believe that the utilization of traditional paternalistic approach furthers their interest in and outside the organization. It should be mentioned that there is a subtle difference in power projection by managers in Islamic societies and large Western organizations. In a privately owned large business organization, the family patriarch, though not involved directly in the business, is the one who yields the ultimate power. In matters related to the appointment of senior executives, reorganization, expansion, and other major decisions, especially in financial affairs, the patriarch almost always has veto power. For example, the patriarch of the Musallam family in Saudi Arabia, Sheikh Ali, is usually consulted and informed about all pending major decisions related to SKAB, a Saudi-based conglomerate. The president and the CEO of the company always discuss major decisions with him. In the last two years, the president and the CEO relocated his residency outside Saudi Arabia, but still manages the company affairs by relying on a network of diverse family members who serve as senior managers.

Generally, the power for making decisions in an organization is centralized at the senior level. The use of power, however, is tempered by four factors: consultation tendency, paternalistic orientation, concern for public image, and Islamic instructions to avoid oppression and abuse of power. These factors individually and collectively motivate executives to show caring, kindness, and responsibility toward those working in the organization. Whether these aspects are translated in practice is a different matter. Nevertheless, executives invariably project the image of a responsible authority consistent with community expectations and religious instructions. Empirical studies conducted in Muslim countries evidence that the majority of managers prefer a consultative style of management (see Ali, 1989; Ali, Taqi, and Krishnan, 1997; Amirshahi, 1997; Muna, 1980). The tendency toward consultation does not necessarily mean an absence of the centralization of authority. Several researchers have found that executives in Muslim countries prefer to hold on to power by centralization of decision-making and by maintaining close control of management affairs. For example, Al-Rasheed (2001) found that there is a clear centralization of decision at the top in most Jordanian-based organizations. Likewise, Ali and Sabri (2001) found that in Jordan-based organizations power culture is found to be the most dominant. That is, executives, though paternalistic, seek personal rather than institutional power and they demand complete submission from their subordinates. Previously, Sabri (1997, p. 205) found that it is a common practice in Jordan-based organizations, as in the rest of Arab organizations, for there to be a high concentration of authority at the top. She quoted a Jordanian manager of a family-owned business saying, "This company to me is like my son. I have founded and developed it. . . . Thus most decisions have to be taken directly by me." She found too that in other state or publicly owned private organizations, most decisions were made under pressure from the most powerful members of the board of directors. Amirshahi (1997) studied Iranian-based organizations and indicated that the consultative style is the most effective and that in the case of the Tehran municipality, institutional power is preferred over personal power. He indicated that the former head of the municipality, Mayor Karbaschi, decentralized decision-making, empowered subordinates and encouraged the dispersion of power. This phenomenon of decentralization of power in organizations, however, is new. Its popularity is widely attributed to the emergence of a new generation of managers who understand today's challenges and the necessity to participate wisely in the global marketplace.

4.   SOCIALIZATION AND SELF-CENSORSHIP

Upbringing and religious norms shape and perpetuate the concentration of power. Perhaps, the socialization of individuals in traditional Muslim societies cultivates a type of culture that tolerates the concentration of power in a few hands and subsequent personal attachment to and reliance on authority. For example, Hofstede (1983) found that employees in Muslim countries generally scored high on power distance. That is, there is a high degree of centralization of authority and a tendency toward autocratic leadership. This finding should be viewed with caution. Empirical research in most of the Muslim countries found that an autocratic style is the least preferred by managers (see Ali, 1989; Ali, Taqi, and Krishnan, 1997; Amirshahi, 1997; Muna, 1980). The application of an autocratic style in most of these countries is different from that in the West. In Muslim countries, the autocracy is almost always exercised in the context of a father figure and it is not impulsive in conduct. The executive is the protector and problem solver for subordinates. The open-door policy, the readiness to lend a helping hand, listening attentively to subordinates, and inquiries about their families and their welfare are part of norms and practices that are sanctioned by traditional values and social relations of kinship and religion.

The early childhood socialization process in Muslim countries provides fertile ground to prepare individuals to listen to elders and authority and to observe and accept what constitutes accepted behavior and ideas of right and wrong. One of the most socially and religiously sanctioned qualities is self-censorship. In this situation, individuals normally avoid disclosing the wrongdoings of others. Even when a person volunteers to talk about the unpleasant activities of others, his group automatically censors him. Individuals in these societies often utter words such as *haram* [not right], fear God, or *Istegfer Allah* [literally God forgives, but in this context it conveys the message that it is not appropriate nor right to say negative things about others]. Subsequently, the exercise of self-censorship becomes an important instrument for being accepted into the group. Religious authorities often remind people not to listen to rumors and allegations unless they see wrongdoings themselves. These authorities rely on the Prophet sayings, "Suspicions are not confirmations" and "Seeing is much better than hearing." Political and business leaders have utilized self-censorship to keep followers in rein and to guard themselves against any possible public outrage. Consequently, those in power take advantage of self-censorship tendencies and reinforce it.

Managers of business organizations, in particular, have found self-censorship mechanisms useful for managing their business affairs. In committee and group activities, criticisms are not freely voiced and conflict is kept under control. Furthermore, followers and immediate subordinates are always reminded of the necessity of cohesiveness and the threat of division. Therefore, attributing misdeeds to authority is considered to be a deviance from accepted courses of action and sanctioned behavior. In the event that managers become aware of a possible threat to their power and that criticism is widespread, they usually appeal personally to the emotions of their subordinates and their friendships. The effectiveness of the emotional appeal is largely determined by the personalized aspect of the relationships and the primacy of social affiliation and acceptance. Frequently, the exercise of self-censorship, individually and collectively, by subordinates has become an important factor in maintaining obedience and control.

5. LEGITIMACY AND CONTINUITY

Continuity in power depends mostly on legitimacy. In business organizations legitimacy is one of the most important sources of authority of the hierarchical superior (see, Hollander, 1978; Simon, Smithburg and Thompson, 1982; Zaleznik, 1971). By designing formal positions for organizational activities and engaging in other related tactics, managers attempt to legitimize their roles and perpetuate their power. While hierarchical status is an important source for legitimacy in organizations, it is not sufficient for companies operating in Muslim societies. Legitimacy has initially rested on the tradition that people occupying certain positions in the organization are legitimate authority. This, however, has to be reinforced continuously. According to Imam Ali, legitimacy is based, too, on the reciprocity between leader and followers and on the perceptions of the followers of the leader. Aside from having some knowledge, managers have to project, if not demonstrate, that they are committed to organizational goals, employees, and community welfare and to behave in accordance with societal norms. One of the most credible threats to legitimacy is avoiding responsibility. Despite the authoritarian political environment, Muslim people have a tendency to recall notable incidents related to shouldering responsibility and demonstrate an admiration of them. Two incidents are indicative of the people's expectations that those in authority must not avoid responsibility. It was reported that during the era of Sultan Suleiman the magnificent (1520-66), soldiers stole sheep belonging to an elderly woman. She complained to the Sultan that while she was sleep, his soldiers had stolen her sheep. The Sultan told her that, "You should take care of your sheep instead of sleeping." Her answer was, "O Master, I thought you were keeping eyes on us so I felt safe and slept" (quoted in Al-Barai and Abdeen, 1987, p. 256). The second well-remembered incident was during the era of the second Caliph Omer (634-44). He reportedly said, "If a person of our community died and was in debt, I would be responsible for his debt. But if he left wealth, then it would belong to his heirs" (quoted in Glaachi, 2000, p. 74). These, and other commonly appreciated stands, reveal that the public's expectation of responsibility is essential for legitimacy.

Behaving according to prescribed societal norms is also significant for maintaining legitimacy. In publicly owned organizations, for example, managers could not stay in power for long if they were perceived by members of the organization or community to behave in a way that is contrary to accepted behavior. In a family-owned business, legitimacy is contingent, too, on the consensuses of the senior members of the family, especially the approval of the patriarch. In the event that several members do not agree with the president or the CEO, there is a high probability that the role of the latter will be marginalized even if he continues to hold on to his organizational title. This situation is further complicated when the patriarch has several sons from different wives. In the absence of an agreed on brother as the ultimate arbiter after the patriarch, conflict takes place and those with organizational positions may lose their legitimacy overnight.

Furthermore, in many Muslim countries, the rulers' blessings are sometimes withheld from executives of private or state organizations. Normally, the fortune of these executives will collapse. Their legitimacy will be in jeopardy and people may distance themselves from them.

Thus, legitimacy in business organizations is contingent upon organizational and non-organizational factors. Managers, therefore, are under constant pressure to reconcile the contradictory demands of various constituencies. Whether these demands are business-related or not, managers have to make sure that their actions and responses are within the boundaries set by societal norms and tradition. That is, what is considered to be operationally legitimate may not necessarily ensure the continuity in power.

6.   EFFECTIVE USE OF AUTHORITY

In highly personalized societies, the effective use of power requires that those in authority have to rely on rational, emotional, and social appeals. In these societies effective application of authority is the result of a complex interplay of the politic, social, and economic. Subordinates seldom respond positively to managers' instructions irrespective of the manager's personal attributes and reputation in the community. Normally, personal considerations permeate organizational operations making it impossible to differentiate between personal and impersonal activities. That is, a manager's personality and style are not separated consciously from his/her actions or roles. Take for example, a manager attending a *Diwaniha* [a place for social gathering in or adjacent to a house of a respected person] in Kuwait. His treatment by the rest of the people is in accordance to his reputation and his family's standing in the community. His position as a manager is credible only if he has cultivated an image of being an honest person. The reputation of his family is essential not only for his place in the community, but also for his role in a business organization. His subordinates may exhibit indifference to his authority. This changes, however, to respect, compliance, and obedience if he manages to convey the image of a socially responsible authority with good community relationships.

For managers to be effective, they have to engage simultaneously in an array of activities that enhance influence and continued acceptance. These activities are grouped into three categories: rational, psychological, and social.

Rational activities These are activities that stem from positions of authority and hierarchical status within the organization. Managers clarify goals and set priorities, grant favors, build alliances, distribute resources, and motivate subordinates. These activities bring them more power and, more importantly, acceptance. In many organizations in Muslim countries, political alliances are continually shifting and power among various organizational groups is not well structured. Effective managers are sensitive to the balance of power among these groups and usually keep abreast of new developments and alliances. Consequently, they use various methods for motivation and recognize that the effectiveness of each depends on circumstances. Nevertheless, they never lose sight of the fact that sustaining and broadening influence requires maintaining a fine balance between firmness and kindness. These managers are sensitive to the macro and micro politics. While the macro political environment is generally autocratic, the environments of business organizations tend to be more open and coercive power is often counterproductive.

Psychological activities Managers are always involved in activities that are psychological in nature. Because of the personalized aspect of working in Muslim countries, these activities take on an added value. While managers in the West are occupied with these activities within the organization, managers in Muslim countries have to be equally concerned with the internal and external dimensions of psychological functions. Their ability to thwart internal and external challenges to their authority allows them to exercise influence and broaden their power base. Thus, managers display behaviors that facilitate organizational goals, while sustaining their influence. For example, managers almost always listen attentively to the concerns and problems of their subordinates and their families and think of ways to reduce their anxiety and uncertainties. In addition, they visit members of the community, motivate them by lifting their spirits and praise their involvement. Furthermore, in the face of serious challenges, effective managers combine reason and emotion to appeal for understanding and cohesiveness. Emotional appeal to internal and external forces is an effective instrument to rally people behind authority.

Social involvement Social activities are an integral part of a manager's job in Muslim societies. As was discussed in Chapter 5, there is no difference between the personal and the official role and there is a high societal expectation that a manager will participate in social functions. Effective managers play multiple roles in the community. They are social workers, mediators in community conflicts and between community and local government and they are expected to display kindness, concern and responsibility. These social activities not only bestow on these managers prestige and recognition, but also strengthen their organizational power.

7. INFLUENCE AND CONTROL

There is a wide range of ways to influence employees to achieve desired goals in organizations. Probably this is true in all organizations. But in organizations operating in Muslim environments, managers have means far beyond the rights of formal authority to guide activities in the appropriate direction. Formal authority relies on rules, procedures, directives, and cultural norms and values to influence behavior and control activities. In many situations, despite existing rules and procedures, managers and employees alike resort to existing cultural norms and the nature of social relations to exercise influence and maintain control. Coercive methods are always mentioned in the literature as one of the most practiced choices for influence (see Kipnis, 1983). In Muslim organizations, the impulsive use of power easily backfires. Thus, managers avoid giving the impression of being coercively oriented. Nevertheless, managers participate in activities that enhance their influence, such as incentives, granting favors, the distribution of resources, persuasion and identification with powerful individuals. In the meantime, they avoid using punishment as an inducement mechanism as it contradicts the desired image of the upholder of justice, mercy, goodness, and kindness. This by no means implies that managers should not be assertive. To the contrary, managers with a broad influence may find assertiveness, tempered with kindness, a very useful method for the achievement of organizational goals and cohesiveness.

Furthermore, managers can rely on alliances and social status to grant concession and favors, thereby enhancing their influence in meeting desired goals. In this context, two points should be clarified. First, managers with less rank in an organization but having a respected social status [being knowledgeable, coming from a good family, piousness, kindness, etc.] exercise more influence than a person with a higher authority, but without respected social status. Second, concession in Muslim societies, especially reciprocal ones, broaden influence and demonstrate that the person in charge is concerned and is willing to cooperate or provide help.

Influence, therefore, facilitates control in organizations. Effective managers are more likely to use cultural norms and values, along with informal approaches than formal rules and procedures to guide employees in desired directions and to achieve stated goals. In other words, means of influence that are not closely linked with an authority level in the organization may appeal more to employees in Muslim societies. In such situations, influence through persuasion, concession, kindness, identification with followers and other means consistent with cultural values seem more reasonable.

8.   CONCLUSIONS

Power and authority in the context of a Muslim environment is examined in this chapter.   It is observed that in the history of Islamic societies the concept and use of power have regressed, rather than progressed in line with the openness and liberalism exhibited during the era of the Prophet Mohamed and his immediate four successors. During the early years of the Islamic state, Muslims differentiated themselves by preaching and practicing openness and democratic principles.   These aspects gradually disappeared from the political scene as Muslims were influenced by the traditions of nearby empires and states. It is argued that both internal and external forces seem to obstruct participative approaches and hinder the progress toward political openness. In business organizations there is emphasis on the consultative approach.   Nevertheless, power is highly centralized at the top of the organization. Managers, however, rely on traditional mechanisms and accepted societal norms to broaden their power and sustain influence. Some of these traditions such as consultation, kindness, and open-door policy could be utilized to improve organizational culture and enlarge participation and full utilization of employees' potentials. They are important, too, in securing legitimacy and influence.

7. Decision Styles and Group Dynamics

In traditional Islamic thinking, the primary intent when making decisions is to ensure justice and social cohesiveness. Both objectives are considered the foundations for stability, public satisfaction, survival and continuity, and economic prosperity. Indeed, both the Quranic teachings and the Prophet's instructions remind the believers that justice is the basis for good governance. The Quran (4:58) asserts, "When ye judge between people that ye judge with justice: verily how excellent is the teaching which He giveth you!" and (5:8) "Be just: that is next to piety." The Prophet told the believers, "I prohibited oppression and make it forbidden among you, thus do not engage in oppression." The Prophet Mohamed considered consultation as a political choice that offers members of his community a wide participation in the decision-making and in governing their affairs.

Islamic teaching obliges leaders to consult and seek advice before making any decisions that effect people - be they organizational or national decisions. There are no exceptions to this rule. The Quran reflects on the story of Queen Sheba who despite her significant wealth and power, and the confidence and respect of her subjects, consulted with her Council when she received a message from Prophet Solomon to espouse the faith of God. Sheba knew that members of her Council were inclined to war. Nevertheless, she had to carry out her decision after consultation, deliberation and transparency. She states (27:32): "Ye advisors! Advise me in my affair, no decision I made without your presence." The Prophet is reported to have said, "He who consults is guarded against regret," "There is no cure for a person who relies solely on his own information" and "A decision that was made without consultation does not produce good outcome." Al-Masudi (died 968, vol. 2, p. 309) reported that the first Caliph, Abu Baker, ordered his new appointed governor to Syria to "be honest and clear when seeking consultation. This guarantees to you honest advice. And do not silence any advisor as the decision will be solely yours." The second Caliph, Omer, considered consultation an obligation for Muslims. He stated, "Muslims must consult in their affairs. People follow those leaders who consult and seek consensus in making decisions." During the early years of Islam, consultation and participation in decision-making were done in the Mosque or in Dar Al-Amaraha, the State House. The ideological fever and nature of social gathering (e.g., regular daily meetings in mosques and state houses, spontaneity, equality, egalitarianism) facilitated democratic practice. The leaders in the early years of state formation (about 50 years) sought to reinforce and follow what was dictated religiously and socially. Their styles of decision-making, despite variances, were within the boundaries of legitimacy and traditions. All leaders attempted to appear that they promoted good and prevented evil. In cases where the community thought that the leader violated justice and did not consult in his decisions, the leader was either warned to correct his practice or be removed. The popular revolt against the third Caliph, Othman, was a case in point. The Caliph was warned to correct his method of governance (relying on his relatives) and style of making decisions (ignoring advice from senior companions of the Prophet). When the deputies of the people from other regions (e.g., Egypt, Iraq) thought that he was not changing, he was removed.

As indicated in Chapter 2, Islamic philosophy long ago postulated that people differ in their behavior and orientations. In terms of decision styles, the early Islamic leaders and thinkers divided people differently. The second Caliph, Omar, recognized three decision-making styles. He stated that " There are three types: a person who relies on his own ideas to make decisions regarding matters that refer to him; a person who consults experienced and wise people and makes decisions accordingly; and a person who is unsure and unimaginative, who has neither his own ideas nor listens to those who give him advice" (quoted in Abu Dawod, 1996, p. 376). Hassan Al-Basry, a medieval Muslim thinker, identified three different decision-making styles as: "Individuals [who]are three types: a perfect man, half a man, and not a man. The first refers to an individual who has ideas and consults others. The second is a person who has ideas, but makes decisions without consulting others. The third is a person who neither has ideas nor is willing to consult others" (quoted in Abu Dawod, 1996, p. 376). Both typologies hold in high regard the process of consultation and the intellectual capacity to understand, retain, and process information. Consultation benefits both the individual and the community. Caliph Omar Ben Abdul Aziz (died 681) was quoted as saying, "Both the ability to consult and debate leads to enlightenment, and are the keys to intellectual clarity and material success."

The emphasis on consultation and openness in making decisions underlie the basic belief that trust, wide involvement, cooperation, and transparency are vital for societal and organizational effectiveness. The Prophet equated determination with consultation. When he was asked about determination his answer was "Consult people with ideas and experience and act accordingly." Long before contemporary behavioral sciences recognized the importance of consultation, Muslim thinkers identified its advantages. For example, Imam Ali stated, "There are seven advantages in consulting: knowing what is right, acquiring new ideas, avoidance of mistakes, being guarded from blame, being safeguarded from regret, a uniting of people, and following a roadmap" (quoted in Al-Mahamy, 1987, p. 172). These advantages have been commonly debated in organizational studies in the West and their practical usefulness has been highlighted.

However, as discussed later, both in managing state and business affairs, Muslims have drifted away from consultation and participative practices and have adopted various forms that differ completely from those that are sanctioned by Islam. Of course, there are forces that have acted to make such changes possible. These forces are discussed throughout the book and some of them are briefly visited in this chapter.

1.   FORCES SHAPING DECISION STYLES

In their quest to better understand managers and their work around the globe, researchers have made significant progress in the methodological and conceptual domains of international and cross-cultural management. They have called our attention to the need for theories and instruments customized to capture attributes of a particular culture or society (e.g., Adler, 1983; Ali, 1988; Hofstede, 1980; Sekaran, 1983). Of particular interest are decision-making styles and group dynamics. Both subjects are crucial for managerial performance and organizational growth.

Rowe and Boulgarides (1983) indicate that the decision-style approach is useful for understanding managers, their decision-making process, their problem solving, and their ability to interact with others in the organization. Singh (1986) suggests that there is a direct relationship between decision-making and attitudes toward risk and performance of the firm. Likewise, group alliances and dynamics are viewed as the foundation of organizational achievement and competitiveness in the marketplace.

Management scholars (e.g., Bhagat and McQuaid, 1982; Miller, 1984) argue that developing and testing culturally relative operational measures of work-related attitudes enhance our understanding of management thinking and practices across nations. The primary focus of this chapter is to identify managerial decision styles and the circumstances that lead to their presence. Six styles have been identified in the literature (see Ali, 1993). These styles are: own decision, pseudo-consultative, consultative, participative, pseudo-participative, and delegation. Cultural and historical reasoning for the emergence of these styles are briefly discussed. Furthermore, an attempt is made to contrast decision styles common in Islamic environment with styles prevailing in other cultures. In addition, the chapter provides an insight into the dynamics of groups in Islamic culture.

Most recent research in cross-cultural studies of management maintains that managers can adopt different decision styles, depending on the pattern of organization and individual characteristics (Ali, 1989; Blyton, 1984; Yukl, 1981) and cultural background (Hofstede, 1980; Tayeb, 1988). Managers may display a variety of decision styles, depending on the situation and the type of decision involved. Furthermore, suitability of decision style depends on a large extent on the cultural conditioning of a leader's subordinates (Hofstede, 1980). Table 7.1 summarizes the relationships between present styles and similar approaches used in prior investigations and in different cultures.

Conventional wisdom and the results of vast amounts of national and cross-national studies suggest that the autocratic style is a common phenomenon in most countries. Disagreement exists, however, on the rise and popularity of other styles (e.g., consultative, participative, etc.).

Table 7.1   Comparison between decision styles employed in this book and similar previous investigations

	Previous research				
Likert (1967)	Heller (1971)	Vroom and Yetton (1973)	Bass and Valenzi (1974)	Muna (1980)	Ali (1993)
Exploitative authoritative (System 1)	Own decision without detailed explana- tion (Style 1)	Manager makes decision him/herself (A1)	Direction (System1)	Own decision (System 1)	Own decision (System 1)
Benevolent authoritative (System 2)	Own decision without detailed explana- tion (Style 2)	Manager makes decision obtaining necessary information from subordinates (A11)	Negotiation (System 2)	Consultation with subordinates (System 2)	Pseudo- consultative (System 2)

Likert (1967)	Heller (1971)	Vroom and Yetton (1973)	Bass and Valenzi (1974)	Muna (1980)	Ali (1993)
Consultative (System 3)	Prior consultation with subordinates (System 3)	Manager shares problem with subordinates; make own decision (C1)	Consultation (System 3)	Joint decision with subordinates (System 3)	Consultative (System 3)
Participative group (System 4)	Joint decision - making with sub-ordinates (System 4)	Manager shares problem with group; makes own decision (C11)	Participation (System 4)	Delegation of decision to subordinates (System 4)	Participative (System 4)
	Delegation of decisions to sub-ordinates (System 5)	Manager and subordinate together arrive at a mutually agreeable decision (G1)	Delegation of decisions to sub-ordinates (System 5)		Pseudo-participative (System 5)
		Manager and group discuss, evaluate, and make a group decision (G11)			Delegation of decision to subordinate (System 6)
		Delegation of decision to subordinate (D1)			

In the context of Arab culture, Ali (1989) and Bill and Leiden (1984) argue that there is a phenomenon of "non decision-making" whereby superordinate-situated managers control the behavior of subordinates through manipulation and control of the environment in which the latter must operate. Both political and economic environments facilitate this tendency. For example, in Saudi Arabia, the government officially advocates strict adherence to Islamic principles. The mere existence, however, of a kingdom system and absolute monarchy is in conflict with Islamic teaching. For example, the Quran (3:159) states, "Consult them [followers] in affairs of the moment, then when you reach a decision trust God" and (27:34), "When kings enter a town they destroy it and disrespect its honorable people." Furthermore, Islam instructs Muslims not to use titles such as Majesty, Highness, and Royal. Muslim scholars assert that Islamic rulers should be elected and that authority should rest on the consent of those governed (Hawi, 1982; Jasim, 1987). This situation has created a tension that centers upon divided loyalty: allegiance to universal principles, while simultaneously observing the demands and orders of the rules.

Doublethink, a term used by George Orwell for holding two contradictory beliefs simultaneously, in Arabia and other Muslim countries, depicts a condition where the ideal (Islamic principles) is held officially, but violated in practice. At the organizational level, this situation produces what Child (1976) calls mental cheating. Managerial behavior, which remains strictly within the framework of the authoritarian and hierarchical structure of the organization, seeks to prepare subordinates to accept decisions already made by managers and to improve the individual managers' images in a society where Islamic and tribalistic values still have some important influence. The intention of managers, in this case, is not to create a situation of real consultation, but rather to create a feeling of consultation by means of the leader assuming a particular style (Pateman, 1970). This style is dissimilar to the consultative concept that prevails in the West. It is appropriate then to call such a style pseudo-consultative, so as to distinguish it from the true consultative one.

The consultative style is the third style often used in Islamic culture. Western researchers have identified it as a common style among managers (e.g., Heller, 1971; Likert, 1967; Vroom, 1984). In the context of Islamic/Arab culture, previous research of Arab managers has been circumscribed to some extent by the cultural values and norms which prevail (Ali, 1990; Almaney, 1981; Al-Nimir and Palmer, 1982; Badawy, 1980). Ali and Swiercz (1986) and Al-Jafary and Hollingworth (1983) found that Arab executives predominantly prefer the consultative style.

The fourth style is participative. Scholars attribute different meaning to participation. For example, Szilagyi (1988) equates collective or participative decision styles with the consultative style, while Likert's (1967) System 4, participative group decisions, implies delegation. Other researchers (e.g., Bass and Valenzi, 1974; Muna, 1980; Vroom, 1984) view participation as a means for making joint decisions but exclude delegation. In this book, participation implies mutual influence and power equalization between managers and subordinates in discussing organizational problems and in making decisions. Cultural experts (e.g., Baali and Wardi, 1981; Hitti, 1964) suggest that an Arab individual is "a born democrat." Empirical research (e.g., Ali, 1986; Ali and Al-Shakis, 1985) provides some evidence that Arab executives display a high preference for participative styles. Contrary to Badawy (1980), it is possible to suggest that the participative style is not an alien concept to Islamic or Arab culture. Many Arab executives show a tendency toward participative management and would prefer to become even more participatory (Al-Jafary and Hollingsworth, 1983).

The fifth style has been a subject of ideological and philosophical debate among Western researchers. The debate centers on the reality of participation. Blyton (1984) indicates that, because of the influence of human-relations philosophy, managers often seek the involvement of subordinates in decision-making, but retain the authority for decision-making. Hofstede (1983) similarly argues that in the United States individual subordinates are allowed to participate in the leader's decisions, but these remain the leader's prerogatives and initiative. Child (1976) agrees with Pateman (1970) that participation is affirmed by word and denied by deed and that techniques are used to persuade subordinates to accept decisions that have already been made by managers. Yukl (1981) suggests that what appears to be participation is really only a pretense. He indicates that a manager may meet with subordinates to make a group decision, but makes it clear that he/she seeks endorsement of his/her own choices. Thus, the fifth style, following Pateman (1970), is called pseudo-participative to distinguish it from the genuine participative style.

In the context of Islamic culture and Arabic culture, in particular, the pseudo-participative phenomenon may exist for three reasons. First, many managers have been influenced by Western management philosophy and by the benefits of the participative approach. In many management textbooks in Muslim countries, the participative approach is considered an ideal form. This has complicated management development as many managers in these countries display an infatuation with ideal forms even when they know these forms to be contradicted by reality (Ali, 1990). The individual is suffering, in general, from a problem of duality in thinking and practice.

Second, the claim that the Muslims and Arab individual is "a born democrat" should be considered in the context of Islamic/Arab culture. The early childhood socialization process in the Islamic culture provides, in almost all Muslim countries, fertile ground to prepare individuals to be oriented toward people rather than toward material gains. Individuals are trained socially to participate in conversation and to take part in social ceremony from early childhood. As a person reaches the age of thirteen or fourteen years, however, the focus is directed more on playing strict social roles and in adhering to societal norms (e.g., obey authority and older persons, listen and show respect). In this context, one would expect some tension to exist between the "ideal" (participative) and the "practical" (authoritarian). It is likely, therefore, that a relatively high portion of

Muslim managers display a preference for the pseudo-participative approach.

Third, Islam is egalitarian and emphasizes social justice, but both features are violated in practice by current political regimes. Typically, Muslims, and Arabs in particular, hold two sets of identity: one – immediate, social, and spatially particular; the other – historical, cultural, and global (Ahmad, 1984). Violation of participative principles, which were cherished in the early days of Islam, is common. For example, Imam Ali (598-661) – the fourth successor of Prophet Mohamed stated (1989, p. 240): "If the presence of the entire people is necessary for the validity of the selection of Caliph, then I swear by my life, there is no way to command such gathering. But those who are eligible should represent those who are absent." Thus, the presence of the pseudo-participative style may represent a symptom of the guilt of not observing "short-lived" tradition.

Tannenbaum and Cooke (1974) argue that, in societies where organizational authority is highly centralized, personalized managers are reluctant to delegate authority. Ali (1990) indicates that the basic aspects of the reality of Arab politics and organizations are the personalized nature of authority, tribalism, and fluidity and alternating fission and fusion of group coalitions and alliances. These features demand an intimate and personal conduct of affairs and, therefore, preclude delegation from flourishing in practice.

2.   DECISION STYLES IN PRACTICE

As indicated above, the decision style scale used in this book includes six statements pertaining to autocratic, pseudo-consultative, consultative, participative, pseudo-participative, and delegative styles. The initial development of the scale did not include pseudo-participative, and participants were asked to select the one style that best described their behavior. Based on input and feedback from various scholars, the original scale (published in 1985) was revised into the current form. Survey participants rated their preference to each statement on a five-point scale ranging from (1) "strongly disagree" to (5) "strong agree." The mean for each statement was generated to indicate the executives' preferences. Ali and Schaupp (1992) and Ali and Swiercz (1986) have used the scale and found it to relate to selected managerial work values and satisfaction respectively.

Table 7.2 shows the results of empirical studies that were conducted in three countries: Iran, Saudi Arabia, and United Arab Emirates (UAE). The table shows managers' preference to each style where 1 is the most preferred and 6 is the least preferred. The strong preference of Muslim executives toward the consultative style is consistent with previous findings. This preference may reflect the influence of Islamic and tribalistic values and beliefs, as both Islamic and tribal laws reinforce consultation in conducting all aspects of life. It is the practice of traditional Islamic/Arab society that members of the entire kinship network or community should be consulted on matters important to their welfare. In fact, consultation mechanisms, a counter-point to autocratic rule, are, for example, a particular feature of traditional Arab society. A tribal sheikh, in the classical nomadic structure, could not rule for long without the consensus of the tribe. Traditionally, the sheikh followed rather than led tribal opinion. He could neither impose duties nor inflict penalties; his authority was not to command but to arbitrate (Lewis, 1966). In addition, Islam presents consultation as religiously positive – "This reward will be for those. . . . who conduct their affairs with consultation among themselves" (Quran, 42: 38).

Table 7.2   Ranking of managerial decision styles

	Saudi Arabia	Iran	UAE
Autocratic	6	5	6
Pseudo-consultative	2	6	3
Consultative	1	1	1
Participative	3	2	2
Pseudo-participative	5	3	5
Delegative	4	4	4

The phenomenon of a pseudo-consultative style deserves special attention because it most directly confronts the issue of cultural bias and misunderstanding. It raises the question as to whether there is a distinction between the appearance of consultation and the reality of consultation. Furthermore, it confronts the crisis of identity that many Muslims experience. The preference for the pseudo-consultative style, among Arab but not Iranian executives, can be traced to the authoritarian element in the Arab political and social environments; an element springing from several factors that have shaped the norms, values, and beliefs of contemporary Arab society. These factors include the primacy of coercive force and instability in the succession process of the Arab state after the death of the fourth successor (Imam Ali in 661) of Prophet Mohammed, the centralized political systems which have evolved since the end of colonialism (Roy, 1977) and the quality of political rulers in the Arab World.

The latter is important as most leaders (political and business) in contemporary Arab society assign relatives and clan members to senior positions in organizations and in government. This is in violation of Islamic teaching. For example, the Prophet Mohammed says, "Whoever is in charge of running Muslim affairs and hires a person on the basis of nepotism, has deserved the curse of God, and God will not accept whatever justice he does beyond that." Likewise, Imam Ali states, "Monitor the behavior of your assistants and use them only after probation. Do not nominate them on accounts of favoritism or egoism. Those two attributes reflect injustice and treachery." Additional factors involved are the fragmented kinship society, generally poor communications and a lack of education in the region for centuries. For example, for more than four hundred years, during the Ottoman occupation (1412-1918), schooling was denied for the Arabs and illiteracy prevailed. Consequently, during these years the Arabs mistakenly treated foreign (Ottoman) practices and orientations as Islamic (e.g., adherence to specified rules, centrality of decision- making, outlawed imagination and independent thinking).

Finally, the majority of the population in Saudi Arabia and the UAE follow Sunni, as opposed to Shiite, Islamic thought. A cornerstone of most Sunni schools is the legitimacy of authoritarian actions by the leaders of society. This particular orientation stems from the fact that most of the religious leaders in the Sunni community in the Islamic world were appointed by the government and they often tend to tolerate and justify the totalitarian actions of existing leaders (e.g., traditional Sunni theologians such as al-Ghazzali, Ibn Jamaa, al-Maward, and al-Bagillani have sanctioned obedience to unjust leaders). In Arabia, in particular, the Umma or Islamic sheikhs have been vital in legitimizing the absolute power of the rulers. It was only in 1980 that King Fahd, under popular pressure, proposed creating a consultative council and built an impressive building for it. But the building has stood vacant with no council or even appointed members for many years. Nevertheless, the religious sheikhs consider it an outstanding achievement. The conflict between authoritative and consultative trends and traditions in Arabic society, indeed within Islam itself, is crucial to the understanding of current tensions in the region, particularly as that tension is manifested in business affairs. Arab managers display a pseudo-consultative style in order to reduce that tension, to enhance loyalty and commitment and to create around them a supportive environment.

The second most preferred style is participative. This indicates that most managers, especially in Iran, desire democratic principles and practice. What should be mentioned is that unlike the clear-cut differentiation between consultation and participation philosophies in the West, in the

Islamic tradition these concepts overlap. In the early years of the Islamic state, both concepts appeared to denote the same meaning. In fact, despite the wide influence of Western concepts and principles of organization in many contemporary Muslim countries, both terms are often used interchangeably. For example, in commenting on the Quran (42:38) that the faithful are those "Who conducted their affairs with consultation among themselves," Jasim (1987) indicates that Prophet Mohamed was guided by a genuine and uncompromising commitment to democratic principles in his life and in the conduct of government affairs. Jasim argues that, for Mohamed, consultation was a primary principle in his life, stemming from his spiritual and rationalistic nature and his rich experience. That is, for Mohamed, democracy was a natural tendency and a solid political choice that he never compromised.

Therefore, the popularity of participative style among managers should be viewed in the context of the condoned practice and general understanding of the broad meaning of consultation. Certainly, it is clear that despite the fact that the general political environment is authoritarian in most Muslim countries, business organizations seem to espouse participation as a useful management approach. Perhaps this situation evidences future tension between the business and political communities. More importantly, it signifies that democratic involvement and participation are not alien to Islamic culture. As Jasim (1987) asserts, democracy at the individual level is strongly associated with the nature and quality of the person. Generally and practically, however, democracy as a system is founded on the principles and laws that govern the state and society that prohibit dictatorship and oppression. Jasim argues that Islam emerged to put an end to all limitations and prohibitions on freedom and choices. That is, Islam intended in its message to liberate human beings from organized restrictions that were imposed by emperors and kings to impede the free will of people and the development of vibrant civil societies. Jasim vehemently asserts that the involvement and participation of people in determining their affairs are the hallmarks of the formative years of the Islamic state and society.

Consistent with the preceding discussion, the empirical evidence in Table 7.2 reveals that the least preferred styles are autocratic, pseudo-participative, and delegative. These results evidence, again, that culture and tradition are crucial in understanding management practices. While this indication seems common sense, a cautionary interpretation is still appropriate. A case in point is Yucelt (1986) who suggests that highly industrialized nations tend more toward participative management (System 4) and less toward the autocratic (System 1) while, in less-industrialized nations, the opposite tends to hold true. This is not the case in the Islamic culture where the tradition and teaching of Islam condones, in principle, consultative and participative practice. The general political environment that prevails in developing countries, including the Islamic nations, is mostly the product of colonial legacy, arbitrary political division and turmoil. All these aspects, along with other forces, have produced a political environment that is neither conducive to wide public participation in the decision-making process nor aligned with traditional culture and principles. In Muslim countries, as in other nations, business organizations are influenced by the general political environment. Nevertheless, managers in these organizations seek to be in tune with trends in the business world and common religious instructions. Therefore, they appear to be receptive not only to the principles of their faith, but also to development in management thought. Assumingly, these managers understand that in today's world, openness and flexibility are necessary qualities for survival and competition.

3.   GROUP ALLIANCES AND DYNAMICS

Group alliances played a special role in Islamic history. Their nature and dynamics significantly altered the course of history in favor of certain groups to the detriment of others. Indeed, the emergence of Islam and the history of the Islamic empire and its demise are closely linked to the formation, development, and dissolving of groups and alliances. This may explain the extraordinary focus of the Prophet and the Quran on cooperation, alliances, and the necessity of groups and group activities in sustaining and promoting the faith. The instructions of both highlight the virtue of cooperation, alliances and group cohesiveness. For example, the Quran specifically warns the faithful against engaging in conflicts. It states (8:46): "And fall into no disputes, lest ye lose heart and your power depart." In this context the Quran asserts that it is the lack of wisdom that induces people to enter conflict and consequently weaken their stand. It explains (59:14): "You think that they are united, but in fact, their hearts are divided; that is because they are people devoid of wisdom." Therefore, it is only in cooperation and understanding that the group can make progress. The Quran (5:2) instructs the faithful to "Cooperate with each other in righteousness and piety, not in sin and hostility."

The Prophet Mohamed initiated alliances with various groups. For example, he entered alliances with several tribes to protect trade routes or to achieve a military goal such as his alliance with Beni Thamra and Beni Mudlage. Likewise, when he had just moved from Mecca to Yathreb (Medina), the Muslims created a pact with the Jewish tribes in the city. The pact, among others, focused on defending the city against outside threats, especially the ever-existing threat of Quraesh and its allies. Karen Armstrong (2002) states, "Very early, he [Mohamed] created a sort of confidence treaty with the various groups of Medina, stating that he would be, as it were, the leader of the community, but no one was to be obliged to convert to Islam. . . . The treaty, or Constitution of Medina, was a purely political arrangement." The treaty's main objective was to create a community where all "the different tribes of the oasis were to bury their old enmity and form, as it were, a new super-tribe. The Muslims and the Jews were to live peacefully with the pagans of Medina, as long as they did not make a separate treaty with Mecca to get rid of the Prophet" (Armstrong, 1992, p. 154). In the early days, the Prophet sought to encourage other people in Medina and surrounding communities to form alliances with the Muslims, but without letting them feel pressured to do so. Among the Muslim groups, Mohamed sought to form an entirely new form of organization; a community called "umma" [in contemporary Arabic, it denotes nation] that was not based on blood relations or tribal identity.

4. THE NATURE OF GROUPS AND ALLIANCES

Before Islam, Arabia was a place that experienced fierce rivalry and fighting among tribes. The primary organization was the tribe. The tribe was organized strictly along the lines of blood relations, and alliances with others were mostly determined by kinship, social relationships, and economic interests among tribes. Mohamed did something quite innovative and original in Arabia at that time. He abrogated the traditional tribal bond and replaced it by an allegiance to Islam. This helped the new Muslims to form the nucleus of a nation and to gradually transform it into a vibrant and respected state.

Tribal loyalty and rivalry had prevented the Arabs of Arabia from establishing a central government, forming a unified nation, and furthering their culture. It should be mentioned, too, that tribal conflicts and disputes and the apparent contradiction between the individualistic tendency of the Arabs and their fierce attachment to a primary group hindered the search for common goals and strategies in dealing with the existing empire to the north and east. Furthermore, each tribe had sub-tribes and powerful families. The latter supervised resources available to their respective groups and were responsible for enacting pacts and treaties with others. The allegiances to these treaties, as well as toward others, were always in a state of alteration. This meant complicated group relations and intensified jockeying and maneuvering to sustain the interest of one's group.

The Prophet Mohamed, while redirecting allegiance and loyalty priorities, capitalized on the dynamics of existing rivalry and channeled it toward promoting the new faith in an unprecedented way in the history of Arabia. This new commitment to faith was a remarkable achievement that made it possible to unify the Arabs and destined them to play a major role in the history of mankind for several centuries. Obviously, Mohamed understood the dynamics of groups and their role not only in sustaining the new faith, but also in building the foundations for an influential state. Mohamed was persistent in promoting his message of justice, law and order, fairness, compassion, universalism and that salvation comes solely from good deeds. The Arabs became gradually receptive; especially when the Prophet reiterated and emphasized that he was just a human carrying the message of God, the Creator, Supreme Power, Most Kind, and Most Merciful. The Arabs accustomed to the abuse of power by their chieftains, the personalized affairs, and tribal divisions and conflicts found this universal and impersonal message appealing and motivating. Their tribal loyalty was profoundly changed and transformed into a loyalty to a new umma that embedded both universal faith and national identity. It is around Mohamed's personality and around Islam that the Arabs felt that their new faith and unity destined them to play a God-sanctioned role to promote righteousness and good deeds and to claim their rightful place in history.

When Islam spread to non-Arab lands (e.g., Persia, Africa, and Indian subcontinent), people there had a different experience from the Arabs. The people in these regions had different cultures and civilizations, but remarkably, they assimilated Islam into their respected cultures. Almost all of them recognized and valued the universal message of brotherhood and equality. This understanding allowed them to transcend their primary group affiliations, be they geographic, religious, profession, or tribal. Like their Arab counterparts, the Muslims in other regions had their own primary groups and established families. Their adaptation of Islam did not render these groups and families completely useless. This is because it was only during the life of the Prophet that Muslims appeared to abandon their previous loyalties for the sake of a loyalty to the new faith and umma. After the death of Mohamed, old loyalties and alliances slowly emerged in different forms. Islamic historians and experts acknowledge that, in subsequent years, many of these groups survived and some acquired additional fame and influence. Indeed, many of these groups and families (e.g., merchants, professional bureaucrats, warrior families, communal groups, sub-tribes and their families, and notable religious families) exercised a tremendous influence on the ruling elites for centuries. Both Islam and the centuries of tested instinct for survival and continuity sustained the ability to make flexible alliances and swift allegiances during the rise and fall of various dynasties.

Since most of the Muslim societies are traditional and since Islam is a powerful force that sustains identity, various groups have flourished or re-emerged under different forms and names. This aspect is both an asset and liability. It is an asset because it allows cultural values and norms to be transmitted from one generation to another and because it facilitates organizational continuity. It is a liability because it might hinder the development of comprehensive organizational and national goals. More importantly, it could lead to fragmentation, apathy and an obsession with minor issues at the expense of what is important and significant. In terms of the Middle East and the Arab world, Ali (1988) identifies four major group characteristics. First, individuals hold concurrent membership in various social and professional groups. Each group, as Riggs (1969) notes, has its own specific range of activities, goals and norms. Individuals usually spend a great amount of time and effort to make corresponding adaptations in their behavior and the symbols with which they identify themselves. Likewise, these groups have considerable fluidity and fragmentation, and are able to attain common goals readily enough to preclude the need for larger groups (Bill and Leiden, 1984). Second, there is continuing rivalry among tribal, sectarian and regional and communal groups. Individuals develop intense loyalties to one of these groups, but usually fail under normal conditions to come up with practical and comprehensive organizational approaches or pan Muslims goals. Third, social groups are characterized by alternating fission and fusion, thus it is possible to divide them and prevent powerful coalitions from forming (Moore, 1970). Finally, most of the group conflict and tension revolve around personal ties, rather than ideology. Often, however, influential individuals camouflage conflict in emotional or ideological terms. In the absence of open and dynamic dialogue, these individuals maneuver to obscure reality and exaggerate their utility to group survival.

5. CONTRADICTION AND IDEALISM

Like many other cultural and religious communities, Muslims often misunderstand their teachings or are not familiar with the principles of their religion. Indeed, the majority of Muslims may not be aware of the pervasiveness of these principles. Perhaps, this phenomenon is almost universal. Nevertheless, in the Islamic World it is common. There are various reasons for its commonality. First, after the death of Mohamed there were upheavals and chaos. This rekindled many old Arab traditions that were forbidden by Islam, such as tribal loyalty, the consumption of alcohol, and autocratic practices. Second, Islam spread to other lands incredibly fast. This happened even before the Arabs internalized its principles. In these lands, though teachers and teaching were highly regarded, the majority of the ordinary people were left only with the ritual aspects of Islam. Third, after the death of the fourth Caliph in 661, the Ommeyade clan came to power. They ended the practice of consultation, openness, and democratic practices. Jasim (1987) asserts that the Ommeyade and the ruling dynasties that followed did not observe and absorb, in practice, the deep message of the Islamic democratic experience. Thus, Islamic principles have become, because of government interference, unrelated to practice. Consequently, an individual is a Muslim only in the performance of ritual, but is prohibited from playing a vital role in managing the affairs of the society and state. Fourth, after the collapse of the Abbasid Empire, the vast majority of the Islamic and Arab lands came under foreign occupations. Furthermore, during the downfall of the Islamic states, many segments of Muslim society adopted foreign practices and rituals as their own. Fifth, after the collapse of the Abbasid Empire, formal education and learning were not held in such high regard as they had been during the Muslim golden age. Foreign powers either did not promote schools or prohibited education all together.

The above reasons helped to accelerate the demise of both the consultation practice and the necessity of group decisions in the organizational and government affairs. In recent years, there have been some attempts to reinvigorate Islamic consultation, openness, and transparency. Various forces, however, have obstructed these attempts. Chief among them is the inability of many Muslims to process the original genuine principles and to abandon the sectarian outlook and formal government Islamic teaching. Indeed, all attempts to sensitize both policy makers and managers that consultation and democratic practices are obligatory in Islam have not been received positively. The general political environment is not only authoritarian, but also seems to impede original thinking and vigorous discourse. It is possible to suggest, therefore, that while consultation and democratic principles have a promising future in improving organizational performance in many Muslim countries, their genuine application in the work environment is still a far possibility.

8. Leadership and Organization

Dramatic events and rapid political changes coupled with a deep sense of vulnerability at home and abroad have brought to the surface the importance of leaders and leadership. Indeed, vulnerability is a result of an absence of effective and trusted leaders. In all aspects of human affairs, effective leadership makes the difference. This is because leadership encompasses both practical and idealistic concerns. Lack of wisdom and a practical vision leads to disaster and setbacks. It is the presence of foresight, responsibility, sensitivity, creativity, courage, and compassion that ensures progress and prosperity.

The history of humankind evidences that leadership has been the pivotal factor in defining reality and designing and shaping events. In fact, the rise and fall of nations and organizations have been attributed largely to the presence or absence of skilled leaders. The importance of leadership stems not only from organizational skills, but also from the ability to motivate, the courage to confront abuses and assume responsibility and the foresight to articulate a purposeful vision and offer possible options to meet goals. Leaders assume various roles and functions. These roles and functions differ in their significance over time and level of existence in an organization or society. Changing circumstances and situations necessitate different leadership roles and functions. Despite this, however, leaders have to coordinate functions and innovatively maintain creativity with order, and order with creativity (Collier, 1971).

In the Islamic tradition, the subject of leadership is given considerable attention. This is because, in Islam, leadership is perceived to be the most significant instrument for the realization of an ideal society. The ideal society is based on justice and compassion. Both qualities are an integral part of leadership. In Islamic thinking, neither creativity nor order can be sustained without justice and compassion. That is, justice "is the mainstay of a nation" (Imam Ali, died 661). Leaders are held responsible for promoting and enforcing justice. The Quran (4:58) instructs its believers: "When ye judge between people that ye judge with justice." Indeed, the thriving of justice is closely linked to the subject of leadership and leaders.

It should be noted that Muslims hold the early period of Islam (about (622-661) as the most just, compassionate, and ideal in Islamic history. Muslim scholars argue that during these early years, an Islamic society most closely resembled the ideal state. Probably, this state did not take place again except during the era of Caliph Omer Ben Abdul Aziz (717-20) and for a short period during the Abbasid Empire. Muslim scholars claim that justice was then fairly meted out and leaders were morally guided and responsible. Therefore, a sense of idealism has evolved in the psyche of most Muslims, resulting in an infatuation with what is termed a Prophetic leader, as opposed to the Caliph model of leadership. Both concepts will be discussed in this chapter.

In this chapter, leadership is defined as the process of influencing a group or followers to engage in certain activities to achieve mutual goals. The chapter provides an insight into the nature of leadership in Islam and the evolution of the concept and its practice under various historical stages. In addition, the chapter discusses different types of leadership and provides a model of the ideal form of leadership.

1.   THE CHANGING NATURE OF LEADERSHIP IN ISLAMIC THOUGHT

At the outset, it should be mentioned that the traditional view of leadership in Islam is that leadership is a shared influence process. Leaders are not expected to lead or to maintain their roles without the agreement of those who are led, and at the same time, decisions made by these leaders were expected to be influenced by input from their followers. The process is dynamic and open-ended and the ultimate aim is to sustain cohesiveness and effectiveness. The Quran clearly calls for a leader to be flexible and receptive to followers and states (88:21-22) "So thou reminding; thou art only a reminder. Thou art not, over them a compeller." The basis for understanding and leading has to be fundamentally based on wisdom and spirited debate, otherwise followers become resentful and dissatisfied. The role of a receptive leader is captured in the Quranic instructions which state, (16:125) "Argue with them in manners that are best and most gracious" as (3:159) "Wert thou severe or harsh-hearted, they would [break] away." The leader is obliged to exemplify openness, a willingness to listen and compassion in dealing with subordinates or followers. For example, during the course of a public meeting, an individual criticized the second Caliph, Omer. Some in the audience thought the criticism was harsh. Omer's answer was that it was the duty of the leader and followers to listen to each other and to voice concerns. He was quoted as saying, "When followers do not participate and provide input, they are not contributing something useful. And we are not useful if we do not consent to their contributions." Omer thought that public participation is fundamental and, as the Prophet Mohamed insisted, that it is a policy choice. Omer, however, pursued the matter further when he informed followers, "When you see me engage in a wrong doing, straighten me out." In this context, the shared influence is not only built on a "two-way influence" through dialogue and debate, but also on the right of subordinates to take a proactive role in confronting and correcting the leader. This foresighted model was possibly founded on Prophet Mohamed's instruction, which made it mandatory that followers not blindly follow leaders: "Obedience is due only in that which is good."

Before discussing the changing view of leaders and leadership in Islamic thought, there are two points that need clarification. The first is that there are imprecise terms such as imam (prayer leader, an authoritative religious scholar), *wali* (governor of a state or region), or emir (a group or regional leader, or a title that is given to a member of a ruling family) that are usually used interchangeably with a leader. People in these positions may exhibit leadership qualities and influence. Nevertheless, they should be differentiated from a leader at the macro or societal level. While the last two terms may have a secular meaning, the term imam mostly implies a religious leadership role. The term often refers to a person who leads the congregation in prayer or to a religious leader. In this chapter, leadership is utilized to convey the art of influence that is exercised by a leader in general.

The second point is that in the history of Muslims, the subject of leadership has been fiercely debated, but there has been no consensuses on what makes up either the qualities of a leader or traits that predict who will emerge as a leader. In fact, the concept of leaders and leadership has evolved across centuries and has been largely influenced by the nature of power structure and sectarian allegiances. Certainly, however, the evolution of the thinking on leadership has been shaped by powerful dynasties, rulers, and individuals. These forces have had a considerable stake in reshaping the image and religious conceptualization of what leaders should be. In traditional Muslim societies, proper religious justifications and assertions are essential for sustaining and validating power and authority.

The perceptions and realities of leadership have evolved dramatically in Islamic thinking. The dramatic change in the concept of what constitutes a leader and leadership has been influenced by the rise and fall of ideology (faith) and openness in the society. As the following discussion shows, the Islamic view of leaders and leadership has been, contrary to other civilizations, in a state of regression. While the degree of strength of faith and openness primarily influences this trend, outside forces and instability have accelerated the trend. Historical evidence and current research suggest that, in general, the changing nature of leaders and leadership went through seven stages: the Prophet era, wise Caliphs, the Ommeyade dynasty, the early Abbasid era, the late Abbasid era, the era of stagnation, and the era of instability. Below is a brief discussion of leadership during each period:

The Prophet Era (610-632)

Mohamed served as a prophet and as a statesman. Under his leadership, profound cultural and political changes took place in Arabia. Karen Armstrong (1992) argues that the immediate spread and acceptance of Islam reflected the unique message of Islam and was clearly a reflection of the genius of Mohamed. She suggests, however, that the Arabs were not sufficiently developed for a sophisticated Islamic monotheism. She states (p. 53), "Christianity took root in the Roman empire where Jewish communities had paved the way and prepared the minds of the pagans. But Mohamed had to start virtually from scratch and work his way towards the radical monotheistic spirituality on his own." Mohamed strongly believed that leadership must be based on three foundations: *rehema* (mercy), *ihasan* (kindness), and *adel* (justice). Once these foundations are met, race should not be an issue in selecting a leader. As Mohamed asserted, "Listen to and obey whomever is in charge, even though he is an Ethiopian [black]." Mohamed developed a pattern of behavior that facilitated the change in Arabia:

1. He developed a vital community of believers and envisioned what this community should look like. While faith was an important instrument in energizing his followers, Mohamed had to engage in dramatic social changes: he established a new form of social association (*muakhat*-two Muslims were paired together and declared brothers, replacing the traditional blood relationship). He announced that faith would replace blood as the base for social relationship (Siddiqui, 1987). Furthermore, Mohamed had a deep understanding that Arabs are highly individualistic and unreceptive to central authority and strict orders. Therefore, contrary to prevailing practices of show of power he declared that he was not a compeller, but a messenger of God; that his job, primarily, was to preach, warn and guide, to do good and avoid vice. This demonstrates how Mohamed understood the unique Arab psyche and situated himself as an impersonal conveyer of the new faith.

2. Initially, Mohamed focused only on promoting the message of Islam and creating an environment to facilitate cultural change. Once the new community became large and a city-state was established instructions regarding law and order were specified. Furthermore, cooperation among members of the Muslim community was encouraged and brotherly relationships were extended far beyond the original Muslim community. When various regions in Arabia and surrounding areas adopted Islam, Mohamed assigned *walis* (governors), local administrators, and market commissioners among others to govern. These were given autonomy in running their affairs (Siddiqui, 1987).

3. Various forms of alliances were established. These alliances were aimed at ensuring safety and stability and that certain principles were observed in an environment that was characterized mainly by the absence of law and order. More importantly, alliances sought to strengthen and spread the faith. The alliance with the Jewish communities and other tribes in different geographical localities were intended to build the foundation of the faith and convey the message to a wider audience (Jasim, 1987).

Mohamed viewed leadership as a process of shared influence. In his general conduct of affairs, whether religious or otherwise, Mohamed utilized a public open forum where members of the community had immediate input and contributed on the spot to civic and administrative matters. He instructed his representatives by saying, "God blesses those who benefit others." That is, leadership is valid only when it results in a benefit to a society, regardless of the setting. He was reported to have said, "Everyone of you is a leader and every one of you shall be questioned about those under his supervision; the Imam is a leader and shall be questioned about his subjects; and the man is a leader in his family and he shall be questioned about those under his care; and the woman is a leader in the house of her husband, and shall be questioned about those under her care; and the servant is a leader in taking care of the property of his master, and shall be questioned about those under his care." In this broad concept of leadership, Mohamed implied that shouldering responsibility is essential for smooth performance and improving the welfare of the society.

The Rightly Guided Caliphs (632-661)

There were four caliphs during this period. The first Caliph, Abu Baker, in his inauguration speech, defined what a Muslim leader should be. He stated, " I have been given authority over you, but I am not the best of you.

If I do well help me, and if I do ill, then put me right. . . . The weak among you shall be strong in my eyes until I secure his right if God wills; and the strong among you shall be weak in my eyes until I wrest the right from him....Obey me as long as I obey God and his apostle, and if I disobey them you owe me no obedience" (quoted in Armstrong, 1992, p. 258). During this period there was a consensus that the quality of a leader was primarily built on three foundations: the approval of subordinates, justice and performance. Imam Ali succinctly stated, "Good leaders are known by what their subjects say about them. So, the best deed is the deed that benefits others." The four Caliphs, in general, reaffirmed that leadership is a shared influence. This was captured by a saying attributed to the second Caliph, Omer: "If you see me doing wrongs, then straighten me." Most importantly, at this stage, despite an attempt to the contrary during the era of the third Caliph, Othman, the Muslims and Caliphs, viewed the role of Caliph as a secular position that represented a successor to the Prophet, but that was neither an heir to his right nor a replacement for him (Arkoun, 1986; Ashmawiy, 1992). In Islam, the government is considered a civic system that is entirely built on the will of the community. The approval of the community of how things should be run is the only validation that the leader needs to be in power. This understanding differentiates the traditional Islamic conception of the leader and government and that of Christianity and leadership. The latter views the leader as having a divine order. This was articulated in (Romans 13:1), "Let everyone submit himself to the ruling authorities, for there exists no authority not ordained by God" and in (Mathew16:19) "And I will give unto thee the keys of the kingdom of heaven: and whatsoever thou shalt bind on earth shall be bound in heaven: and whatsoever thou shalt loose on earth shall be loosed in heaven."

Ommeyade Dynasty (661-750)

The Ommeyade dynasty's ascendance to power was a turning point in Islamic history and in terms of the definition and rationale of leaders and leadership. First, the Ommeyade appeared to invoke a modified Christian concept of the source of power and leadership. Theologically, Christians believe that "God is the one who appoints leaders" (quoted in Milbank, 2003). It is possible that the Ommeyade leading members were influenced by the Christian theological perspective. The founder of the Ommeyade State, Muawiyah (died 680), for example, was the governor of Syria for many years and had close contact with the Byzantine Empire and its representatives. The Ommeyade dynasty abrogated the Rightly Guided Caliphs' tradition by viewing the Caliph not as a civil institution, but as a divine system. Therefore, the Caliph was treated as the vice-regent of God and people had no say in his election (Ashmawiy,

1992). In order to sustain this new system, Muawiyah relied on coercion, rewarding followers and severely punishing enemies. In addition, he surrounded himself with close advisors and associates who were blindly loyal to him, or related by blood. Al-Masudi (died 968, vol. 3, pp. 41-43) reported that in recruiting soldiers, the Ommeyades relied on people who had no knowledge about Islam and the politics af that time. Indeed, according to Al-Masudi (p. 101), during the Ommeyade era, people were ordered to fear and obey the Caliph, rather than God. This was embedded in the behavior of many Ommeyade Caliphs and their representatives. For example, Al-Masudi (p.151) reported that Al-Hajaj ben Yousef Al-Thaqafi, one of the most feared military leaders of the Ommeyade State, was quoted saying, "God says 'fear God as you could.' This concerns God and has exception. And God says 'listen and obey.' This specifically meant the servant of God, Caliph, and the favorite of God, Abdul Malik [the fifth Ommeyade Caliph]. I swear in the name of God that if Abdul Malik ordered the people to move into this valley and they went somewhere else, I would shed their blood." In the Ommeyade era, a leader had absolute power, and legitimacy was based solely on authority and coercion.

The Early Abbasid Era (750-833)

In the early years of the Abbasid state, two remarkable yet different perspectives on leadership appeared to exist simultaneously. The first was that the Caliph position was considered to be a consanguineous position, descended from the Prophet and religiously sanctioned. As such the Abbasids were harsh with their enemies, but generous and accommodating toward their supporters and non-Arab Muslims. The second revolved around the fact that the dynasty encouraged spiritual and philosophical discourse. They built a network of scholars who were closely linked to the Caliph's palace. While this development was essential to provide religious and legal justifications for the Caliph's position, it, however, created an environment characterized by openness and tolerance for diverse ideas. In this environment, opposition and loyal groups alike questioned the role of the Caliph and the reasoning for its existence.

Ibn Abed Raba (died 985, p. 38) reported that one time Abu Gafer Al-Mansour, the second Caliph (754-775) told his advisor: "A hungry dog follows his master. A healthy dog will eat him." Al-Mansour meant that in dealing with people, the leader should not be generous with his followers. One of his advisors did not agree suggesting, "When there is another person willing to feed the dog, the dog follows him." This implies that a leader must keep a balanced and just approach to his subjects. The Caliph after careful consideration decided to follow the advice of his advisor. So in the early era of the Abbasids, though the Caliph's position derived its legitimacy from perceived religious reasons, the Caliph gave considerable attention to the welfare of the people and maintained an open-door policy in dealing with friends and foes.

During this era four views on leadership emerged. The first proposed that, "If a society is just and there are no corrupt people, there is no need for a leader." This was advocated by some of the *Mutazila* (Al-Masudi, xol. 3, p. 236). This perspective was shared too by a faction of Al-Khouraj (a Muslim group that refused to obey the fourth Caliph around 660).

The second perspective was represented by the majority of *Mutazila* who followed the *Tafwiz* school. This school stated that the choice of a leader is solely the collective responsibility of the community or nation. At any time, the chosen leader must be from people who are known to be just and faithful. The leader can be from any racial group as long as he promotes justice and shows concern for the general interest of the people.

The third view was represented by the *Jabria* school. This view asserted that a leader has the right to dictate what is right and wrong. Followers have to obey their leader whether he is an oppressor and corrupt or not. The underlying assumption of this perspective is that authority is the most important foundation for leadership. The existence of other qualities (e.g., justice, virtue) is perceived to be good, but their absence does not constitute illegitimacy. This view gives the leader a religious justification and, thus, a leader is beyond criticism and is not accountable to others. Surprisingly, this view slightly resembles traditional Christian thinking. President Bush, for example, asserted this when he stated (June 27, 2002), "As a matter of fact . . . we received our rights from God."

A counterpart to the *Jabria* school is the *Ikhtiar* school. In the context of leadership, the original premise of this perspective was based on a representative approach. This was evident when Imam Ali stated, "If the presence of the entire people is necessary for the validity of the selection of the Caliph, then, I swear by my life, there is no way to command such gathering. But those who are eligible should represent those who are absent." During the Abbasid era and due to repression committed by the Abbasids' authority against this approach, a new element was introduced- twelve direct descendents from the family of the Prophet Mohamed had the religious right to assume the position of Caliph. In general, however, under this school, the community must agree upon the leader who must be just, knowledgeable, courageous, generous, wise, humble, and fear God (Al-Masudi, p. 236, vol. 3). Unlike the *Jabria* perspective, this view affirms the rights of people to remove a corrupt leader and, if necessary, use force in doing so.

The Late Abbasid Era (833-1242)

This era was characterized by the rise to power of non-Arab armies (Turks and Persians) and that of the first w*azir* (equivalent of a prime minister) relative to the Caliph. It was during this period that two dynasties of Persian (Buwaihid, 932-1062) and Turkish (Seljuks, 1038-1194) origins dominated the government and eventually the position of Caliph, as an institution, was reduced to a mere figurehead. The more notable development in terms of administration was the growing importance of bureaucrats in the management of the empire. Previously, they were an extension of the Caliph's palace. But during that period their influence became so dominant that it has never been matched in the history of the Islamic state.

Miskawayh (died 1043, vol. 1, pp. 2-3) reported that when the Caliph al-Muktafi (902-8) was about to die, the *wazir* consulted the directors of *diwans* (executive branch) on the successor to Caliphate. One of these directors suggested "Do not appoint somebody who has been in society and knows to whom this and that thing belongs; someone who has met people and who people have known, has knowledge and is shrewd, and takes into account what people say." The *wazir* asked, "Whom do you suggest?" The director answered, "Jafar the son of al-Mutadid" [a Caliph, from 892-902]. The *wazir* was astonished, exclaiming, "Jafar is a child." The director explained himself, stating that they did not need a man "who gives order, knows what we are doing, governs affairs, is in charge and regards himself as independent. Why not appoint one who will let you administer the empire?" Subsequently, the thirteen-year old boy was appointed and named al-Muqtadir [the able, 908-32].

During this era, two distinct theories of leadership evolved. The first one was in line with the *Jabria* school. It was developed and articulated by Abu al-Hassan Ali ben Habab (died 1058) who was known as Al-Mawardi. Al-Mawardi gave a theoretical justification for selecting and maintaining a leader; avoiding crisis and chaos. He went further by proposing that the caliphate was a divine institution. The functions of Caliph were "to guard the religion and world affairs." Therefore, obeying the Caliph was a religious obligation. This led Al-Mawardi to assert that order is more important than justice. The latter is essential, but order must take precedence to ensure the continuation of the institute of the caliphate. Al-Mawardi differentiated among three primary leaders: the Caliph, *wazir*, and emir. In terms of Caliph, he argued that it is the duty of the existing caliph to name his successor (Crown Caliph). Likewise, the existing Caliph has the absolute power to select a team, even one person, to nominate the incoming Caliph. He differentiated between two types of *wazir*: delegation and execution. The first is broader and has more authority and encompasses the functions of the intellectual and the military. The *wazir* in this case is given the authority to run the caliphate and affairs of the people. The second was concerned with opinion and resolve regarding the Caliph's affairs only. The *wazir*, however, has to implement the Caliph's orders and policies, and advise and clarify things to him.

In terms of emir, Al-Mawardi described two types of authority (emirate): by appointment (assigned) and by seizure (acquired by force). When the Caliph assigned a person to represent him in conducting the state and religious affairs of a particular region, the authority was legal and called delegated. In the second case, the emir controlled a region and imposed his conditions on the Caliph. In both cases, the functions of emir were: establishment of justice, enforcement of law, maintaining the military, the appointment of employees, and taking care of the financial affairs.

The second theory of leadership in this era was espoused by *Ikhwan-us-Safa*. This theory emphasized knowledge, generosity, selflessness, and justice as the foundations of power. Leaders must be qualified intellectually and display an unwavering commitment to justice. In their third volume, *Ikhwan-us-Safa* elaborated on three groups of qualities that a leader needs: qualities for the hereafter, qualities for life, and qualities for sustaining power and governance. Table 8.1 presents qualities of leaders under three situations.

The Era of Stagnation

This era was initiated with the collapse of Baghdad after the Mongol invasion in 1258 and continued until early 1900. While this era was primarily characterized by the fragmentation of the Muslim World, it represented, until its late years, the retreat of the liberal thinking and the ascendancy of the *Jabria* school. In terms of leadership, the thinking of Ibn Khaldun (1332-1406) and Ibn Taimiya (1263-1328) became generally accepted. Ibn Khaldun (p. 112) argued that goodness and inclination for collective or group feeling are a prerequisite for any leader. Lacking of these qualities, he asserted, "would be like appearing naked before people." He prescribed several qualities needed by leaders to ensure acceptance by subordinates. These are: generosity, forgiveness of error, tolerance toward the weak, hospitality toward guests, support of subordinates, maintenance of their indigent, patience in adverse circumstances, faithful fulfillment of obligations, liberty with money for the preservation of honor, respect for the religious law and for the scholars who are learned in it, thinking highly of religious scholarship, belief in and veneration for men of religion and a desire to receive their prayers, great respect for old men and teachers, justice for those who call for it, fairness to and care for those who are too weak to take care of themselves, humility toward the poor, attentiveness to the complaints of supplicants, fulfillment of the duties of the religious law and divine worship in all details and avoidance of fraud, cunning, deceit, and shirking of obligations.

Ibn Taimiya (died 1328) witnessed the era of fragmentation, chaos, and foreign invasion of the Arab and Muslim lands. Naturally, at the time of defeat and humiliation, security becomes a more urgent concern and people tend to be more inclined to accept a pessimistic and simple view. Ibn Taimiya's thinking captured the essence of that period. He recognized the qualities of good leaders like his Muslim predecessors (e.g., honesty, compassion, enforcement of justice, etc.) but gave considerable attention to restoring stability. Therefore, he asserted the need to obey a leader even if he is an oppressor, corrupt, and unjust. Ibn Taimiya believed that how a leader obtained his power was less important than how he used it and "even if the leader [ruler] 'was unjust or impious,' it was generally accepted that he should still be obeyed, for any kind of order was better than anarchy" (Hourani, 1991, p. 144). Ibn Taimiya strongly advocated the obedience to an unjust leader or ruler as obligatory, therefore, deviating from clear Islamic instruction exemplified by the Prophet's sayings, "Obedience is due only in that which is good" and "When one sees a wrongdoing, he has to change it by force, if he cannot, then by voicing concern, and if he could not then by denouncing it in his heart; this however, is the weakest faith." It is quite possible that circumstances and political development subverted ideals. That is, Ibn Taimiya was influenced by the need for protecting the community and self during foreign invasion and national chaos. Ibn Taimiya stated, "It is obvious that the [affairs of the] people cannot be in a sound state except with rulers, and even if somebody from among unjust kings becomes ruler, this would be better than there being none. As it said: 'Sixty years with an unjust ruler are better than one night without a ruler'" (quoted in Enayat, 1982, p. 12).

At the end of this era, around 1900, there were several attempts at revivalism. The revivalism movements were a genuine response to rising Western challenges, the dramatic decline of the two Muslim states, the Ottoman and Safavi, and the further fragmentation of the Muslim countries by foreign invaders. Most of the revivalists were influenced by their contact or their studies in the West. Nevertheless, their attempts did not produce any significant new leap in the thinking on leadership. In fact, Ibn Taimiya's perspectives gained a widespread acceptance and were promoted tirelessly by existing rulers. Enayat (1982) asserts that such justification of tyranny in the name of religion was responsible for stagnation of political thought among Muslims.

Table 8.1   Qualities of leaders under three situations

Qualities for the hereafter	Qualities necessary for this life	Qualities necessary to reform authority and sustain power
1. Acknowledgment of the unity of God 2. Belief and acceptance of all prophets 3. Belief in their books 4. Protection of the book, the Quran, and diplomacy in dealing with people 5. Humbleness and avoidance of pride 6. Avoidance of brutality and oppression 7. Avoidance of spending time alone with women 8. Avoidance of drinking alcohol 9. Generosity and extending a helping hand to friends and enemies alike 10. Truthfulness and rendering back trusts to whom they belong, whether the owners are honest or corrupt people	1. Right conduct 2. Good manner 3. Fulfillment of promise and adherence to commitment 4. Forgiving when capable 5. Avoidance of jealousy and the development of responsible people 6. Avoiding having enemies, but if you have an enemy make your kindness to him his punishment 7. Do not spend unwisely 8. Temper your passions by generosity 9. Do not indulge at the expense of the hereafter 10. Do not interfere in things that do not concern you	1. Follow up on and be concerned with the affairs of the people in order not to overlook their problems, whether these problems are related to the young or old 2. Treat people according to their deeds 3. Justice should encompass all with no exception 4. Do not be brutal 5. Reward the knowledgeable and ignorant people accordingly in terms of position and compensation 6. Select and appoint your representatives and subordinates who have the best reputations and are independent to supervise and conduct people affairs 7. Select your advisors from those who share your faith and outlook 8. Select a *wazir* who is the best in terms of faith and worldly affairs 9. Protect the rights of the weak and the oppressed people 10. Make sure that people who were subjected to wrong are given justice

The Era of Instability (1914- present)

This era was inaugurated with the colonization by the Western countries of most of the Muslim world. It has continued even after the emergence of national governments in newly established Muslim states. Since the early years of the twentieth century, there has been no genuine attempt to develop a theory of leadership responsive to new challenges and raising the expectations of the people. The colonial powers (e.g., Britain, France, Italy, etc.) brought with them their conceptualizations of leaders and leadership, which revolved around power and its implications. The direct colonization, however, did not last long enough to initiate genuine transformation in the perceptions and practice of leadership. The post-colonial era, therefore, has been primarily characterized by cultural discontinuity and mistrust of Western conceptualizations and ideas. Absence of critical evaluation of the colonial legacy and reasonable familiarity with the Islamic classical perspectives remain a persistent problem.

This does not preclude serious attempts by both secular and religious intellectuals to indulge in the development of leadership theories that are applicable to today's affairs and are based on Islamic principles. These attempts, however, have not been successful in gaining popularity and acceptance. Both cultural discontinuity and the mediocrity of most educational programs hinder the progress of leadership research and the appreciation of the role of effective leaders in societal development. Some of these perspectives are briefly discussed in the pages that follow.

2.   LEADERSHIP TRAITS AND SKILLS

Hawi (1982) attempted to synthesize the most desired traits and qualities of leaders in Islamic thinking. He relied on history and the early years of the Islamic state to come up with an all encompassing list. He described the attributes of an Islamic leader as having the ability to reason or act rationally, to be knowledgeable, mentally stable, courageous, in control of desires, generous, wise, in control of his temper, forgiving, caring, flexible, relying on evidence, abiding by promises, honest, able to keep secrets, acting decisively, being cunning, humble, free from hatred and envy, patient, thankful, diplomatic, not listening to slanderers and backbiters, not appointing the non-faithful as deputies, following up and processing work, receptive and willing to give advice, attentive, a good organizer, rewarding and recognizing achievers and respectable in their appearance.

In the context of business, Asaf (1987) provided two categories of traits and qualities that a leader must have: moral discipline which includes eight attributes identified under moral categories; goodness, patience, forgiveness, an ability to make peace among conflicting parties, selflessness, cooperative, a sense of responsibility, and tenderness and kindness in conversation. These attributes must be accompanied by the avoidance of lies, arrogance, enviousness, anger and suspicion and spying. In addition the traits of a leader deemed to be essential for effective conduct in business are: experience and knowledge, justice, caring, exemplary behavior, willingness to consult, a trust in God and persuasiveness through goodness. Those leaders who exhibit these qualities are assumed to show kindness, moderation, a willingness to consult and delegate and not to inflict intentional damage on others, as well as a commitment to the development and growth of the organization.

Most of the above qualities and traits stand in sharp contrast to qualities that were recommended by Machiavelli (1469-1527) and which seem to be practiced in a contemporary world. The latter asserted that cruelty is essential for keeping followers "united and faithful," that it was safer to be "feared than loved," and that a leader must imitate "the fox and the lion." These qualities are perceived in Islamic thinking to be destructive and are impediments to nurturing thriving and healthy organizations. Those who espoused such qualities during the history of successive Muslim states have been labeled as oppressors and aggressors, simply because these qualities are more likely to violate the foundations of leadership: mercy, kindness, and justice.

While most of the qualities identified above seem to be essential leadership traits, not all leaders display these qualities simultaneously. Furthermore, the absence of any of them does not necessarily preclude leaders from being effective or ineffective. There are, of course, certain situational factors that may give more weight to some attributes over others or that may lead to the neglect of sanctioned qualities. For example, during the Mongol invasion and the fragmentation of the Islamic world, honesty, kindness, and openness were often overlooked as essential qualities for leaders. An ability to maintain law and order, protection of the land and decisiveness were appreciated by most of the people. But Muslim perspectives on leadership and leaders have always been linked to the nature of followers. Indeed, according to a Muslim saying: "The leader reflects the quality of his people." That is, in a situation where followers are educated and responsible the leader will be receptive and participative. But in a situation where followers are dependent and avoid initiative and responsibility the leader has to be decisive and in control. This dialectic relationship between leaders and followers was captured by Imam Ali. He stated (1989, p. 244), "Constituencies will prosper only if they have a responsible leader, and for a leader to be great, the constituencies must be upright. When both the constituencies and leader observe each other's due, right is strengthened, religion tenets are respected, justice prevails and the society will benefit."

3. MODEL OF LEADERSHIP

Islamic teachings and Quranic instructions have been instrumental in maintaining rich traditions across generations and vast and dispersed geographical areas. The teaching, however, has created an inclination among most Muslims, especially the religiously informed ones, to be infatuated with the ideal forms, even when they know that these ideal forms are contradicted by reality. This situation should be differentiated from having beliefs conflict with facts. For example, in the United States, Davies (2003) reported that many Americans avoid having an experience of cognitive dissonance when presented with facts that are inconsistent with their beliefs. In this situation, people are not infatuated with the ideal; rather, they blindly follow and trust leaders. They disregard facts that contradict information provided by leaders, thereby strengthening the leader's position. On the other hand, people who are infatuated with ideals consider a leader who has deceived them to be corrupt, thus enlarging the psychological gulf between themselves and the leader.

In the context of leadership, the Muslim infatuation with ideals has hindered the development of sound and practical leadership theories. This is because when the ideal is treated as identical to practice, rather than merely constituting the criterion by which practice is to be judged, disappointments and frustrations take place. Furthermore, the infatuation with the ideal in an authoritarian environment solidifies autocratic tendencies among individuals in authoritative positions. That is, the feeling of indispensability finds a fertile ground in this environment.

One of the most promising Islamic-derived leadership models that successfully captures the interplay of personalism and individualism and leadership was developed by Khadra (1990). Indeed, Khadra's prophetic-caliphal model is an attempt to cast light upon a phenomena in the Arab world where contradictory forces constrain leaders and obstruct societal development. The model has four elements, personalism (a subjective, egocentric view of the relationships of an individual to others), individualism (a tendency to make decisions irrespective of the opinion of the group), lack of institutionalization (lack of institutional arrangement to address the issues of accession, succession, and conflict), and the importance of the "great man' (see Figure 8.1). The last two are perceived to be the output of the interaction between the first two elements. The model depicts a situation where qualities of personalism and individualism undermine the quest to build institutions. Lack of institutionalism is thought to create a vacuum in society. As such, neither the overriding concept (ideology) nor an overriding group is essential in filling the vacuum. Khadra suggests that the role and quality of the individual leader takes on an added value. If the leader happens to be an ordinary person, the model that emerges is the "caliphal model" - an authoritarian leadership model. If the leader happens to be a great person (visionary), a prophetic model emerges - a compassionate, attentive, flexible leader who displays a remarkable confidence in his behavior and action. Khadra, however, over looks the role of the infatuation with the ideals in the rise of either the authoritarian or the visionary leader.

This model is useful in calling attention to important societal and organizational problems in the Arab world. Nevertheless, the model needs to be modified to be applicable to broader Islamic culture. Unlike the Arab world, not all Muslim countries exhibit strong personalism and individualism, simultaneously. That is, while almost all Muslims display the quality of personalism, not all of them are individualistic. Nevertheless, the infatuation of Muslims with the ideal and their longing for a just leader and society play a significant part in their daily lives. Idealism in the Arab and Islamic culture is considered a necessary social element. In fact, despite their current relative economic and political failure, people in Muslim countries still bemoan the loss of a glorious past and hope for a bright future. Muslims' infatuation with idealism is a powerful force that prevents them from dealing effectively with contemporary world events. It could be, however, a potent factor in energizing their activities and revitalizing their economies.

4. TOWARD AN ISLAMIC MODEL OF LEADERSHIP

Since both the Quran and the Prophet's teachings place emphasis on social cooperation and idealism, there is a need for a model that reflects the essence of the Islamic message, while capturing the nature of leadership in the Muslim world. In this section, a leadership model is proposed (see Figure 8.2). The suggested model explains how two primary types of leaders come to exist. The model has four elements: personalism, idealism, great expectation, and culture. Personalism here is viewed as the tendency among people in a society to relate to each other in a warm, friendly, and subjective manner. That is, people place a high value on personal relationships and relate to individuals in the context of their reputation in the community and societal norms.

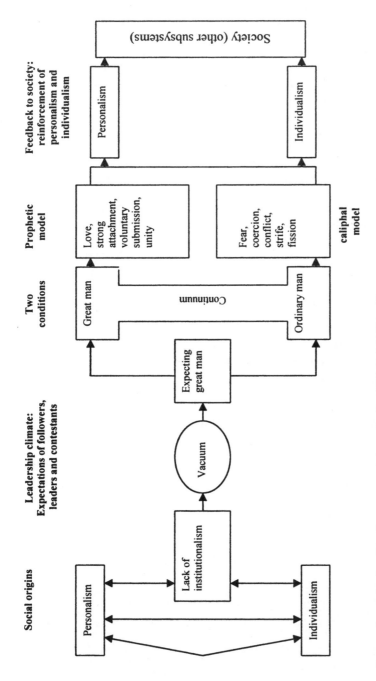

Source: International studies of management and organization, 1990, Vol. 20(3), p. 38. Reproduced by permission of M E. Sharpe, Inc., publisher of ISMO.

Figure 8.1 The prophetic caliphal model

149

The personalized aspects have certain advantages. Chief among them are that problems can be solved directly through intermediaries, that concession and compromise are the norm, that there is ease in social interactions and formation of group/team work, that this results in strong loyalties and cohesiveness if applied intelligently, that it is easy to enhance commitment to goals and that, in many cases, clients' needs can be satisfied in a friendly manner. Personalism, however, can have a devastating impact as it may facilitate fragmentation and divided loyalties thereby allowing minor problems to linger.

Idealism is defined as an aspiration to attain and an infatuation with the highest possible state of existence or perfection. In idealism, absolute perfection is sought and considered to be a virtue. Both personalism and idealism produce great expectations within society. In a culture that is characterized by deeply held and widely shared beliefs and values the great expectation generates an environment conducive for positive and clear vision, involvement and cohesiveness, receptiveness and tolerance. Consequently, the leader that emerges is a "great person." The great person exemplifies the ideal qualities (e.g., openness, thoughtfulness, foresight, articulation of vision, caring, confidence in subordinates, optimism, accountability, etc.). The resulting leadership model is prophetic. Under this model there is a two-way interaction between the leader and subordinates and caring, respect and love govern relationships. The leader is committed to the interest of the people and the latter trusts and shows affection to the leader. The mutual trust and understanding between the leader and the people eventually institutionalizes the rules of law.

A prophetic leader not only highlights the advantages of establishing traditions and institutional procedures, but also induces a continuing commitment. Once a commitment is made and a tradition is entrenched, transformation to a healthy environment can be realized. Many scholars believe that, despite the existing bleak economic and political situation in the Arab and Muslim world, most societies are on the verge of major changes and circumstances will inevitably lead to an ideal state. Such optimism is based on two assumptions: an awareness of the fundamental Islamic cultural elements will increase in the years to come, and the societal conditions will eventually improve leading to better cohesiveness and higher cultural identity.

In a weak culture where beliefs and values are not widely and deeply shared, great expectations are more likely to translate into empathy, indifference, frustration, and fragmentation. More likely, the emerging leader is a type of "ordinary man." That is, the leader does not exhibit any superior quality and is feared and mistrusted by subordinates. With the absence of respect and love from the populace, the leader resorts to coercion and authoritarian practice to maintain power and submission. Thus, the emerging leadership model is "caliphal." Under this model, law and order are contingent upon the will of the leader. Therefore, there will be a lack of institutionalism.

The caliphal model has been common in government, but it is rarely found in business organizations. In contrast, the prophetic model is rarely found in contemporary Islamic governments. Nevertheless, variations of it can be found in family-owned and small-business organizations. The effectiveness of either model is difficult to judge. But using institutionalism as a desired end, the prophetic model is certainly preferred. The economic stagnation and the lack of technological advancement in Muslim countries have been attributed to the determination of the leaders, lack of institutionalism, and lack of public participation. For example, in the context of the Arab world, the United Nations' *Arab Human Development Report 2002* (2002, p. vii) noticed that "the predominant characteristic of the current Arab reality seems to be the existence of deeply rooted shortcomings in Arab institutional structures. These shortcomings pose serious obstacles to human development and are summarized as the three deficits relating to freedom, empowerment of women and knowledge. They constitute weighty constraints on human capability that must be lifted."

5. IDEALISM AND REALISM

When the French philosopher, Maxime Rodinson (1981), wrote that many sayings attributed to the Prophet Mohamed sound like contemporary liberal thoughts and, thus, must have had to be written in an era of openness and liberalism not in the environment of Arabia around 620s, he raised an intriguing issue. He stated (p. 59), "There are some *hadiths* [the sayings of the Prophet] that clearly reflect contemporary thinking rather than tendencies dating from the time of the Prophet. For example, many *hadiths* deal with the problem of racism." Rodinson's astonishment, however, should be attributed to the state of Muslim societies today. Most of these societies are backward, authoritarian, and behind other countries politically, socially and technologically. Their social and economic progress has been disappointing and has led to deep frustration among people of these societies. It is possible that scholars, especially in the West, may attribute such mediocre achievement to religion without a careful understanding of the tenets of the religion and the internal and external conditions that have led to societal stagnation.

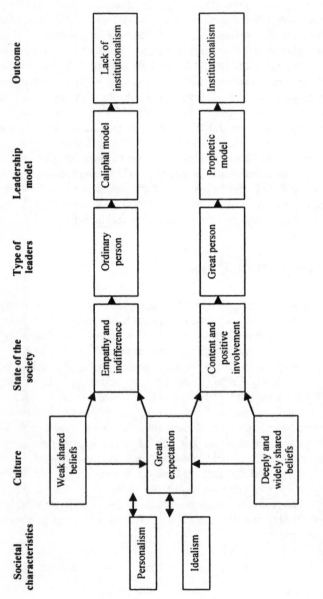

Figure 8.2 Islamic model of leadership

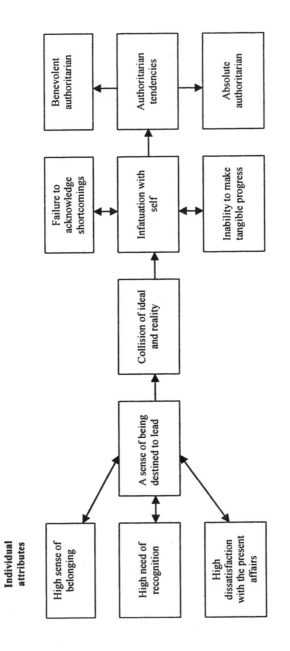

Figure 8.3   Factors influencing authoritarian tendencies at the individual level

For a Muslim, "Exalted values are the fundamental components of his essence; they are inherent to his being, his living, his thinking, his loving" (Shariati, 1979; p.123). It is more likely, however, that in an environment of greed and political corruption and foreign domination, confusing ideal with reality becomes permissible and gradually habitual. Furthermore, most Muslim societies are still traditional in nature. In these countries religion is not separated from other aspects of life. In his investigation of the Arab culture, Patai (1983, p. 165) noted that the Arab preference " for thought - wishes, ideas, ideals, aspirations, and the like - over factual reality should not be confined to the era of religion, but should penetrate, together with religion, all other aspects of life." Such interplay of ideals and reality in actual life serves magnificently in sustaining hope and continuity under adverse conditions. Nevertheless, in the context of leadership, it may facilitate the emergence of authoritarian practice, especially in the absence of ideological clarity and widespread social cohesiveness.

The rise of autocratic leaders in both political and business organizations is not something peculiar to Islamic culture. All cultures and civilizations have experienced authoritarian rule in their history. In Muslim societies, however, authoritarian rulers in recent history have been more commonly in power despite Islam disapproval of oppression and authoritarian tendencies. The Quran, for example, condemns oppression (2:217): "Tumult and oppression are worse than slaughter and (3:159): "Wert thou severe or harsh-hearted, they would have broken away from about thee: so pass over (their faults) and ask for (God's) forgiveness for them; and consult them in affairs. Then, when thou hast taken a decision, put the trust in God."

Leaders in Muslim countries, like those in other cultures, display various styles of leadership. In the business world consultative, paternalistic and autocratic are more common than other styles. Muna (1980) conducted a study on managerial practice in the Arab world and found that most managers espouse a consultative style. Ali (1989) found that most managers preferred consultative and pseudo-consultative styles. The latter is a mixture of consultative and autocratic styles. It is an attempt by individuals in a position of authority to give the impression of a commitment to a sanctioned tradition. That is, some leaders display a pseudo-consultative style to reduce the tension between authoritative and consultative trends and create a supportive and cohesive environment around themselves. Its existence can be traced to the authoritarian element in most Muslim societies - an element springing from several factors that have shaped the norms and practices in contemporary Muslim states. These factors include the primacy of coercive force and instability in the succession process of the Islamic polity (Hudson, 1977), the centralized political system that has evolved since the end of colonization of some

Muslim countries, foreign occupation and cultural discontinuity (Ali, 1995), the domination of the Jabria school of thought in many Muslim states which legitimizes authoritarian action and the quality of leadership (Watt, 1961).

The persistent presence of authoritarian leadership in both politics and business is an intriguing subject. In Figure 8.2 the focus was on the societal and cultural factors, which under certain conditions either produce great leaders (visionary) or ordinary leaders (authoritarian). There are various personal factors, too, that facilitate the presence of the latter. In this part, the most important personal attributes are identified. These attributes are shaped to a large extent by internal (societal) and external (foreign) forces. Indeed, the interplay of all these qualities and factors, in the absence of openness, creates a hospitable environment for authoritarian tendencies. These attributes encompass a high sense of belonging, a high need for approval, a high dissatisfaction with the current affairs, a high need for recognition, and a sense of being destined to lead. Description of each attribute follows.

High Sense of Belonging

An individual in an Islamic culture feels, due to Islamic teaching and socialization, that he/she is part of a wider social organization called "umma" or community. The self "exists as the sum of its interactions with others" (Raban, 2003). The sense of self as an autonomous unit separated from other members of the society is seldom appreciated in Muslim societies. It is considered neither a virtue nor is it sought after. Those who show a high sense of belonging to this *umma* normally display a higher involvement in the affairs of the society and are inclined, more than others, to champion societal causes.

High Need for Approval

Those who seek approval for their actions, even for small matters, usually display deep frustration and disappointment when they do not get immediate approbation for their actions. When individuals with a high sense of belonging, however, display simultaneously a high need for approval, they tend to engage in several manipulative acts to capture the attention of others and hopefully win their approval.

High Dissatisfaction with the Present Affairs

When a person perceives that current affairs are unsatisfactory or inconsistent with their perception of the interest of the society, they may feel a need to change the status quo. The slow change or the failure to make progress to alleviate personal, societal, or organizational problems often motivates people in this category to actively advocate change.

High Need for Recognition

People with a high need for recognition are always anxious and restless. Their persistent quest for recognition underscores an uneasiness and a desire to influence others. Normally, they are involved in various activities and networking to build support at any expense. Their quest for power and influence, however, revolves around selfish interest.   Societal or organizational matters are useful only as long as they facilitate their goal for recognition.

A Sense of Being Destined to Lead

When a person displays a high sense of belonging, believes that the state of the society or organization is not satisfactory and that they have the vision to make a difference, that person perceives that they are destined to lead. That is, individuals in this case overestimate their ability to lead and believe that their vision will lead to ideal outcomes. This perception is strengthened when the person believes that the rest of the people are not adequately qualified to either articulate their demands or meet existing challenges.

The irony is that when individuals with these qualities assume a leadership position and find themselves incapable of making positive changes, they cling to power. Here, the ideal and reality collide leaving leaders concerned more with their own interest, rather than with the interest of the organization or the society at large. Often, the leaders attribute failure to outside forces and to the inability of followers to appreciate their vision and purpose. As time passes and problems persists, the leaders genuinely begins to believe that they are visionaries or great leaders and that the general public is not yet sophisticated enough to value their contributions. This combined with the failure to acknowledge their shortcomings, and a general lack of empathy and lack of cultural identity among followers sustain authoritarian tendencies. Depending on the leader's sense of belonging to the community and the degree of commitment to general interest, the leader is likely to exhibit either a benevolent or absolute authoritarian style (see Figure 8.3). The first style incorporates traditional qualities of informality and caring in conduct. The leader, however, behaves as the ultimate protector, caregiver, and the one who shoulders all responsibilities. The absolute authoritarian leader spends a great deal of energy to project the image of the most capable and knowledgeable individual, but relies on coercion and brutality in maintaining power.

The infatuation with the ideal and the tendency to project the appearance of greatness, despite an inability to articulate a vision that rallies followers, may be considered the most significant factors in nurturing authoritarian tendencies. That is, when leaders aspire to be great leaders but lack the necessary qualities, they are probably inclined to limit freedom and liberty in order to conceal their deficiencies. This may explain the rise of authoritarian rulers in the Muslim world since the death of the fourth Caliph in 661. Indeed, the conflict between the desired ideals and reality is crucial to understanding the current tensions in the Muslim countries. Rulers and managers alike manipulate events to perpetuate the appearance of greatness and moral clarity in order to create a supportive and cohesive environment around themselves. Failure to stimulate popular support and respect induce them to utilize coercive and dictatorial mechanisms.

6.   CONCLUSION

In this chapter the concept of leadership in Islam was discussed. The chapter provided a historical perspective on the evolution and importance of leaders and leadership. The chapter showed how the concept and understanding of leaders and their roles have evolved across centuries. This historical survey evidences that contradictory conceptualization and justification for leaders and leadership have existed across the history of the Muslim people. The evolution of leadership concept has departed from the concept that was advocated during the very early years of the Muslim state (622-660). The departure is a remarkable regression from the relatively liberal understanding of that early period.

A model of an Islamic leadership was presented and the conditions that led to the presence of authoritarian role were highlighted. It was argued that these conditions have greatly shaped leaders' orientations in governments and in the realm of business. Nevertheless, it was suggested that the Islamic model of leadership offers a better understanding of the situational and cultural factors that exist in Muslim societies. More importantly, the model and its underpinning assumptions may be highly appropriate for managing twenty-first-century organizations.

Leadership concepts and practices in Muslim societies suffer, therefore, from a serious crisis. This crisis can be solved when managers and policy makers in the Muslim world become more pragmatic, reconcile the differences between what is ideal and what is reality and when they internalize the principles of their faith. This demands an honest and deep rethinking about the role of followers, participation in the decision-making process, the rights of individuals, and the whole issue of accession and succession.

9. Organizational Structure

Around the 1950s, organizational structure gained momentum in the business world as a vital instrument for effectively coping with a changing business environment and for improving corporate performance. Since then, organizations have sought various forms of structure to achieve goals and tackle complex relational and job issues. Organizational structures have evolved accordingly. Indeed, the significance that has been attached to organizational structures has been associated with the rise or fall of great corporations and the nature of the challenges they have faced in the marketplace. Corporations that have made remarkable achievements in the market have been regarded highly, or at times, even envied by other companies. Their structures and strategies have been imitated. That is, organizational structure has been viewed as instrumental to the survival, growth, and evolution of corporations.

Prior to the1950s, the prevailing view was that organizations were merely mechanical entities characterized by a centralized authority, departmental specialization and division of labor, and strict rules and regulations with clear lines of authority and responsibilities. Bureaucratic behavior and norms dominated in both public and private organizations. The model of a bureaucratic organization was developed as a reaction against the "personal subjugation, nepotism, cruelty, emotional vicissitudes, and capricious judgment which passes for managerial practices in the early days of the industrial revolution" (Bennis, 1965, p. 31). The 1950s witnessed six major developments that challenged the mechanical view of the organization. These developments are: advancement in behavioral studies and approaches, technological progress, the rise of professional managers, increasing economic uncertainty and insecurity, widespread adoption of corporate alliances and merger and acquisition strategies and fierce competition among corporations at home and abroad. These developments accentuated the need for improving corporate performance and the quality of life for employees and the rest of the stakeholders. Restructuring of organizations, therefore, has been thought of as a practical and an effective approach to enhance organizational ability to cope with change and to facilitate an optimal implementation of strategies. Consequently, organizations have experimented with various forms of structure. The primary objectives are increasing flexibility and adaptability and maximum utilization of resources, especially human capital.

Structure is not an objective in itself. Rather, it is a means to an end. Simply and practically, organizational structure (generally represented by charts) is the framework that depicts job arrangements, lines of influence, and coordination mechanisms. It is the hierarchical and purposeful arrangement of positions and jobs that aims at facilitating the performance of organizational activities. Since firms pursue a variety of goals and are involved in numerous activities, structure varies among organizations. Scholars have argued that structure influences individuals and group behavior (Cummings and Berger, 1976; Gibson, Ivancevich and Donnelly, 1988) and relates to organizational effectiveness and change (Bate, Khan and Pye, 2000; Duncan, 1979; Miles, 1997). The literature, however, does not evidence consensus on the factors that determine structure. Earlier studies (see Woodward, 1965) have asserted that the structure of organizations sharply differs due to the type of technology. Other researchers have highlighted the role of the environment in determining structure. In fact, Duncan (1979) considers environment as the most influential factor in effective structuring of organizations. Previously, Lawrence and Lorsch (1969) identified three sub environments: market, technical-economic and scientific. They found that differences in organizational structure are due to differences in the environment. Other researchers have given considerable attention to strategy. They argue that structure is an instrument to achieve strategies. Therefore, strategy determines structure. This was exactly what Chandler (1962) suggested. He found that most companies that progressed from volume expansion to product diversification altered their structures from simple to product diversification structure. Other studies evidence that structure follows strategy (see Fredrickson, 1986). Corporations in formally planned economies have different institutional and environmental challenges. Nevertheless, their strategies for survival and growth appear to influence their structures. For example, Peng and Heath (1996, p. 521) suggest that firms in countries in transition exhibit limited financial and managerial resources and, thus, they adopt a distinct model of organizational growth than that prevailing in the West. Corporations in transitional economies achieve growth by "pooling resources and coordinating activities among members of the network while avoiding the politically difficult task of ownership transfer." That is, these corporations use boundary blurring organizational forms to achieve the necessary adaptability to survive and prosper.

There is an increasing understanding among scholars and managers alike that structure is an instrument for implementing strategies and achieving goals. The meaning of structure, therefore, stems from specific attributions that are given to it by the corporate community, managers, and employees. Consequently, corporations are inclined to select those structures that facilitate their operations globally. The meaning and significance of structure vary according to attributions attached to it. Useem (2002), writing in *Fortune* magazine, captured this fact when he traced the evolution of chief executive officers (CEOs) in the United States over 100 years. Useem stated that organizational structure was drawn only in the second half of the 1800s after the rise of large hierarchies and a sudden growth in the pace of business. Before that there were not that many subordinates and business organizations were staffed with few clerks. Useem classified CEOs into eight categories: tyrant, administrator, faceless, number machine, statesman, neutron bomb, celebrity, and destroyer. The meaning of and the significance of structure under each typology of CEOs differs. Under the *tyrant*, the owners and managers are one and the same. It is a one-man rule; things are done subjectively and arbitrarily. Structure, therefore, is simple and mechanical. The situation is different, for example, under the *administrator* and the *number machine*. The first creates a multidivisional structure along with a committee system to free him/her to set company policy. The *number machine* is interested in managing diverse assortment of businesses; thus, creating conglomerate structures. Useem's typology links the evolution of structure to the nature of the life cycle of the economy and the accompanying orientation of the CEOs. This view is inconsistent with Hofstede's (1983) hypothesis. Hofstede argues that societal culture, more than any other factor, is responsible for shaping the structure of organizations. Consequently, organizations in different societies develop different structural configurations.

In this chapter, forces that shape and influence organizational structure in Muslim societies are discussed. In addition, a historical survey of types of structure in Muslim societies, since the inception of Islam, is provided. High-density and high-diversity social networks characterize Islamic societies. This generates an environment conducive to an effective alignment of all employees with the strategic intent of the organization and several options to structuring organizations. The chapter addresses, too, whether structure is culture-free or culturally bound. Furthermore, the chapter examines structure in terms of social and instrumental conceptualizations.

1.   STRUCTURE AND CULTURE

Whether or not organizational structure differs across cultures has been the subject of extensive debate. Generally, two theories stand out: culture-free and culturally bound. The first theory postulates that relationships between the structural characteristics of work and variables of organizational context are stable across cultures. Consequently, organizational structures are culture-free (Hickson, Hinings, McMillan and Schwitter, 1974). The second theory suggests that organizational structures vary across societies. Furthermore, the meaning of structure to organizational members in each society might be different (Inzerilli and Laurent, 1983). In studying social structure and bureaucracy in the United States and Iran, Conaty, Mahmoudi and Miller (1983) provide a strong support for the culture-free theory. They found that the structure of organizations appears to be similar in the United States and Iran and that the structuring of organizations in Iran was patterned according to Western principles of organizational design. In contrast, de Kervasdoue and Kimberly (1979) found that despite similarities in objectives, technologies, and size, hospitals in the United States and France have different structural configurations. They assert that structural configurations are not culture-free.

While it appears that there is no conclusive evidence of the impact of culture on organizational structures, the meaning of structure and its significance are certain to be different across cultures. People's orientations and group relations give specific meaning to organizational symbols, characteristics, arrangements, and goals. Social systems within organizations appear to be influenced by technology and the possible transfer of ideas and systems from other organizations and cultures. Nevertheless, the social system within organizations is always the product of its own societal culture and the organizational culture that evolved under the founder. Therefore, the meaning of structure has particular meaning for each social group, even though organizational structures appear to be similar across societies. That is, the framework of organizations may appear to be familiar and the same in different countries but the influence and coordination mechanisms, along with the routine and daily interactions within the organization remain specific to that organization, and easily differentiated from others.

In traditional societies, like the Muslim world, the social system is dynamic and easily absorbs new developments without the weakening of its foundations. Over centuries, waves of foreign invasions have broadened its capacity for renewal and solidified its resilience. The system might borrow Western technique and frameworks, but molds them to fit its needs. In Iran, for example, the government before 1979 imported almost every possible

Western business techniques and procedures. The influence of Westernization on the government and business organizations, however, proved to be inferior to the depth and strength of the social system. The Iranian businesses adopted the Western structure of organizations but approached business according to the accepted societal norms and values. The same is true in Indonesia, Malaysia, and Saudi Arabia.

2   STRUCTURING IN AN ISLAMIC SETTING

The preceding discussion demonstrates that formal organizational structure is an innovative form characteristically linked to and associated with the emergence of large business organizations in the second half of the 1800s. Furthermore, it demonstrates that the meaning of structure is derived primarily from what members of organizations attribute to it. This means that structural arrangements can be transferable, but the meaning of these arrangements is localized. This by no means implies that structure did not exist before the second half of the 1800s. Indeed, for centuries government, business, and social organizations had their own structures, but probably, these structures were not well articulated and formalized. What should be emphasized is that earlier civilizations in Persia, Iraq, Egypt, and China, for example, had complex organizations and built large projects. In Mesopotamia (Iraq), the ancient Assyrian and Akkadian civilizations were credited with the establishment of the first written laws that governed agriculture, irrigation, trade, and industrial matters. In ancient Persia, the empire built a highly sophisticated system of classifying administrators. There were elaborate procedures for the King's court and engagements. Furthermore, the ancient civilizations in the Middle East established a system of complicated canals along with other navigation projects, while Egypt built the pyramids. These projects could never have been carried out without planning and organization. Likewise, the trade volume and activities during the Roman and Persian era required careful planning and organized efforts. None of these activities could have been possible without some sort of hierarchical arrangement in the workplace.

In Arabia, the birth place of Islam, and in nearby Yemen, some forms of organization existed but probably not on a level of sophistication as that which flourished in Iraq and Iran. The fact is that the aristocracy of Mecca was divided into two councils: Al-Mal'a, representing the most important families that were responsible for trade and war, and Majlis Al-Nadwa (the Seminar Board), a board that determined social and military affairs. These two councils are evidence of organizational arrangements in the immediate pre-Islamic society. A pre-Islamic poet, Al-Afwah Alawdi, captured the necessity for organization and leadership when he stated long before Islam: "A house can not be built without posts and there will be no posts without an even foundation. If there are posts and a solid foundation, people can reach their goals. With anarchy and the absence of a vision, people will not make progress and there will be no coherent vision if the ignorant lead."

During the early years of Islam and the start of the Islamic state, the Prophet Mohamed gradually organized the state and economic affairs. The state organization was simple. There were the military, civil administration, financial, and religious affairs (see Siddiqui, 1987). Civil administration affairs (see Figure 9.1) were divided into two departments: central administration (deputies, advisors, secretaries, envoys, commissioners, poets and orators, petty officials) and provincial administration (governors, local administrators, and local representatives, judges and market administrators). Administrators and officers were given autonomy in running their affairs, but had to consult with the Prophet when they faced difficulties. Indeed, the structure, though appearing hierarchical, was loose as all officers, regardless of their level in the organization, had the right to approach the Prophet or his deputies and report their problems. Siddiqui (1987, p. 261), for example, indicated that governors were quite independent in managing the affairs of their respective regions, relying on the general instructions given upon their appointments.

Business organizations at the time were family-owned and extended family affairs. Most of the existing businesses were in trade. The merchant-owners conducted business with a few representatives or agents and several guards for the caravans. The latter were either local part-timers or subcontracted groups throughout the caravan routes. The situation changed slightly after the phenomenal growth in commerce and industry during the Ommeyade and Abbasid dynasties. As indicated in Chapter 1, both dynasties encouraged economic participation and trade. Most of the business organizations, therefore, grew and covered vast regions. The number of employees increased dramatically and envoys and secretaries (Kitabs) were added. All available information tends to suggest that the organization of the business was done in an informal cooperative way.

The publication of *Ikhwan-us-Safa,* (Vol. 1, p. 280) recorded that industry and trade houses were common in the Islamic World during the medieval time. In terms of the industry, the publication listed several types (e.g., metal, oil, pottery, music instruments, instruments used for astronomy, glass, carpentry, sugar, textiles, banking, jewelry, furniture, perfume, drugs, chemicals, etc.). In these activities the businesses were either family-owned or partnerships. In either case, the owner-manager performed the work with the help of subordinates or directly supervising subordinates. Subordinates were classified into two categories: scribers (responsible for correspondence and recording transactions) and those who carry out the core work. Those include both the *Ista* (senior craftsman or superintendent) and workers. The latter were classified into three categories: *tilmidth* (pupil), *ghulam* (apprentice), and *ajir* (journeyman) (Goitein, 1967, p. 93). The pupil could provide some help, but mostly learned through observation. The apprentice assumed part of the work under direct supervision. The journeyman was a permanent worker or craftsman. Depending on the size of the business, there might be representatives of the business in other cities and envoys. The envoys could be any of the people working in the business or a designated person within the organization. Figure 9.2 depicts the organizational structure of a company during that era. What should be stated again is that the lines depict only those in authority as relationships and lines of communication were open and lacked formality.

In terms of trade, the publication of *Ikhwan-us-Safa* identified various types and reflected on their importance to the welfare of society. There are no details on the nature of such enterprises. The emphasis was on the qualities and behavior of those who engaged in commerce and industry. Goitein (1967, p. 149) indicates that Al-Dimashqi, in his twelfth-century handbook on the technique of commerce, divided merchants into three categories: "the hoarder," the monopolists who kept commodities and sold them when prices were high; "the peregrinator," those who transported wares from one country to another; and "the shipper," those who traded shipments abroad. Goitein (p. 150), however, argues that the reality of commerce during the period of Medieval Islam was far more complex than what was described by Al-Dimashqi. He provided five categories of merchants: producers and dealers - those who engaged in producing and selling of a commodity; retailers and wholesalers - simultaneously engaged in retailing and wholesaling; diversified and specialized - those who concentrated on a limited line or on a great variety of goods; itinerant and stationary - those who engaged in international commerce or operated only in a metropolitan city; and brokers, auctioneers, and other middlemen - those who worked on commission. Goitein indicates that, regardless of their business type, these traders operated in a friendly and cooperative way and almost all of them employed agents and scribers to record their correspondences and transactions.

3. COMPLEXITY IN ORGANIZATION

Geographical expansion of the Islamic state and intense interaction with and openness to other civilizations accelerated the adoption of a new form of organization, especially at the state level.

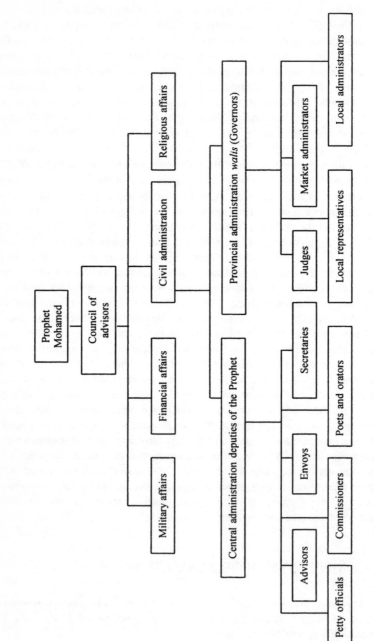

Figure 9.1   Administration structure during the Prophet era

It was during the rein of Ommeyade Caliph Abdel Al-Malik (685-705) that Muslims recognized that a new and a more sophisticated system was needed to manage the vast empire. According to historical reports a translation of the Persian and Byzantine laws and systems was undertaken and adopted in administration. Financial, taxation, post services, and the army had to be reorganized to smooth operations and meet rising economic and military needs. In addition, the language of the administration was altered to Arabic (Hourani, 1991). Furthermore, it was Abdel Al-Malik who ordered the establishment of a uniform currency to be used in all provinces, thereby replacing the Persian and Byzantine currencies in the Muslim state (Al-Maqrizi, died 1442).

Years after the death of the Prophet Mohamed, the complexity of the state was exemplified by the rise of a professional class of secretaries and their deputies. These secretaries exercised significant influence in managing the affairs of the state that exceeded, at some points, the power of the Caliph. Indeed, Miskawayh (died 1030) recorded in his book, *Experiences of Nations*, how secretaries and/or the *Wazir* manipulated events and Caliphs to their advantage in the second half of the Abbasid era. Historians reported the existence of several *Diwans* (Departments) of the state administration. Figure 9.3 depicts the likely structure of central government. For example, Al-Khwarazmi (a tenth-century mathematician and a bureaucrat) divided *Diwans* into: taxation, treasury, postal services, army, state land and resources, water regulation, and correspondence (see Bosworth 1982). Previously, Omero Ben Mustafa, the chief *wazir* of Caliph Al-Mutasim (833-42), divided secretaries into five categories: correspondences, taxation, Justice, army, and police (see Saraj, 1986). Even though the power of secretaries varied according to existing power structures at the time and the individual personality, they all seemed to acquire and display certain qualities. Al-Khwarazmi argued that secretaries must have two general types of qualities: requisite and complementary knowledge. The first category encompassed the knowledge of religious sciences including the Quran, principles of government, the poetry and proverbs of the Arabs, orations of eloquent persons, the history of former dynasties, grammar and rhetoric, and professional skills such as calligraphy, formation of letters, and the use of implements needed for writing. The complementary qualities were divided into two subcategories: foundational knowledge and manners in dealing with people. The basis included knowledge of legal thought, logic, various religions and sects, metre and prosody, solving codes, mathematics, agriculture and surveying, optics and mechanics, weaponry, astronomy, medicine and veterinary sciences, and zoology and falconry. The subcategory of manners included interpretations of events and omens, ethics, statecrafts, public management, and an ability to read faces and intentions (*firasa*) (see Bosworth, 1982). Previously, Abdel Hamid ben Yahya, Prime Minister of Caliph Marwan II (744-50) provided more general qualifications in addition to the prerequisites. The prerequisites included an inclination for justice, tolerance, flexibility, braveness, decency, discretion, commitment in crisis, a willingness to learn the art and science of doing things and familiarity with religious instruction. The qualities for secretaries included knowledge of literature and art, religion, the Arabic language, calligraphy, poetry, the history of the Arabs and foreign nations and mathematics. They should exhibit high moral character while keeping a strong commitment to the profession and its members (see Saraj, 1986).

Unlike the structure of most of today's governments, secretaries (head of Diwans) in Medieval Islam differed from those who supervised them, the *wazir* or Prime Minister. To start with, they generally evolved into a recognized profession with social/political prestige. This gave them considerable autonomy in managing their departments' affairs. While secretaries had a wide range of professional qualities, the Prime Minister was expected to display limited professional skills and qualities. According to Al-Mawardi (died 1058), the *wazir* had to have two qualities: protection of the Caliph, the state, the self, and the constituency; and bravery in acquiring benefits and preventing misdeeds. Furthermore, Goitein (1968) argues that the power of the Prime Ministers was continually expanded or restricted according to the inclination of the Caliph and occasionally it was altogether suspended. Consequently, secretaries and their senior clerks were a powerful class that evolved gradually from being an extension of the Caliph's palace to a power in its own right. The secretaries in this later stage, argued Mottahedeh (1981, p. 35), became "an order in society, almost a caste, of technical experts. They were men of some inherited status and of long apprenticeship, who tied together networks of local interest with the passing parade of military regimes." The existence of a professional administrative class during that era matches contemporary technocrats in many of today's governments. In the United States, for example, though each new administration in Washington has its own political appointees to run federal offices, the majority of the federal administration staff are career-oriented professionals. The reputation of the indispensable independent professional bureaucrat in the contemporary world has been largely associated with democratic transformation, the rise of civil society, and/or government stability. During the second half of the Islamic state, which ended about 1258, the rise to prestige and influence of the professional administrative class was mostly the outcome of the power vacuum and the declining power of the sovereign, the Caliph.

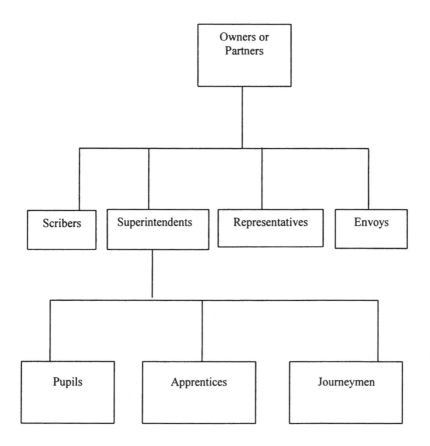

*Figure 9.2   Structure of a manufacturing organization during the
medieval era*

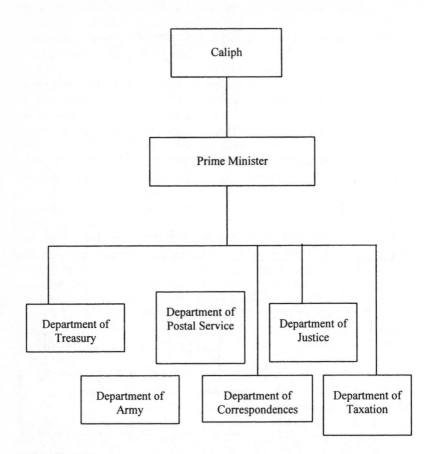

Figure 9.3   Organizational structure of a government in the medieval era

It should be mentioned, too, that the transformation of the bureaucrats from being an extension of the Caliph's palace into an autonomous professional group led to a less hierarchical method of public management (Mottahedeh, 1981). This aspect differentiated it from Max Weber's model of bureaucracy. In Weber's conceptualization of bureaucracy, hierarchical levels are more likely to increase rather than decrease. The professional bureaucrats in the medieval state were dissimilar to the new form of bureaucrats that evolved during the Ottoman Empire, especially in the Eastern part of the Arab world. Due to the authoritarian characteristics of the Ottoman rulers, their infatuation with detailed and cumbersome procedures, along with the supremacy of the individual in charge, a career-oriented personnel gradually emerged. This form of bureaucrat is called *Maslaki* (literally it means a career-oriented, go-along, professional). This form differed from that which prevailed in the second half of the Abbasid Empire and Weber's bureaucratic model. The *Maslaks* do not seem to have had power independent of the sovereign or their immediate *wazir* and though they strictly follow the rules, they might be impersonal with their clients but not with their peers and supervisors. They existed as faceless, subservient bureaucrats with no deep convictions and were content to follow what they were instructed to do. Their distinctive qualities were: avoidance of any creative conduct, a high sense of survival, strict observance of instructions, obedience to supervisors, loyalty to those in power, insecurity, slow processing of work, and treatment of rules as contingent upon the wishes of the boss. To reduce insecurity, *Maslaki* personnel almost always sought approval from various levels in the hierarchy. Therefore, the organizational structure tended to be a taller rather than flat hierarchical arrangement.

Unlike *Maslaki*, a phenomenon which was common at the middle and lower levels of management bureaucracy, a hybrid form emerged in recent decades. This form, called *sheikocracy,* is often found in some organizations in the Arab world and surrounding countries. Its existence in other Muslim countries, under a different name, is possible. *Sheikocracy* is a product of the interaction of a colonial bureaucratic, Ottoman autocratic system and paternalistic orientations and behavior (see Ali, 1990; Al-Kubaisy, 1985). Due to industrialization and integration in the world economy, managers have had to reconcile and adapt to conflicting demands: managing for performance, division of labor and detailed rules and procedures, while simultaneously observing traditional values and norms. Organizations, therefore, attempt to incorporate these conflicting orientations into their culture. They pursue a system that clarifies authority and responsibility, is efficient and productive and, at the same time, maintains traditional values and norms. The latter sanctions personal relations, open-door policy, and caring. The primary characteristics of *Sheikocray* are: hierarchical authority, rules and regulations contingent on the personality and power of the individuals who make them, an open-door policy, subordination of efficiency to personal relations and personal connections, indecisiveness in decision-making, informality among lower-level managers and a generally patriarchal approach. Nepotism is often evident in selecting upper-level managers, but qualifications are emphasized in the selection of middle- and lower-level personnel. Furthermore, there is an apparent emphasis on unity of command, scalar principles, and division of labor.

Executives under *Sheikocray* may share a similarity to the *Tyrant* executives who existed during what Useem (2002, p. 84) calls the founding generation of many of United States' great corporations. In both cases, the executives consider the organization to be their fiefdom; an extension of the office. Nevertheless, they differ in projecting their power. According to Useem, the *Tyrant* is an "arbitrary one-man rule" who rules by "intimidation and occasional arson." At the National Cash Register, an executive learned of his dismissal by 'finding his desk and chair aflame on the company lawn." Under *Sheikocray* this behavior is not only unacceptable, but also unthinkable. Aggressive behavior is avoided and caring is projected within or outside the organization. While executives under *Sheikocray* may share a similarity with the rest of the executives in Useem's typology (administrator, faceless, numbers machine, statesman, neutron bomb, celebrity, and destroyer), their behavior is always tempered by consideration of what is acceptable or not acceptable by the community.

4.   CONCEPTUALIZATION OF STRUCTURE

Inzerilli and Laurent (1983) argue that, depending on cultural assumptions and underpinnings, organizational structure is perceived in either instrumental or social terms. Under the instrumental conception of structure, positions are related to the task to be performed independent of the person in charge. That is, the various positions within the firm are defined by the functional interdependence of the tasks corresponding to positions. Simply, organizational structure represents a system of tasks. In contrast, social conceptualization implies positions within an organization that are not independent of the people performing the task. That is, an organizational chart manifests a system of status and positions of authority. Consequently, the relationships in an organization are not functionally bounded, rather they are personally based; a superior-subordinate relationship. The two conceptualizations imply that there are two distinct types of organization that are structured according to either functions or social status.

Inzerilli and Laurent (1983) studied how two concepts of structure among American and French subjects are perceived. They found that the proportion of French managers who agree with statements pertaining to a social conception of structure is greater than that of American managers. American managers show greater preferences to structure as instrumental conception than French managers. The authors concluded that in each culture people adapt more easily to patterns of work interaction corresponding to the patterns by which organizational positions are ordered and differentiated in their conception of structure. That is, societal norms and values considerably influence how people perceive organizational arrangement and structure. In societies where traditions and personal relations are admired, social concept of organizational structure is more likely to endure.

In Islamic countries, tradition plays a significant role in the life of individuals and groups. Extended families, friendships, personal relationships, and religion, reinforce group orientations and duties. In Islam, work is devoid of meaning and has no significance if it is not aimed at serving society. Members of business organizations have duties and responsibility to their communities. Indeed, the cornerstone of Islamic teaching is that the benefit of work stems largely from its benefit to mankind. In an organizational setting or in daily life, relations with people are the measure of goodness. This was exemplified in the saying of the Prophet Mohamed, "*Al-Din Al-maamala* (Religion is found in the way of dealing with other people)." Consequently, members of organizations are likely to show preference to social rather than instrumental conceptualization of structure. To find out which conception is given more preferences by Muslims, questionnaires related to structural issues were administered, as part of a larger study, to managers in Saudi Arabia and the United Arab Emirates (UAE). The questionnaires encompassed 12 statements. The first ten statements were taken from Inzerilli and Laurent (1983) and relate to the instrumental and social terms of structure. The last two statements were taken from Laurent (1981) and relate to the issue of minimizing conflict within organization and the extent to which the manager controls the activities of his subordinates if he gave them freedom of initiative. Participants were asked to indicate their agreement or disagreements with each statement using the Likert scale: (1) strongly disagree, (2) disagree, (3) have no idea, (4) agree, and (5) strongly agree. Table 9.1 shows the overall rates of agreement (agree and strongly agree).

The results in Table 9.1 evidence that managers in Islamic environments are highly committed to social connotations of structure. The first two statements underlined the importance of hierarchical relations within organizations and both statements are highly approved. The first statement views structure as identifying, "who has authority over whom." The statement is invariably consistent with the social view of structure as a system of persons rather than a system of functions (instrumental view). The second statement, "no organization could ever function without a hierarchy of authority" implies that organizational arrangements are essential characteristics of organizations.

Respondents in both samples agreed with the social connotation of the message. It should be noticed that even though Islam is an egalitarian faith, it does acknowledge that people differ in their abilities and knowledge. The Quran (46:19) states, "And to all are [assigned] degrees according to their deeds." Islam, too, acknowledges that everyone assumes responsibility according to their social role. This is evidenced in one of the Prophet's sayings, "Every one of you is a leader and every one of you shall be questioned about those under his rule."

Table 9.1   Percentage of managers in Saudi Arabia and the UAE agreeing with statements related to structural issues

	Saudi Arabia (n = 134)	UAE (n = 163)
1. The main reason for having a hierarchical structure is so that everyone knows who has authority over whom	87	91
2. No organization could ever function without a hierarchy of authority	81	91
3. The notion of subordination always has a negative connotation	39	69
4. In order to maintain his/her authority, it is important for a manager to be able to keep a certain distance vis-à-vis his/her subordinates	28	39
5. Most managers seem to be motivated more by obtaining power than by achieving objectives	37	49
6. It is desirable that management authority be able to be questioned	72	75
7. One should submit to all of a superior's demands if he/she has legitimate authority	79	86
8. It is important for a manager to have at hand precise answers to most of the questions that his/her subordinates may raise about their work	72	81
9. An organizational structure in which certain subordinates have two direct bosses	83	83

should be avoided at all costs		
10. In order to have efficient work relationships, it is often necessary to bypass the hierarchical line	46	62
11. Most organizations would be better off if conflict could be eliminated forever	74	86
12. If a manager gives his/her subordinates more freedom of initiative, he/she must at the same time reinforce the extent to which he/she controls their activities	73	72

Participants, however, were not consistent in answering the third statement. Managers in the UAE agreed that subordination has a negative connotation. Subordination is viewed as a relationship among people, rather than as positions in an instrumental conception (Inzerilli and Laurent, 1983). Saudi managers appear to subscribe to the notion that subordination in formal organizations should not be viewed with contempt. This may reflect the fact that in Saudi Arabia, unlike the UAE, the majority of the population is Wahhabi. The cornerstone of Wahhabi belief is strict adherence to rigid instructions that uphold complete submission to authority. In both countries, participants did not agree with the fourth statement, "to maintain authority, it is important for a manager to be able to keep a certain distance vis-à-vis his subordinates." The statement is consistent with an instrumental conception of structure. The message of the statement violates the friendly, personal, and family environment that prevails in most Muslim countries.

Inzerilli and Laurent (1983) assert that agreement with the fifth statement, "Most managers seem to be motivated more by obtaining power than by achieving objectives," manifests a social rather than an instrumental conception of structure. This might not be accurate culturally and conceptually. In Islamic culture, managers and organizations set goals and avoid being perceived as power hungry. Indeed, setting goals in Islam is a virtue. Whether the goal is to prosper or to improve the welfare of a family or community is still a process of achieving a desirable outcome. The Prophet Mohamed instructed Muslims, "Once you set your goal, work on it" and "You have a goal, so proceed to your end." Conceptually, the statement is not clear either in terms of objectives or power motive. There is a wide range of objectives (e.g., profit, harmony among members of the organization, cohesiveness, firm's competitiveness, market share, etc). In some cultures, these goals are prioritized differently. Similarly, the attributes of power and the process of acquisition of power differ. For example, in the United States, individuals purposefully and deliberately seek power, but publicly they shy away from acknowledging it. Therefore, when participants of the questionnaire did not give great preference to the fifth statement, it does not imply they are committed to the instrumental conceptualization of structure.

Similarly, when participants indicated a high agreement with the sixth statement, "It is desirable that management authority be able to be questioned," it does not necessary mean they are committed to the instrumental term of structure as Inzerilli and Laurent (1983) claim. Rather, it reveals that in Islamic culture, leadership is viewed as a shared responsibility. Leaders and followers alike have duties toward each other. Furthermore, this result may underscore the fact that the consultative aspects of Islamic societies influence how members of organization relate to their supervisors. Most importantly, the result evidences that in Islamic culture people believe that legitimate leaders should answer their people and should be held responsible for their actions. This is confirmed in the seventh statement, "One should submit to all of a superior's demands if he has legitimate authority." A high proportion of participants agree with the statement. Legitimate authority, in Islamic thinking, conveys the message that leaders are agreed upon collectively and openly. Consequently, heeding to their command is a duty.

Participants agreed, "It is important for a manager to have at hand precise answers to most of the questions that his subordinates may raise about their work." This is consistent with the view in most Muslim societies that those in responsibility should have general knowledge sufficient to perform their managerial jobs. Having sufficient knowledge does not necessarily mean, however, as Inzerilli and Laurent (1983) claim that managers are superior to their subordinates. The agreement with the statement may, too, uncover some cultural peculiarity. In both Saudi Arabia and the UAE, referring problems to the superior may intend to engage him/her in the solution or may be subtle attempt, on behalf of subordinates, to shift responsibility to supervisors. In many cases subordinates feel that an issue may have far-reaching implications for a community or government and it is more appropriate to seek input from others or to broaden responsibility.

The issue of applicability or desirability of multiple command structures in an Islamic setting was represented in the ninth statement, "An organizational structure in which certain subordinates have two direct bosses should be avoided at all costs." Participants agreed that unity rather than multiple commands in formal organizational relationships should be maintained. It is not clear whether Islamic teaching or organizational traditions are the reason for avoidance of multiple hierarchical relationships. What is clear, however, is that in the medieval Islamic state one center of command was preferred. It was perceived to lead to unity of direction, consistency of instructions, and the strength of the government.

Nevertheless, it should be mentioned that this commitment to the maintenance of a direct manager does not preclude members of organizations being involved in lateral and hierarchical informal consultation. In fact, it is customary in an Islamic setting that members of the organization exchange ideas or reflect on issues regardless of hierarchical arrangements. That is, informal bypassing is part of a common socialization process and is not a deliberate or an intentional violation of the unity of command. In other words, the connotation of bypassing authority in Islamic thinking may not resemble the one common in the West. In the West, bypassing authority may convey an attempt to undermine vertical hierarchies. But this is not the case in societies that are governed by personal and informal relationships. Likewise, when participants rated the tenth statement, "In order to have efficient work relationships, it is often necessary to bypass the hierarchical line," managers in the UAE, rather than those in Saudi Arabia, displayed greater agreement. It is possible to attribute the difference in the rating to the focus in the statement on "efficient work relationships." In fact, there is a widespread understanding in and outside organizations that the personalized aspect of work and frequent interactions among employees are detrimental to efficient work. That is, participants in the UAE may focus solely on the necessity of efficient work relationships, rather than on the literal meaning of 'bypassing' in their rating of the statement. It is doubtful that members of organizations think of such 'bypassing' the hierarchical line as a threat to the status and authority of those who are bypassed.

Statement eleven suggests that, "Most organizations would be better off if conflict could be eliminated forever." Participants showed strong agreement. Laurent (1981) asserts that conflicting issues are often dealt with or avoided by formalization of roles and arbitration by a single authority. That is, regulating behavior through rules and formalization, and the presence of a clearly identified authority reduces variation in behavior and expectations and ultimately conflict. This might be true in the West, but in most Muslim countries avoidance of conflict is a goal by itself - a state of harmony and cohesiveness. While the formalization mechanism might be a useful means for minimizing conflict, organizations often rely on self-censorship and cultural tradition as primary mechanisms to eliminate or avoid conflicts. In Islamic environments, conflict-oriented individuals and conflict itself are not looked upon positively. Despite changing conditions since the early days of Islam and the fact that Muslim history has been filled with political conflicts, in the psyche of most Muslims and in their collective memory, conflict is a dysfunctional development. There is always a common belief in Muslim societies that the presence of a just leader helps to eliminate conflict and to spur prosperity. This may explain, too, the positive rating accorded to the last statement, "If a manager gives his subordinates more freedom of initiative, he must at the same time reinforce the extent to which he controls their activities." Early Islamic thinking and practice sanctioned giving subordinates the autonomy and freedom to take initiatives. Furthermore, the emphasis at the time was primarily on performance rather than on activities. Nevertheless, morally guided activities were considered essential for performance. For example, it was reported that when the Prophet Mohamed appointed Muaz ben Jabal to be a governor of Yemen, he asked him a series of questions about how he would decide on running things. The governor told him that he would decide according to the Quran and the Prophet's way of doing things. Then Mohamed asked him "Even if you do not find anything there, then?" His answer was, "I shall, then, formulate an independent judgment of my own" (quoted in Siddiqui, 1987, p. 261). More explicitly, the emphasis on performance was elaborated on in a letter by the fourth Caliph, Imam Ali (1989), to his governor in Egypt. The letter stated (pp 319-324).

> Show recognition of their [subordinate's] good deeds. Repeat your appreciation of the achievements of those who do well. That will encourage the valorous. and entice the reluctant . . . Give each of them the appreciation he deserves. Do not attribute one's good deeds to another, and do not give him less than what is his due. Do not overestimate one's deeds on account of his position or ancestry, or underestimate one's deeds on similar grounds. . . . Monitor their performance and use for this purpose people who are known for their truthfulness and loyalty. Your discreet monitoring of their work will ensure that they remain honest and considerate to their subjects.

In both instances, performance was considered to be the main criterion for evaluation. Activities, however, were monitored to make sure they were consistent with principled conduct. The end objective was to motive subordinates, while optimally serving the public. That is, work process and activities were left to the discretion of subordinates as long as they were morally guided and did not intend to harm society.

The results in Table 9.1 demonstrate that, in Muslim countries, managers are inclined to view structure in terms of social conception. Nevertheless, the meaning that was attributed to some of these statements by Inzerilli and Laurent (1983) may not necessarily be, as our discussion shows, valid in an Islamic setting. Cultures differ not only in their values and norms, but also in the meaning and symbols attached to certain terminologies and actions. For example, Inzerilli and Laurent argue that French and other European managers subscribe to social conception of structure, but American managers endorse the instrumental conception. The French and American cultures differ from each other and from the culture in many Muslim countries. The general tendencies, however, among French managers and those in Saudi Arabia and the UAE to agree with the general social connotation of structure does not mean that their views of organizational structure are identical that is., personal hierarchy versus. personal network of influence. In addition, Inzerilli and Laurent's claim (p. 100) that when superior-subordinate relationships are defined as personal, they defiantly imply general superiority of one person over another. This claim may not be adequate culturally. In the Islamic culture, most of the relationships at the workplace are personal, but equality among people remains the hallmark of the organizational and societal culture.

5. STRUCTURE IN PRACTICE

The proposition that management problems remain the same over time, but their solutions have differed from society to society (Hofstede, 1999) may be relevant to the issue of structure. Over the years, formal organizational structures have changed dramatically to effectively cope with problems in the organization and the marketplace.   Theoretical justifications have constantly evolved giving more options and better insights for managers and leaders alike.   In the Muslim world, organizational problems are not different from other countries and have evolved around performance, sales or profit decline, employees' satisfaction and turnover, competition, politics within organization, etc. In coping with these problems, structuring or restructuring is often utilized, among other solutions, to ease difficulties and enhance effectiveness.

As indicated in the preceding discussion, even when structure is not influenced by national culture the meaning that is attributed to structure differs from one country to another. Empirical studies that have been conducted in the area of organizational structure in the Muslim world provide valuable insight on the issue of structure. Sabri (1997) studied companies in Jordan and found a relatively higher tendency toward structuring of activities and concentration of authority at the top level. Like Conaty, Mahmoudi and Miller. (1983), who compared structures of organization in the United States and Iran, Sabri, provided a support for the cultural free hypothesis of structure. That is, Sabri argued that Jordanian manufacturing companies were subject to the same contextual constraints as their counterparts in Britain, Japan, and Sweden. Al-Rasheed (2003) investigated institutionalism among Jordanian organizations. He reported that even though hierarchy is observed in the decision-making process, work is not assigned according to function and specialization. This, too, was reported by Sabri who indicated that job description and specialization were not strictly adhered to. Previously, Al-Rashhed (2002) investigated the structure of Jordanian organizations and found that in most organizations top managers closely supervise their subordinates, are directly involved in gathering information they use in making decisions, and have a tendency to control the execution of decisions. Atiyyah (1993) indicated that in terms of structure, management in the Arab world is characterized by a high centralization of decision-making and absence of formal organizational structure and clear job descriptions. Similarly in Iran, Amirshahi (1997) indicated that most of the Iranian corporations have centralized authority and a pyramidal organizational structure with many layers of management. It should be mentioned, however, that organizational structure is not strictly viewed as part of a map of hierarchical authority. Indeed, as El-Tayeb (1986) argued, in many cases the organizational structures and designs are superficial, but on occasion are literally used in conducting activities.

To understand the variation in practice of organizational structures and whether or not organizations in Muslim countries adopt different or peculiar organizational charts than those that exist in other countries, thirty organizational structures were collected for corporations from four countries in the Muslim world. Furthermore, two publications that contained hundreds of organizational charts in the Arab world were used, as well. That is, approximately 140 organizational charts were reviewed. Table 9.2 shows that most of the organizational charts were structured according to functional departmentalization, product or geographical divisional structure existed but were not that common and the mixture of functional and divisional structure were the second most popular structure after functional. The review of these structures reveals that unlike in the United States, the term CEO is not common. Rather, general manager is the common term. Furthermore, there is a frequent utilization of committees in structure and the presence of tall rather than flat structure even in small organizations. Samples of organization charts are shown in Figures 9.4 – 9.8.

Figure 9.4 depicts a functional structure of the Qatari Al-Aahli Bank in 2000. The general manager supervises directly all functional areas (e.g., human resources, credit and international relations, legal, administration, customer services, finance, operations, and computers). The general manager is assisted by three committees (credit, personnel, and procedures and systems) and an assistant general manager. The usefulness, utility, and effectiveness, however, of these committees are subject to speculation. In many instances, these committees are not utilized to facilitate decision-making. Rather, they are established to legitimize decisions made by the general manager.

Figure 9.5 shows a functional structure of the Jordan Institute for Export Development and Commercial Centers. The structure is divided into two major functional areas: financial and technical affairs. The structure is further organized into functional and area divisions. That is, there is a combination of geographical and functional divisions. Here the company's primary focus is on functions and the two main markets: the Arab markets and foreign markets.

The structure of the Saudi Lebanese Modern Construction Company is presented in Figure 9.6. Since the primary business is construction, the company is structured by projects, along with supportive functions. There are various layers and clear and detailed departmentalization. These details might reflect the nature of work and its needs for specific task description or the fact that the company is owned and managed by two nationalities. It is possible that clear delineation of structure is aimed at reducing uncertainty and possible management conflict.

Table 9.2   Classification of contemporary organizational structure

Type / Industry	Functional	Product Division	Area Division	Mixed	Matrix
Manufacturing	30	1	1	6	
Service	63	6	2	26	
Non-Government	2			2	
State	1				
Joint-ownership					

A structure for a marketing company in Egypt is shown in Figure 9.7. The company is structured according to area division. Again, since marketing and distribution is the main activity of the company, the structuring of the organization is intended to optimize activities in each geographical area.

A strategic business unit structure along with functional activities is presented in Figure 9.8. This is the most complex structure and certainly reflects the depth of business activities of the Saudi Basic Industries Corporation. The company is one of the largest corporations in Saudi Arabia. It produces a wide range of products including basic chemicals, polyolefin, polyester, fertilizers, and metals. It has about 16,000 employees and serves customers in over 100 countries. There are six strategic units and four functional divisions. All report to the vice chairperson and the CEO.

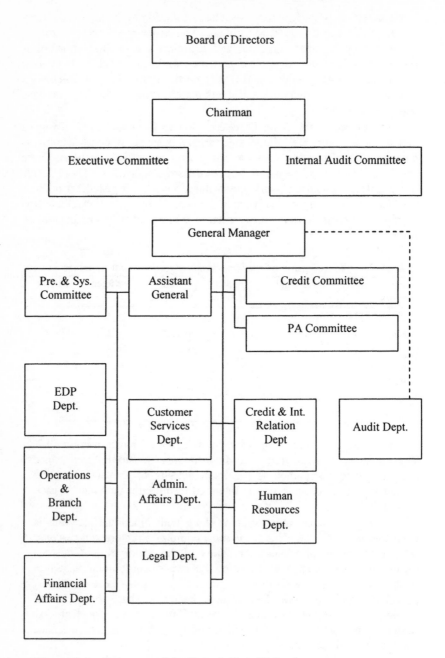

Figure 9.4   Structure of the Qatari Al-Aahli Bank

Figure 9.5 Structure of the Jordan Institute for Export Development and Commercial Centers

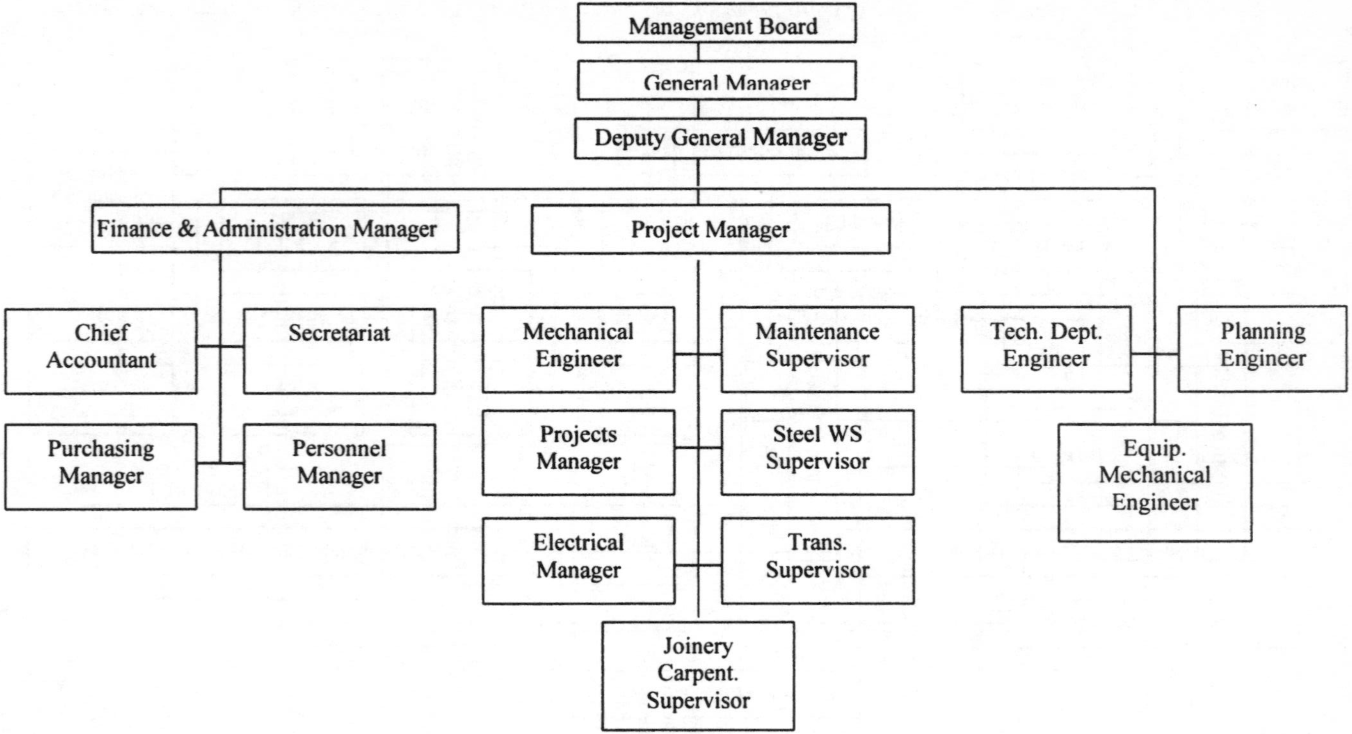

Figure 9.6   Structure of a Saudi Lebanese modern construction company

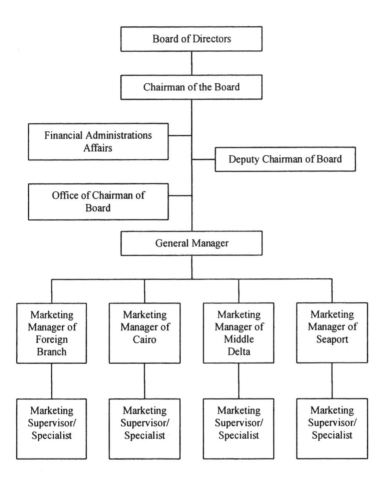

Figure 9.7   Structure of a marketing company in Egypt

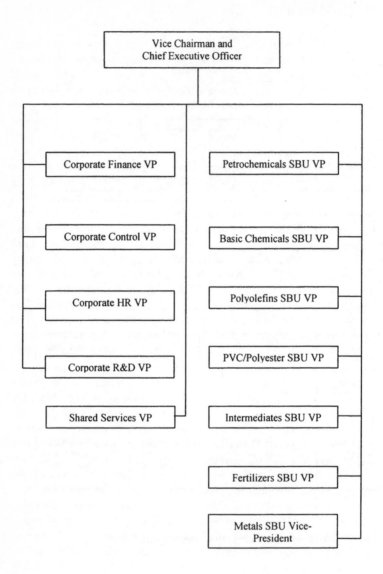

Figure 9.8 Structure of Saudi basic industries corporation

6. CONCLUSION

The evolution of formal structures of organizations in the Muslim World resembles that of the rest of the world. The nature of the evolution, however, has been influenced by two factors: sudden and rapid integration in the world economy and the religious emphasis on maintaining order. Unlike Britain or the United States, for example, most Muslim states have not passed through a gradual economic progress and integration in the world after building sound economic and legal institutions. Their involvement in the world economy was induced mostly by colonization and the exploitation of their natural resources by Western corporations. These corporations established offices and subsidiaries in the colonized countries. The structure of organizations followed that of the parent company. Furthermore, indigenous corporations that were established during that time were influenced by Western views and procedures of organization. Thus, structural arrangements have been based on models that were borrowed mainly from Western countries. While organizations were found in the Muslim world long before Western colonization, structure existed but was not formally drawn. That is, structure was implicitly understood in terms of hierarchical professional arrangements and cultural norms. Types of relationships and arrangements were determined by form of ownership (individual versus partnership), seniority in the craft or profession and instructions that were dictated by owners or their representatives.

Because of the Islamic emphasis on order and *Rehema* (mercy), *ihasan* (kindness), and *adel* (justice) in formal and informal relationships, the structure may be less harsh, relative to other civilizations. Since its early days of inception, Islam has placed a unique emphasis on the necessity of order in life and work. This might be the most significant factor that motivated early Muslims to organize the state and business to avoid chaos and lack of direction. In the early years, and particularly during the golden age of the Muslim state, the emphasis on order may have been intended to ensure growth and flexibility in dealing with ever changing challenges. As the Muslim state started to disintegrate and its economy experienced stagnation and fragmentation, order was considered essential to minimizing uncertainty. In both cases, one can infer that since, at that time, roles were assigned based on expertise, functional departmentalization might have been utilized. The *Rehema*, *ihasan* and *adel* foundations which were discussed in Chapters 5 and 8, have a different implication for organizational structure. Senior managers, because of the societal norms, attempt to give the impression that they are committed to cherished values, encourage the less fortunate members of the organization or those with problems to bring their problems directly to their attention. Outside the organization, some senior managers may have a *Majlis* (open informal meeting) in their houses or neighborhood to hear requests and solve problems outside the formal organizational channels. In some cases, these informal channels are more efficient in solving complex problems on a timely basis.

The preceding review of a large number of organizational charts proves without doubt that contemporary organizational structure in many Muslim countries is determined by factors relevant to organizations and their environments. Possibly, these factors range from strategy to type and the nature of business and management orientations. Indeed, the organizational charts that are presented in the previous section resemble organizational frameworks that exist in other countries, especially in the United States. This may lend support to the proposition that in technical and structural matters, firms, regardless of their home culture, seem to adopt whatever means necessary to facilitate their operations and provide a fit between their goals and environment. At the end, it is the members of the organization, especially its management, that give meaning to structure. The degree to which members of organizations in traditional Islamic environment adhere strictly to hierarchical arrangements as they are depicted in the formal structure is more likely to differ from one country to another and from that in Western industrial nations.

10. The Human Resources

Whether in government or in business, accomplishing organizational objectives depends solely on having skilled, talented, committed, and disciplined personnel. Without the involvement and active participation of human resources, neither capital nor technology finds adequate and functional application. The history of civilization is the record of humankind's endeavors to control their environment and to improve their welfare; their positive involvement, aspirations, and potentials. As in the past, human contribution has been the result of organized efforts and a testimony of the human capability to overcome difficulties and to improve the welfare of the world community. Organized efforts do not take roots in a vacuum. They require planning and development of human resources. In recent years, this function has become more important than ever. Fierce competition, globalization of the world economy, and the continued search for the improvement of quality of life places the human resource function on the top list of managers' jobs. Consequently, there has been an increasing focus on the utilization of employees' and managers' talents to engage creatively in performing their tasks.

As in other civilizations, the Islamic civilization focuses primarily on humankind. It addresses their limitations, potentials, and aspirations. That is, there is a focus on people as the end and means for doing well on earth. As such, it gives considerable attention to the role of individuals and groups in building a desired society. Furthermore, as indicated in Chapters 2 and 5, Islam views people as "free agents." This perception of the human being, if fully and reasonably understood, enables employees to creatively engage in furthering the goals and objectives of organizations they freely join. In addition, the nature of personal relationships, personal networks, responsible behavior, and the viewing of organizations as part of people's lives have far-reaching implications for human resource management. In this chapter, the function of human resources is discussed in terms of early Islamic perspectives, as reflected in the teaching of Islam and current organizational practices.

1.   FOUNDATION OF HUMAN RESOURCE ISSUES

The issues dealing with human resources have been given considerable attention from the inception of Islam. Islam places tremendous emphasis on business conduct and day-to-day dealings. It focuses on the pragmatic aspects of life, while asserting the humanistic and spiritual needs. The emphasis, however, on business conduct and proper relationships with other people uniquely highlights the centrality of human resources in an organization. Therefore, in the early years of the emergence of the Islamic government and community, selection, retention, and motivation of the workforce were given special consideration. Just after the establishment of the Muslim state, the workforce of the state or that of the business was not large. Indeed, in the case of the state and especially in the military, membership was mostly voluntary. Nevertheless, there were certain instructions regarding staffing, training, and motivations that were specified and became guidelines for subsequent governments and private business. In particular, elements pertaining to recruitment, training, and development, evaluation, and wages and compensations were sanctioned.

Recruitment and Selection

This is one of the most complicated tasks in organizations, yet one of the most significant responsibilities. In traditional societies and in family-owned businesses the task takes on an additional importance. In a situation where there are few options to select from, the problem of favoritism is held at a minimum level. Most often, the organization may not have enough qualified individuals to select from. Its options, therefore, are limited for hiring adequately competent individuals. In a case where there are plenty of choices to select from, favoritism and nepotism may influence staffing practices. Islam provides strict guidelines to minimize favoritism in selection decisions. For example, the Quran advises (28:26), "Truly, the best of people for thee to employee is one who is competent and trust worthy." Prophet Mohamed asserts, too, that "He who is in a leadership position and appointed knowingly a person who is not qualified to manage others, then he violates the command of God and His messenger" and "when a person assumes an authority over people and promotes one of them because of personal preferences, God will curse him for ever." Furthermore, Mohamed instructs Muslims not to hire those who are weak or not qualified (see Chapter 6). The second Caliph Omer emphasized behavioral and moral aspects along with performance potential in selecting employees for jobs. He is reported to have said, "When a person is in charge of Muslim affairs and appointed for reasons of favoritism or kinship relationship [nepotism], then he cheats God, the Prophet, and the community" (quoted in Asaf, 1987, p.346).

Two documents that were written in the seventh and ninth centuries on general management affairs sheds light on the issue of hiring and selection. The first one is in a letter that Imam Ali (656-661) sent to the governor (Al-Asthar) of Egypt, hereafter referred to as the Al-Asthar document. The document sets out not only the moral boundaries and rules that an administrator must abide by, but also the conditions for selecting and monitoring subordinates and the principled conduct for treating followers and constituents. In selecting subordinates the document states (p. 322), "Do not nominate them [subordinates] on account of favoritism or nepotism. Select from among them those who have experience and decency, who are known for their good ancestors. . . . Your selection of them should not be based solely on your own intuition and confidence. . . You should rather scrutinize their record of service under previous good governors, and select those who leave the best impression with the people and who have a reputation of honesty." The second document was written by Tahir Ben Al-Hussain, a chief administrator during the Caliph al Mamun's era (813-33), herein refer to as Tahir document. The document was adopted as guidelines for good governance across the vast Abbasid Empire. It states, "Employ subordinates to manage the affairs [of people] those who are known for their sound ideas and management, who have experience and exhibit talent, justice, wisdom, and decency" (quoted in Abd El Hadi, 1990, p. 264).

The criterion set for recruitment and selection primarily encompasses experience and competency in carrying out the job. While these criteria may be different in practice, Muslims over generations have held them in high esteem. As indicated in Chapter 9, Prophet Mohamed, in selecting personnel for government positions, appeared to take into consideration job specifications and task requirements. For example, in selecting governors, most of his appointees were from influential clans. The reason underlying this is that at that time Arabian communities appreciated personnel who were known for their braveness, assertiveness, and noble social affiliation. In selecting market administrators, those who were selected were known to be pious. Market administrators dealt with issues that demanded empathy and sensitivity to and identification with immediate daily problems. This situational aspect in selection seems to influence Muslim thinkers even during the era of decline. For example, Ibn Taimiya (1263-1328) argued that in selecting an employee, task requirements should be taken into consideration. In a situation where the primary job involves maintaining wealth or treasury, then the appointed person must be trustworthy. In case of generating and maintaining wealth, both competency and trustworthy attributes are prerequisites. This is applied, too, in case of war or national instability; a decisive rather than a pious leader is recommended.

In contemporary Muslim countries, the selection of employees is affected by several factors. These factors range from a scarcity of qualified personnel, nepotism, rigid bureaucracy, to rapid growth in the number of private and state enterprises that have been established since political independence and the official end of the era of colonization. The most important factors that render the selection process to be subjective and sometimes worthless are personalized relationships or personalism; kinship, regional, or neighborhood favoritism; and the presence of a large number of guest workers and employees in some Muslim countries, especially the oil-producing countries. As was discussed in Chapter 8, personalism phenomena undermines objectivity and sanctioned procedures. Despite the lengthy procedures for interview and testing, those who are involved in the selection process are more likely disposed toward subjectivism and arbitrary judgment in deciding who is going to be hired.

Likewise, despite public denouncement of nepotism, kinship, regional, or neighborhood relationships shape the selection process. While this practice is found even in Western countries, it is more common in developing countries, including the Muslim states. A politically correct term for it is friendship networks. This is found not only in institutions in small towns and communities, but also in large corporations or government agencies. Keller (2002), for example, provides a detailed account of how, during his long federal government career, Paul Wolfowitz, deputy secretary of defense, always recruited friends to work in his office. He offered the number three position in the Defense Department to his friend Richard Perle. When the latter declined, it was offered to another friend, Douglas Feith. In Muslim countries, however, the recruitment of friends and relatives is a widespread practice and is not limited to senior positions. Branine (2001, p. 166) asserts that in Algeria, friendship and kinship "can take precedence over qualifications and skills as managers feel obliged to support their relatives and friends."

The presence of guest workers and employees also constitutes an obstacle to objective recruitment and selection. In countries like Saudi Arabia, the UAE, and Kuwait, companies have under their disposal a larger number of workers from other countries to select from. These workers, by law, do not have or are not qualified for permanent residence and work permits normally issued for a specific occupation or employer. This makes it easer for corporations to seek employment of those who were willing to work for the lowest possible wages and more likely under conditions that would otherwise not be accepted by national workers. Corporations hire and dismiss these guest workers as they wish. This increases the propensity to be subjective, to ignore vital human resource development issues, and to not be concerned with long-term perspective in selection.

Training and Development

In today's business environment training of employees has become essential for any institution longing for a healthy position in the marketplace. Various techniques have evolved and emerged to sharpen employees' skills and prepare them to confidently and competently perform their tasks. Training objectives are numerous; chief among them are improving employees' performance, preparing employees to assume a new job or more responsibilities, and immersing organizational culture and aligning individuals goals with that of the organization. In the early days of the Muslim state both business and government affairs were simple. Like their contemporary rivals in nearby states, the Muslims saw the training as something that was instrumental in improving image and proper conduct. Ibn Khaldun, the medieval Arab sociologist, considered skilled workers as the creator of profit and prosperity in a society. Furthermore, he asserted that capable employees, even when they are not trustworthy, are preferable to trustworthy but not unskilled employees.

The Quran generally places emphasis on having general knowledge, good listening, and observation skills. In particular, it highlights the importance of apprenticeship. Devoted Muslims in authority, therefore, have given these attributes close attention for training and development. The second Caliph, Omer, is reported to have said to one of his subordinates, "I appointed you to test you. If you did well, I will promote you; but if you did not, then I will dismiss you" (quoted Abu-Doleh and Ayoun, 2001). Furthermore, in the Al-Asthar document, there is a great emphasis on probation aspects, shouldering responsibility, learning and reasoning, and decent dealing with people. Similarly, the Tahir document highlights experience, justice, honesty, and logic. In the years that followed most of the middle-level jobs and state's bureaucracy relied on professionally trained individuals, which in turn evolved into a professional class that was handed down in families from generation to generation (e.g., *Al-Jabi*, collector of tax; *Al-Khazin*, warehouse director; Al-Katib, scribe).

At that time, it appears that apprenticeships were common practice in business and commerce. Those who mastered the profession were maintained and promoted. In recent years there have been a flourishing of private and government institutions that are specialized in training and management development in almost all Muslim countries. Three types of training and development institutes are found in Muslim countries: employees training (e.g., Saudi Royal Institute for Human Resource

Development, Institute of Public Administration); management development (e.g., Center for Management Development, Iraq; Industrial Management Institute of Iran; Bangladesh Institute of Management); and employees and management development (e.g., Arab Administrative Development Organization; Bangladesh Institute of Bank Management; Institute of Banking Studies in Kuwait). In addition, large companies, too, have their own training centers. Both on-and off-job training are common (e.g., Askari Bank in Pakistan; Sabic Companies in Saudi Arabia, National Bank of Kuwait, Housing Bank for Trade and Finance in Jordan). The National Bank of Kuwait, a major corporation, has its own training center. Senior-level managers and those who need special skills are sent to outside institutes to acquire knowledge and skills. Internal training is mostly confined to operational and technical aspects. This type of training is either carried out by internal staff or by contracted professional consultants and experts. Charles Wilson (1993), the Training Manager at Emirates Airline, indicated that in training managers in the United Arab Emirates (UAE), there was a special emphasis on converting middle and senior managers to new management ideas. Both inside and outside experts served as trainers. He further reported that in training managers in the UAE the emphasis was placed on motivational factors "doing something for my country," and on improving work ethics and enhancing work discipline.

The appeal for training and the spur of training institutions reflects an understanding of the importance of the organizational and job-specific skills for economic development. There are, however, two major drawbacks in most of the training programs in the Muslim world: heavy reliance on Western techniques and methods with no adequate attempts to decipher their relative cultural appropriateness and an emphasis on theory at the expense of application. These weaknesses combined with bureaucratic tendencies, to a large extent, are responsible for the lack of notable management innovation and organizational effectiveness in many Muslim countries.

Performance Evaluation

In today's business environment, performance evaluation generally serves four objectives: measuring organizational progress in meeting goals, enabling senior managers to know what has been done, providing feedback to and developing subordinates, and allocating rewards. These general objectives have evolved over centuries. Their ambiguity, articulation, specificity, and enforcement have been influenced mostly by the degree of task specificity, the nature of jobs, and the evolution and progress of management and organizational thought. The latter seems to be the most important factor in shaping the seriousness of and commitment to performance evaluation.

Two considerations have influenced performance evaluation in Islam: normative instructions and the practice of the Prophet Mohamed and his immediate four Caliphs. The normative realm is revealed in Quranic instructions. These general instructions can be viewed as relevant to work aspects and employees' activities. Whether or nor they are followed literally in practice is not clear. What is clear, however, is that people at the workplace fondly utter them. These normative judgments can be grouped into three categories: contractual arrangement, self-responsibility and control, and the Almighty's assessment of performance. In terms of contractual aspects, Islam views the employment of a person as a reaffirmation of an obligatory relationship between the organization and the employee. Both the company and the employees have expectations that must simultaneously be fully met. The Quran (17:34) instructs Muslims that any promise or engagement is a contract that must be met by participants: "And fulfill engagement [promise], for the engagement will be enquired into." Indeed, the Quran (5:1), presents the fulfillment of obligations as a command "Fulfill all contracts."

Under self-responsibility, the Quran clarifies that what one does is solely his/her responsibility and no one should be held responsible for the mistakes of others. While the normative responsibility is clearly specified (74:38), "Every soul will be held in pledge for its deeds," the Quran articulates that individuals are aware of their deeds and are capable of initiating corrections (75:14), "Nay, man is a witness against himself." That is, employees are expected to have a moral duty to monitor their performance. These intrinsic aspects, however, are more likely to transform into action in an environment of reciprocal trust and understanding of religious principles. Both contractual arrangement and self-assessment are verified in the hereafter. There is a warning that God monitors what one does. Here the Quran seems to be specific (11:112), "for He seeth well all that ye do" and (16:91) "Indeed you have made God your surety; for God knowth all that you do." Therefore, the normative aspects make the assessment of performance first and foremost a responsibility of the employee. This responsibility is transcended to the hereafter, when a person is presented with a record of his performance in the world (17:14), "sufficient is thy soul this day [of Judgment] to make out an account against thee."

Furthermore, the company has a moral responsibility to see that things are carried out according to the agreed upon direction. There are mutual obligations and entitlements between employees and the company. Obligations and entitlements reinforce each other. In both cases, the premise is that the action of each party in the contract is monitored by God and is measured in the next life (4:1), "for God ever watches over you" and (2:234) "God is well acquainted with what ye do." Presumably, the performance and evaluation of performance are an interactive process that is ever verified by an omnipresent power. Figure 10.1 depicts the normative aspects of performance evaluation.

The sayings and practices of Prophet Mohamed and his immediate four Caliphs also influence the outlook toward performance evaluation. Mohamed commands that "Muslims shall be bound by the conditions which they make." Furthermore, he makes it obligatory for employees to perfect their work and be responsible for what they do irrespective of their position or social and organizational hierarchy. The second Caliph, Omer, used three approaches to monitor performance: directly reviewed public complaints and asking subordinates for accountability, sending monitors to assess the performance of public officers, and giving assessment and feedback to governors and subordinates during the session of pilgrimage. In the Al-Asthar document, Imam Ali specified that evaluation of subordinates must be strictly based on deed and behavior toward the public. There were two approaches in carrying out the evaluation; direct and indirect. The direct approach was done by the Caliph himself for those who were working around him or those who were asked to bring their records with them to be evaluated. The second was done by sending monitors to far regions to evaluate governors and other employees. The document (p. 325) states: "Monitor their [subordinates] performance and use for this purpose people who are known for their truthfulness and loyalty. Your discreet monitoring of their work will ensure that they remain honest and considerate to their subjects. Beware of your close assistants. If you have reliable information from your agents that one of them has committed treachery, then that should be sufficient evidence to impose punishment."

In the Tahir document, the view on performance evaluation is similar in direction to the preceding one. Specifically, it articulates two methods. The first is to have a trustworthy agent to monitor the behavior and performance of subordinates in regions far from the main office. The agent reports on subordinates' conduct and action. The second is to review the action of those subordinates and subscribers who work in the superior's office. The document specifies that a daily meeting has to take place to evaluate each subordinate's concern and performance. The instructions in the document highlight that the assessment meeting has to be taken seriously and that the superior must show attentiveness, alertness, and be careful and diligent in looking at issues evaluated.

In recent years, performance evaluation has become an integral part of human resource function. Both state and private enterprises officially specify it for tenure, rewards, and promotion decisions and for development assessment. In countries like Iraq, Kuwait, Iran, Pakistan, and Turkey organizations have detailed forms and procedures for evaluation. These procedures are often time consuming and bureaucratic in nature. In fact, in many cases the evaluation outcome is ignored or not seriously taken into consideration in making human resource decisions. In small businesses, however, the utilization of formal evaluation is not that common. Informal personnel assessment appears to be preferred. This can be done because of the limited resources and skill or because of traditional habit of relying on personal judgment.

Factors influencing performance evaluation

Despite the usefulness and appreciation of performance evaluation, close adherence to its procedures and goals is not always found. It is plausible that those responsible for its implementation value its contribution but encounter difficulties in literally following its aim and steps. While this concern is found in almost all societies, in the Muslim world there are several factors that shape and influence attitudes toward performance evaluation and subsequently hinder its implementation. Three factors stand out as having the most lasting impact: religious consideration, personal relationships, and bureaucratic tendencies. In terms of religion, there are at least three issues that often render performance evaluation irrelevant regarding punishment or disciplinary actions. The first issue pertains to the common understanding and religious edict that firing employees may constitute a violation of spiritual guidelines and commitment to the community. That is, managers rethink the consequences and adverse impact on the family of the fired employee. The second revolves around *Rehema* (mercy), *ihasan* (kindness), and *adel* (justice). These tendencies are religiously sanctioned, and have become an important part of organizational culture. The religious instructions emphasize the goodness of forgiveness and communicating good news (64:14), "If you would pardon, overlook, and forgive, know that God is All-forgiven and All-merciful" and (2:83) "Speak fair to the people." The last religious concern is related to what was discussed in Chapter 4; the intention rather than the outcome is the primary basis for treatment. In this context, there are several factors to be considered before one is subjected to a disciplinary action. If there is evidence that circumstances have prevented satisfactory performance and there is no bad intention, forgiveness and understanding is likely to be the case. This tendency is strengthened by the belief that God is the ultimate evaluator and He will judge people in the hereafter.

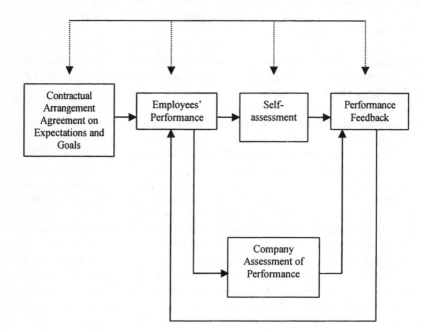

Hereafter Assessment

Figure 10.1   Normative realm of performance evaluation

The second factor that influences performance evaluation is personal relationships. The primacy of the person and personal aspects of business conduct makes it almost impossible to strictly observe the performance process and the desired outcome of the evaluation.   Those who are responsible for making recommendations avoid being seen as harsh or inconsiderate.   Beside the religious considerations presented in the preceding discussion, managers also take note not only of the person under consideration but also his/her friends, relatives, and neighbors and their possible reactions.   That is, the managers' options for giving negative evaluations are conspicuously limited. The third factor, bureaucracy, gives managers responsibility for evaluating an exit strategy. The bureaucratic aspects of the evaluation enable managers to follow specific guidelines and procedures. They allow them to produce recommendations regarding the subject under consideration.   These recommendations, however, are filed in the personal folder but there is no intention of implementing them. The employees are either not informed about them or are informed informally about them with a clear signal that they will not be implemented.

Methods of Evaluations

Behavioral studies and measurement advancement in recent decades provide managers with a variety of techniques for conducting performance evaluation. These techniques were implemented after the Second World War and have continued with the subsequent growth in international business and multinational corporations (MNCs). Indeed, in recent decades there have been several tools available for performance evaluation. They range from the type of judgment (relative or absolute) to the focus of the measurement (trait, behavior, or outcome). The degree of using these techniques differs across organizations and countries. Consequently, in contemporary business, the use of complex performance measurements has been on the rise. The simple performance evaluation is found in small, mostly family-owned organizations. Previously, most of the performance evaluation methods were modest in procedures and aims.

In early Muslim states, references in documents to and instructions pertaining to performance evaluation of subordinates were common. The frequency of references to performance may have underscored, at the time, the importance that Muslim leaders attributed to moral conduct and satisfying and meeting the demands of constituencies. The emphasis on one's deeds was consistent with the general instruction to the faithful that no one should bear the action of others. Furthermore, people were treated in accordance with their work contribution. In fact, it is customary for Muslims to recite the Quran (46:19), "And to all are ranked according to their deeds." Therefore, responsible Muslim leaders usually showed an inclination toward objectivity in evaluation. For example, Imam Ali in one of his instructions stated (p. 386), "you will do them justice and be more objective if you confine yourselves to the description of their [subordinates] deeds and the nature of their condition." At the time, the work operations were not as sophisticated as today's businesses and objectives were stated in general or vague terms that make measurement precision impossible. Nevertheless, two methods of evaluations appear to have been used: judgment-based and behavioral-based evaluations. The judgment-based approach normally used statements related to trait, attributes, and characters of employees. These attributes included decency, truthfulness, kindness, shouldering responsibility, maturity, justness, decisiveness, reliability, dedication, and so on. In both Al-Asthar and Tahir documents, these attributes were highlighted.

The aspects of behavioral-based approach are asserted in available historical documents. It was reported that the second Caliph, Omer, consistently used to focus on how his deputies and subordinates carried out their work and the reaction of constituencies to their behavior. He gave priorities to the following questions: did the deputy visit the sick people, did he take care of the slaves, and how did he treat the disenfranchised? If the answer to one of theses question was negative, Omer would remove the subordinate from the position (Abu-Doleh and Ayoun, 2000). The Al-Asthar and Tahir documents generally address the behavioral-based approach that could be verified through desired results. In the Tahir document, there was an emphasis on "behavior and actions." Likewise, the focus in the Al-Asthar document was on behavior and performance.

In contemporary organizations, whether they are state or private enterprises, a mixture of the above methods are used. In fact, large and medium-sized organizations in countries like Algeria, Iran, Iraq, and Saudi Arabia, Western forms and evaluation techniques have been used widely. While the judgment approach is common, it is always combined with one or two of the focus methods: traits, outcomes, and behavior. Corporations have used these methods intensively and have invited consultants and experts to design and train human resource personnel on using modern business performance evaluation. The National Bank of Kuwait, the Arab Bank in Jordan, Delta Life Insurance Companies in Bangladesh, and ARAMCO are pioneers.

Compensation

The issue of wage and compensation has a special place in Islamic thinking on human resource management. The issue is closely linked to and examined in the context of justice and responsible behavior. The compensation in the early years of the Muslim State was based on the following foundations:

a.   Employment is a contractual agreement. The fulfillment of such a contract is an obligation that both the employer and employee have to meet. The Quran not only instructs believers to meet conditions, but also to avoid any attempt to go around the contract (7:85), "Nor withhold from the people the things that are their due."

b.   Compensations differ according to expertise and situation. The Quran states (46:19), "And to all are ranked according to their deeds" and (39:9), "Say: 'Are those equal, those who know and those who do not know?'" Kurd Ali (1934) reported that the second Caliph, Omer, used to arrange wages for his subordinates and deputies according to hardship, living standard in a region, nature of task, and needs of subordinates (e.g., family size).

c. Compensations must be determined in advance and that wage has to be given immediately once work is completed. It was reported that Prophet Mohamed asserted that "if one hires an employee, he must inform him of his wage" and "the employee must get his wage promptly after the work is done" (quoted in Asaf, 1987, p.362).

d. Compensations can be either cash or/and in kind. This practice was followed in many Muslim states for many centuries.

e. Wages and compensations are based on prior agreement and should be increased according to circumstances. It was reported that the first Caliph, Abu Baker, requested the senior members of the Muslim community to increase his base pay as he had to quit his business, commerce, after assuming the leadership position, Caliph. To this end he argued, "Increase my base pay. I have to support my family and the Caliphate role prevents me from engaging in trade" (quoted in Abu-Dole and Ayoun, 2000).

f. Wages and compensation should be sufficient to provide a decent living. This point was clearly illustrated in the Al-Asthar document. It was stated (p. 50) "Give them [subordinates] decent remuneration. This will give them the power to resist temptation and make them less susceptible to abuse that which they have been entrusted with."

In recent years, companies have adopted pay and compensation systems that are similar to what is found in Western countries. There is a use of base compensation, incentives, and benefits. In fact, it is common to have a base salary, cost of living allowances, special bonuses, and benefits in almost all business and government institutions. For example, ARAMCO and Sabic Companies provide base salary, lump-sum annual amount, housing allowances, insurances, and other related incentive plans. In addition, monetary and non-monetary rewards have been espoused. Nevertheless, there is a widespread use of the seniority system in compensation determination. While this may simplify the administration of the compensation system, it helps to frustrate competent and achievement oriented personnel. Furthermore, equity issues and the just compensation system that was highly cherished in the early years of the Muslim state are often violated. In this context, it should be noticed that the colonial legacy and contemporary foreign occupations have reinforced a system of wage differentiation that may constitute a discrimination based on ethnicity. For example, in Saudi Arabia pay scales differ according to national or ethnic backgrounds. In this case, "natives are paid the highest salaries, followed by Americans and European, Arabs, Filipinos, Koreans, and at the bottom of the scale, Indian subcontinent national" (Mellahi and Wood, 2001, p. 146). This situation is part of the British colonial legacy and exists, too, in other Arab Gulf countries. Since the occupation of Iraq in 2003 by the United States, the American occupational authority has adopted an employment salary scale that differs across ethnicity. For employees in the central and southern parts of Iraq (mostly Arabs) the average salary is between $100 and $300 while that for the northern part (Kurds), the range is between $400 and $700 (Azzaman, 2003).

Reward Systems

Organizations offer a variety of rewards. These rewards are distributed to employees to serve various objectives. Individual employees have different views concerning rewards and seek to satisfy specific personal needs. For example, individuals may seek recognition, and appreciation, equity relative to performance and skills, compatibility to similar jobs in the marketplace, and/or meet other personal needs such as comfortable living standards and positive involvement in organizational affairs. On the other hand, organizations grant rewards to employees to enhance loyalty, motivation, commitment to work, retention, performance, and planning for managerial career and management succession.

Rewards in Islamic teaching are based on the following foundations:

a. The reward must be linked to performance and behavior. The Quran admonishes (27:90) "Can you expect any recompense other than what you deserve for your deeds," and (37:131) "Thus indeed we reward those who do right."
b. The reward must be generous to reinforce the good deeds. The Quran states (6:160), "He that doeth good shall have ten times as much to his credit: He that doeth evil shall only be recompensed according to his evil." In the Al-Asthar document, it was stated that the reward must be decent (p. 323) in order to enable employees "to resist temptation and make them less susceptible to abuse that which they have been entrusted with."
c. The leader's reward of subordinates is an obligation and an ingredient of the job. In the Tahir document, the instructions to an appointed administrator encouraged him to consider generosity and reward "as an ethical obligation and as a philosophy and practice . . . Decent remuneration should be given as such that God made it easy for them [subordinates] to overcome their urgent material needs and strengthen them, thus they will be more obedient and loyal to you."

d. The reward is both monetary and non-monetary. In the case of the non-monetary reward, the leader must show recognition and appreciation. In the Al-Asthar document, it was (p. 319) stated, "Show recognition of their [subordinate's] good deeds. Repeat your appreciation of the achievements of those who do well. That will encourage the valorous and entice the reluctant."

e. The reward should be given to those who deserve it. The Al-Asther document succinctly made this point when it stated (319), "Give each of them [subordinates] the appreciation he deserves . . . Do not overestimate one's deeds on account of his position or ancestry, or underestimate one's deeds on similar grounds."

It should be noted too that in Islamic practice, the reward was administered according to elitism and egalitarianism principles. During the era of the first and fourth Caliph, Abu Baker and Ali respectively, egalitarianism was espoused in practice. The elitism principle was practiced during the era of the second and third Caliphs, Omer and Othman respectively (see Glaachi, 2000; Kurd Ali, 1934). In contemporary business practices, however, there is no clear principle or unified policy regarding the appropriate way for distributing rewards. Both circumstances and institutional specificity appear to play a significant role in determining the amount of and approach to reward. Nevertheless, there are a few observations that might be essential for understanding the management of the reward systems in many Muslim societies. First, almost all business organizations uniformly grant rewards at the end of the year as a bonus or an increase in salary. While companies in Bangladesh and Iran seem to give a cash reward, firms in other countries like Saudi Arabia, Kuwait, and Lebanon give an annual bonus or a percentage increase in salary in addition to other forms of rewards. Second, management are more to likely recognize and reward employees especially those who are perceived to be decent and who are respected by other employees or the community at large. Reputations and social position in the community are important considerations in giving the reward. That is, reward is seen mostly as a public gesture rather than a tool for improving productivity or performance. Third, in giving rewards, senior managers often seek to solidify their authoritative positions and enhance personal loyalty. Lastly, documentation of performance evaluation does exist in most organization, but the distribution of rewards or the amount of the reward may be arbitrary and is not necessarily linked to performance.

2.   CHALLANGING ISSUES

The current practice of human resource management in Muslim societies lags behind relative to other aspects of management. Furthermore, the practice is neither in line with the rapid development in most of the industrial societies or with the tradition of the early Muslim state. In particular, two areas pose a serious challenge to the management of organizations in these societies: diversity and women in management. Tackling these two issues successfully may boost sound management practice and qualitatively advance the practice of human resource management. Concerns pertaining to both issues are intertwined with other aspects of management and probably underline deep organizational problems. In this section, these two issues are addressed.

Diversity No issue at the workplace that exemplifies the contradiction between idealism and reality likes diversity. As we saw in Chapter 1, diversity is one of the most distinct hallmarks of the Islamic faith. Not only the religious edicts sanction diversity but also generally for the first seven centuries of Islam, the practice of diversity in employment and leadership was the rule rather than exception. The Quran sanctions diversity and considers it a way of life. For example, the Quran (10:99) states, "If it had been thy Lord's will, they would all have believed, all who are on earth! Wilt thou then compel mankind, against their will to believe!" and (16:93), "If God so willed, He could make you all one people." Furthermore, Quran instructs believers that men and women are equal. Quran (3:195) states, "I do not neglect anyone's work, be he male or female: ye are members, one of another" and "If any do deeds of righteousness, be they male or female and have faith, they will enter heaven, and not the least injustice will be done to them." The Prophet Mohamed asserted that there are no differences among people except in their commitment to their faith. In that regard, he vehemently rejected discrimination among people because they were Arabs or non-Arabs, white or black.

Perhaps, it was only in Muslim societies that the slaves [Mumluks] rose to power and became heads of state. Indeed, after the eleventh-century non-Arab rulers governed most of the Islamic world. Non-Muslims, especially Christians and Jews, assumed higher places in the court of Caliphs. They served as prime ministers, special envoys and advisors, and heads of important bureaucratic and professional offices. The end of the Muslim golden age brought with it not only political, economic, and scientific decline, but also intolerance and foreign traditions. The qualities of openness, inclusiveness, tolerance, and flexibility that once made Muslims influential on the global stage gradually disappeared.

In recent years, there has been a phenomenal growth in the labor market in the Muslim world. Depending on the situation, some countries have become a recipient of workers from all over the world (e.g., Arab oil countries). Other countries have become an exporter of cheap labor (e.g., Bangladesh, Egypt, Morocco, Pakistan, etc.). In countries that have become a destination of workers, discrimination in terms of wages, pay scales, benefits, and rewards become the norm in both public and private institutions. In Saudi Arabia, for example, *Amnesty International* (2000) asserts that Saudi sponsors of Asian workers "often confiscate their passports and they are forbidden to change jobs or travel from where they work. Many suffer at the hands of their employers on whom they are completely dependent. Some are not paid and are vulnerable to abuse by employers." In addition, non-citizen workers have been either placed in special compounds or are subjected to ill-treatment that is inconsistent with Islamic teaching (forcing workers to do things that are not specified in their contract, limiting their freedom to switch employers, or treating them with contempt). These issues, along with other policies related to recruitments, training, promotion, and tenure, significantly curtail human potential and adversely impact diversity and human resource development. Confronting them, therefore, becomes an organizational imperative.

Women in Management

The role of women in management and the workplace in general is considerably restricted. Historically, women played important roles in social networking, socialization, and motivating men to do their best in their endeavors. There were women who served as market administrators, advisors, arbitrators, poets, and narrators in various parts of Muslim states. Probably, at that time, women in Muslim societies played a relatively more active role than their counterparts in other societies during the same period. In recent years, women in business have gradually assumed a corresponding role to that in other fields such as politics and literature. For example, women in Muslim societies, rather than in the United States or Japan, have become heads of state in countries like Bangladesh, Indonesia, Pakistan, and Turkey. Likewise, in the field of literature there are prominent women poets and novelists in many countries. Women literary clubs have been established for a long time in Iraq, Syria, and Lebanon. Generally, in countries that have espoused social liberalism and placed limited social restriction on women, females have more opportunities for education and employment (e.g., Iraq, Syria, Tunisia, Turkey, etc.). In these societies women have actively pursued political and educational involvement and subsequently played a leading role in the construction of their societies. For example, Nazeha Al-Delamey, in the late 1950s assumed a cabinet level position in Iraq, while in Sudan Fatama Ibrahim served several senior positions including the head of the International Women's Union.

However, in some countries like Kuwait, for example, women do not have the right to vote.   Nevertheless, because of the educational opportunities that have been available for them since the early 1960s, they have participated in the labor market and some of them serve on the board of directors of major corporations and or have established their own businesses.   Women in Kuwait, however, prefer to work in the government and relative to men most of them are placed in non-supervisory jobs (Abdel-Halim and Ashour, 1995).   The authors attribute these results of their studies to the need for job security, which is offered in the government sector, and to the largely male-dominated society of Kuwait respectively. Recent studies in Kuwait indicate that women owners of small firms tend to have more education but less business experience than their male counterparts. Furthermore, businesses owned by women are found to suffer from the liability of newness and their financial performance is significantly lower than men (Alowaihan, 2004).   Similar situations may exist in Jordan and Tunisia.   But in Iraq, Syria, Lebanon, Turkey and most recently in Bahrain and the UAE women have been actively engaged in businesses.

Five major developments have recently spurred women's participation in the business world. First, after many years of public participation in political, literary, and art affairs, women have felt more confident about entering a sector that has been traditionally dominated by men.   Second, with the dramatic increase of public sector institutions after official independence of many Muslim countries, governments sought to recruit women to fill vacant jobs.   After the recent privatization trends of public enterprises, these women either retained their jobs or actively sought to be part of the privatization movement. Third, the flourishing of public education, especially at the university level, opens new opportunities for women to be positively involved in the economic development and to venture beyond the traditional fields - education, art and health.   Fourth, circumstances (e.g., illness, family feuds) and deaths of the patriarch in established business families in Muslim societies often leave women in charge directly or indirectly in the business affairs.   This gives them not only the experience but also the confidence to run some or all parts of the business. Finally, between the 1940s and 1980s, various Muslim states espoused socialism and state capitalism. A cornerstone of socialist ideology is the equity between women and men.   In these countries, women are provided with opportunities to venture in various areas of public affairs thereby given them the experience and skills to manage organizations.

Nevertheless, there are four prominent factors that limit women participation in the workplace in general and management in particular. First, the care of children and household duties are considered the women's domain.   Second, the lack of the availability of affordable childcare facilities in most of the Muslim societies often impedes the desire to look for jobs. Third, narrow interpretations of Islam place certain restrictions on the full participation of women in the workplace. In countries such as Saudi Arabia and Afghanistan rigid interpretations of Islam have conspicuously limited the role of women in the business world.   Finally, in terms of management, most management responsibilities are held by men.   Most women in the workplace, despite their achievements and potentials, have served as clerks and non-supervisory roles.   In addition to these major factors, there are two other reasons that influence women's participation in the formal workplace. In rural areas, in many Muslim countries, schools are not available or are strictly for boys.   This lack of education has limited women's options for work and advancement. Furthermore, after the sudden increase in oil revenues that was started in the early 1960s and the initiation of many Muslim countries of ambitious economic development plans, people migrated in large numbers from rural areas to urban centers. Previously, in the rural areas women participated openly and actively in agricultural and related work.   These same women suddenly find themselves in a different environment where men leave early morning to work and return late home. Furthermore, they are no longer surrounded by relatives and friends.   These developments limit their roles outside the home and intensify their social insecurities.

3. HUMAN RESOURCE MAMNAGEMENT AND TYPOLOGY OF ORGANIZATION

In the preceding discussion the evolution of human resource thinking and practices has been addressed.   The discussion was general and aimed at providing a coherent review and analysis of human resource management in the Muslim world. In that context, contemporary human resource management practices in countries and organizations are tackled.   In this section, human resource dimensions across three typologies of organization are investigated.   The three typologies are: autocratic, traditionally group-centered, and spiritually enlightened organizations.   These organizations were identified in Chapter 5.   As it can be seen in Table 10.1, human resource practices differ across theses typologies.   In autocratic organizations, the culture seems to place an emphasis on the economic aspects and the importance of senior managers. Employees and workers exist to serve the organization economic interests. Their existence is justified by economic considerations. Therefore, they have neither job security nor the competitive opportunities to acquire new skills and knowledge. Under the traditionally group-centered organization, concerns about group harmony and the viability of the organization are not divorced. Thus, in such cultures human resource management is utilized to foster cooperation and understanding among employees while working to meet organizational goals. For spiritually enlightened organizations, human resource management functions serve not only to ensure harmony between employees' and organization's goals but also to align organization interests with the welfare and viability of the community. All these forms of organization exist in Muslim countries. Perhaps, the most prevailing form is the autocratic and to a lesser extent the traditionally group-centered. The mere existence, however, of the third form demonstrates that certain fundamental values and behaviors are persistent and their presence leads to establishing organizations that are appropriate for managing in the twenty-first century.

Table 10.1   Human resource management across three forms of organization

Human resource dimensions	Autocratic	Traditional Group Centered	Spiritually enlightened
Recruitment	Facilitates the implementation of economic objectives	Facilitates employees' harmony while meeting organizational goals	Enhancing company's role in the community and improving its welfare
Training and development	Is not useful unless it is initiated by senior managers and used to coping with a crisis	Important to enhance group coordination and identification	Important to accumulate human capital, enhance cooperation, and strengthen organizational involvement in the community
Performance evaluation	Enforces regulations and takes action to correct deviations from performance standards	Necessary for the alignment of individual and organizational goals	Ensures clarity of goals and direction and optimally serves organizations and society

Human resource dimensions	Autocratic	Traditional group- centered	Spiritually enlightened
Compensation	Should be limited and is a base pay; it's an economic burden	Instruments for fostering cooperation, loyalty, and identification with the company	Instruments for improving the welfare of employees while enhancing their involvement in the community
Firing and layoff of employees	Essential to keep the organization economically viable and force employees to obey management	May cause group fragmentation, disharmony, and resentment. It should be used as a last resort and be undertaken with utmost caution	Unnecessary act, that ultimately leads to negative consequences and destroys the alignment between organizational and community goals
Rewards	Necessary to ensure employee commitment to economic goals and to bring about personal loyalty to senior managers	Instruments for recognizing positive involvement and harmonious functions	Necessary for recognizing and appreciating achievement, spiritual involvement, and alleviating hardship
Diversity	May lead to dysfunctional activities and conflicts	May motivate employees and enhance their dynamic spirit to meet organizational goals	A natural situation and necessary to enhance spiritual dialogue, involvements, and innovation

4. CONCLUSION

In this chapter, the perspectives and practices of human resource management were discussed. The discussion focused on the variation in perspectives and practices over centuries and across organizations. The nature of recruitment and selection, training and development highlights the diversity of thinking and the regression that has taken place in these areas.

In terms of performance evaluation, compensations, and rewards, the chapter underscored the profound variation in practices and how current practices seem to reflect Western thinking and influences on organizations in Muslim societies. The chapter also attempted to shed light on the unique Islamic perspectives and how these perspectives can be relevant for today's organizations. In particular, the chapter underscored the fact that as in all other functions of management, human resource function could be more productive in an environment of openness, receptivity, and tolerance.

Organizations are typed as autocratic, traditionally group-centered, and spiritually enlightened. Human resource practice differs across these organizations. It is suggested that the spiritually enlightened organization represents the ideal chamber for effective application of the human resource management. This form of organization, however, is not widespread. Instead, the autocratic form appears to be the most common in today's Muslim environment.

11. Organizational Development and Change

The pillars of Islam and its tenets have been at the center of international attention in recent years. Issues related to Islamic views on work and organization are neither known nor researched in the management literature. Cross-cultural negotiations and organizational development activities are, therefore, carried out in a less than optimum manner. This chapter addresses the application of organizational development (OD) in the Islamic world. It specifies the necessity of change in the Islamic business environment. In addition, the chapter identifies certain norms and qualities and their implications for OD practitioners/consultants.

1. ISLAMIC PERSPECTIVES ON ORGANIZATIONAL DEVELOPMENT

Understanding organizations and their environment has been an important goal for scholars and practitioners alike. Without it, neither organizational effectiveness nor national economic development can be satisfactorily realized. One of the most important factors that influence organizations and management is religion. Simpson (1991) argues that religion is a major ingredient that must be taken into account in order to understand the evolution of the contemporary global situation, including business organizations. He indicates that the oneness of the world is embedded in the story framework of religions. Simultaneously, these religions reflect the thematic disunity of the world. The impact of Christianity and Judaism on business and organizations has been relatively well covered in literature (e.g., Green, 1997; Friedman, 2001; Weber, 1958). However, the Islamic influence and role in business has not been given adequate attention. This chapter is designed to address Islamic perspectives on OD. Islam, like Christianity and Judaism, provides adherents with a spiritual reference framework. Furthermore, Islam provides identity, pride, continuity, hope, and a way of life for millions of its followers across the globe. Its social and economic instructions are closely observed by many of its adherents.

Familiarity with Islamic perspectives on OD and related organizational matters will more likely enable researchers and practitioners to decipher certain organizational difficulties that arise in the Islamic setting. An awareness and sensitivity to Islamic general guidelines can contribute to minimizing business blunders and stereotypes. Both can facilitate cross-cultural understanding and narrow the seemingly increasing misunderstanding in international relations. Eventually, this will enhance business conduct and effectiveness.

In today's business world, management knowledge and techniques are easily available for examination and use in different cultures and places. This is made feasible by three major developments: rapid advancement and revolution in information technology, advancement in the material world, and improvement in behavioral science. The first makes knowledge and new discoveries easier and less costly to transfer across cultures and nations. The second makes prosperity a reachable goal, especially in the Western world. The third, allows scholars to develop methodologies and tools not only to explain the world, but also to change it. It was during the last five decades that change and growth managed to capture the minds of social scientists and practitioners. It is no wonder that OD became a familiar term in business and education circles.

Since OD was developed in the United States and since the United States became the dominant global economic power, OD theories and techniques have found a receptive audience all over the world. In addition, the demand for other "American-made" theories has become global in nature. For almost 50 years now, management experts and consultants have roamed the globe advising government personnel and business executives on ways to apply specific U.S. management techniques and theories. OD, management by objectives (MBO), and participative management have become common names in the global business literature. OD, in particular, has assumed a prominent place in the business world and in scholarly efforts in the United States and abroad.

The phenomenal demand for American management theories has, of course, helped to satisfy the curiosity of scholars and practitioners abroad. Serious questions regarding the applicability of these theories to foreign cultures have been raised. Many theorists argue that management theory is influenced by specific societal values, beliefs, norms, work, and social experiences. Hofstede (1993), for example, argues that the "export of Western-mostly American-management practices and theories to poor countries has contributed little to nothing to their development." He attributes such failure to the fact that local management practice is part of the cultural infrastructure and, therefore, cannot be imported in package form. It is true that the debate over the transferability of Western theories to non-Western civilizations is far from over. Nevertheless, Hofstede's statement is supported by empirical research (Hofstede, 1981). Additional research projects in various countries lend support to his observation (see Davila and Samper, 1994; Jones and Blunt, 1993).

In the context of OD, Jaeger (1986) concludes that there are "a large number of cultural configurations, particularly in the developing world, that conflict with OD in general and with the values underlying most interventions in particular." He recommends a broader repertoire of interventions that can bring about necessary planned organizational changes without violating societal values and norms. Golembiewski (1993) suggests that OD designs/approaches are not homogeneous, and neither are organizations or nations applying them. Therefore, he argues that OD can be successfully applied in foreign cultures. That is, OD is a flexible approach for organizational change. He suggests that OD practitioners should become sensitive to different cultural settings and thereby improve their judgments about the advisability of making OD interventions. Srinivas (1992), on the other hand, concludes that OD has fallen short of the promise for positive change toward national development. He analyzes 100 OD cases across 35 countries and indicates that the results cast a shadow of doubt on the applicability of OD.

This chapter seeks to address issues related to Islamic perspectives on OD. In particular, it argues that OD, in theory and practice, should be molded to fit Islamic outlooks and tradition as a frame of reference. This does not mean that OD should be Islamicized. Rather, it calls for developing an OD perspective that is culturally relevant and effective in dealing with peculiar aspirations and problems. This chapter is organized into three major parts. First, it examines the Islamic influence vis-à-vis OD. That is, it clarifies the meaning of organizational changes and development in Islamic thoughts. Second, it identifies cultural elements and their OD implications. Finally, the chapter identifies major assumptions of organizational changes in the Muslim-Arab world, discusses the relevancy of OD interventions, and sets guidelines for OD practitioners.

2. ISLAMIC THOUGHTS AND OD IMPLICATIONS

Scholars of organizations have long recognized that OD is a value-based process. French, Bell and Zawacri (1983), note that OD theory and practice focuses primarily on the human and social aspects of organizations. Likewise, Bennis (1969) argues that OD "'almost always concentrates on the values, attitudes, leadership, organizations climate - the people variables.'"

Golembiewski (1993) and Srinivas (1992) argue that OD focuses on feelings and emotions, ideas and concepts and places considerable importance on the individual's involvement and participation. Previously, Burke (1982) indicated that the values on which OD is based are: (1) a humanistic orientation; (2) the belief that feelings are important and need to be treated as data; and (3) the belief that conflict needs to be surfaced and dealt with directly rather than ignored. OD almost always focuses on "people variables" to advance organizational goals and induce positive change toward the achievement of these goals.

Thus, OD approaches and content are necessarily linked to forces in societies that shape and influence value orientations and attitudes. One of the most influential forces molding and regulating individual and group behavior and outlook in Islamic societies is religion. Religion is an influential force in these societies because: (1) most of the Islamic societies are still traditional in a sense that commitments to honor, honesty, respect to parents and older persons, loyalty to primary group, hospitality and generosity are held deeply by the majority of the population; (2) religious institutions and mosques play a significant role in Muslims' lives. They are not only a place for religious rituals but also a community salon where social, political, and economic issues are formulated and debated beyond the ritual context; (3) family and other social institutions still command the respect of almost all individuals regardless of their social backgrounds. These institutions utilize religion to sustain their endurance and influence; (4) Muslim people in their daily lives, either to make a point in a debate or to show humbleness, normally quote from the Quran; and (5) Islam is a comprehensive religion that regulates not only the asceticism but also worldliness. Almost all social, political, and military precepts are covered in the Quran along with the piety of the soul and moral aspects of individual behavior.

Quranic principles and the Prophet's prescriptions serve as a guide for Muslims in conducting their business and family affairs. During the golden age of the Arab/Islamic Empire, the first six centuries of Islam, knowledge, trade, industry, agriculture, and the construction of complex organizations flourished. It was during that time that various schools of thought were developed. Syed Ali (1964) identifies these schools as *Jabria, Tafwiz, Ikhtiar, Mutazilas, Averroes (Ibn-Rushd)* and *Ikhwan-us-Safa* (Brothers of Purity). A brief description of each (for more details see Chapter 3) follows.

The *Jabria* emphasizes compulsion or predestination. This school asserts that man is not responsible for his actions, and that followers must heed to the leader, whether the leader is just or corrupt.

The *Tafwiz* school emphasizes free will and unqualified discretion in the choice of wrong and right, because rules and regulations constrain human and organizational life. In the organizational context, employees assume different tasks and duties, and collective responsibility is preferred.

The *Ikhtiar* school shares the Tafwiz emphasis on free choice, but differs in the beliefs about man's capacity to turn evil into good. A human being is solely responsible for his actions. Man is believed to be a responsible social actor striving to work with the group and to achieve the group goals in harmonious and cooperative environment.

The *Mutazilas*, or the rationalistic school, believes that all knowledge must be attained through reason. This school holds that nothing is known to be wrong or right until reason has enlightened us to the distinction; and, further, that everything is liable to change or annihilation. In business and politics, the school promotes participative approach and transparency.

The fifth school of thought, advocated by Ibn-Rushd (or Averroes, c. ad 1126), holds that actions depend partly on free will and partly on external environmental forces that serve to restrain and/or determine individual and collective actions. The school appears to promote contingency view in judging business and societal affairs.

The sixth school, the *Ikhwan-us-Safa* (Brothers of Purity) advocates rationalism, self-discipline, and self-control. Ikhwan-us-Safa believed that faith without commitment to work and knowing without practice were futile. The School espouses the belief that human beings are able to make progress and control the environment. In an organizational setting, the school asserts that liberty of intellect is an essential precondition for a creative and healthy society. Furthermore, the school suggests that there is a correlation between autocracy and corruption.

These schools have had a profound influence on various political and economic structures in Islamic and Arab states (for more details, see Ali 1990). These schools differ in their view of the world, including business, and offer profound insights into the richness and diversity of Islamic thinking. In addition, these schools of thought have several implications for OD. Table 11.1 clarifies these implications.

Ali (1990) argues that after the Arabs and other Muslims gained their independence in the twentieth century, they established authoritarian regimes in the new nation-states (e.g., Algeria, Indonesia, Iraq, Kuwait, Pakistan, Saudi Arabia, Syria). Thus independent thinking, concepts of liberty, and power of mind were condemned, and Jabria principles were sanctioned in every aspect of life. The Jabria is, therefore, the dominant school in contemporary Muslim world. The other schools with the exception of Ikhtiar and Mutazilas have no influence on the daily life. The Mutazilas appeal to highly intellectual individuals and groups. While Ikhtiar still commands respect among some religious figures and some enlightened merchant classes such as in Bahrain, Lebanon, Iraq, and Iran.

Since the Iranian Revolution in 1979, the Muslim world has experienced a profound rethinking of certain Islamic issues and debated the necessity of revitalization. An early attempt, however, for genuine reform and revivalism has faced serious obstacles. Authoritarian governments, foreign powers, and traditional religious establishments consider new revivalism as a threat to the status quo. Despite monumental obstacles, the grassroots revivalism movement has stimulated new thinking and created psychological conditions for dramatic future change. The underlying motivator for the new Islamic revivalism is the quest for understanding Islamic principles and their theoretical foundations. This has strengthened the inclination toward change. That is, many people in the Islamic world, especially the young professional and intellectuals, have become more than ever receptive to changes that improve the welfare of their respective communities. This is more apparent in the realm of organizational performance and effectiveness. As such, organizational renewal efforts would be viewed positively.

Indeed, in the work environment there appears to be a steady but gradual change among educated groups including managers. Unlike the less educated, members of the more educated groups are seriously debating societal ills and advocating changes. The rank and file, to a large extent, however, are not expected to initiate change. After several hundred years of foreign occupations and current political dictatorship in almost all Muslim countries, the majority of the people fear government reprisals. Consequently, there is a hesitation to openly express dissatisfaction with current affairs. This common political fear outside the workplace hinders openness in organizational culture. Nevertheless, people informally debate issues and voice concerns. But under normal conditions, they are reluctant to convey their concerns through formal channels. Thus, the role of catalysts or leaders in initiating change assumes significant importance.

3. ASSUMPTIONS OF ORGANIZATIONAL CHANGES IN ISLAMIC SETTINGS

In Islam, a human being is considered the master of the earth and is endowed with free will. As the Quran states, "It is He [God] who created everything on earth for you . . . We have made you inhabit the land and provided you with the means of sustenance" (Quran 2:29, 7:10). From the Islamic perspective, humans are considered to be the vicegerents on earth. The Quran declares that after the creation of Adam, God tested the knowledge of the angels and man asking them to (2:31-34) tell Him the inner nature and quality of things and creatures on earth. While the angels could only reply, "You are glorious indeed! We do not know more than what You have taught us," Adam "was able to reveal the qualities and nature of the creatures on earth . . . [and] God told the angels to . . . prostrate [themselves] before Adam. They all obeyed except Satan who refused and was haughty: He was of those who reject faith." As the story illustrates, Islam views man as God's trustees in the universe. The Quran (33:72) clearly states that God, ". . . offered the trust to the heavens, the earth, and the mountains; but they refused to undertake it, being afraid thereof. But man undertook it." Being the vicegerent, man (male or female) has been gifted with the ability to be creative in maintaining harmony and growth on earth (Shariati, 1980). Nevertheless, people are held responsible for their action. The Quran (99:6-7) warns, "On that Day [day of judgment] will people proceed in groups sorted out, to be shown their deeds. Then shall anyone who has done an atom's weight of good see it. Anyone who has done an atom's weight of evil, shall see it" and (59:18) "And let every soul look to what it has done for the hereafter. Fear God, for God is well-acquainted with what you do." Individuals who act wisely and engage in good deeds, their reward is multiplied. This is succinctly stated in the Quran (6:160), " He that doeth good hall have ten times as much to his credit; he that doeth vice shall only be recompensed according to what had done." Humans employ multiple strategies in their quest for optimum fulfillment of their needs. The Quran specifically declares (92:4), "Verily, (the ends) ye strive for are diverse." Human beings are endowed with free will to determine what is good or bad for them. The Quran states (17:15) "Whoever receives guidance receives it for his own benefit: who goes astray does so to his own loss" and (6:164) "Every soul draws the meed of its acts on none but itself; no bearer of burdens can bear the burden of another."

Thus, Man possesses four unique qualities over angels and other creatures: knowledge, trust, having multiple goals and free will, and accountability. Furthermore, it should be pointed out that in Islam, humans are regarded as the sole agents for change. The Quran (13:11) states "God does not change the condition of people unless they change what is in their heart." Change is undertaken to enrich the universe and capitalize on opportunities. However, the change should be in complete harmony with nature and not at the expense of other fellow men and women. That is activities and work should be carried out to enhance human welfare. Prophet Mohamed clarified this by saying "The best kind of work is the one that generates benefit and the best people are those who benefit others" (quoted in Al-Barai and Abdeen, 1987). Since change produces consequences that affect others, the objective of change should be articulated with no ambiguity. In addition, Islamic traditions highlight the

Table 11.1 *OD applications under various Islamic schools of thought*

OD	Jabria	Tafwiz	Ikhtiar	Mutazilas	Ibn-Rushd	Ikhwan-us-safa
Initiator of change	A leader who has answers to all questions	Individual, but collective responsibility for implementation is a virtue	Individual with consultation with agreed upon leader	Any person regardless of position in organization	Collective responsibility	Any person regardless of position in organization
Self-reliance	Is not a virtue. It may open the door for chaos	Individual capable of assuming responsibility	Is a virtue as it facilitates continuity of the community	A necessary quality for growth; a virtue	A quality that everyone has regardless of gender	Necessary to ensure liberty and growth
Possible self-development	Predestination is the norm	No limit for self-development	No limit for self-development	Man is capable of growth and development	External environment may constrain individuals from achieving their full potential	Man is able to make progress and control environment
Possible organization change	Is due only to crisis and the wish of the leader	Is a normal course in serving people's interests	Is a normal process that should be encouraged by the leader	Everything is liable to change or annihilation	Is a contingent process	Is a healthy trend towards growth and community

Human training	Is not useful unless it is initiated by the leader and for coping with a crisis	Essential to reduce uncertainty and to allow a person to develop various expertise	Essential to achieve the group's goals in a harmonious and cooperative environment	Is a prerequisite for improving performance and achieving goals	Essential to achieve perfection in life	Essential to do the right work in a right way
Conflict	Unhealthy situation as it is a threat to cohesiveness and conformity	Openness in dealing with issues reduces expense of unhealthy conflict	Voicing concerns through spirited debate prevents unhealthy conflict and reinforces consensus	Debating issues is essential for societal welfare. Difference in ideas should be appreciated	Conflicting ideas are the source for positive change	Voicing concerns to increase awareness is essential to prevent stagnation
Systematic planning	Not a virtue as it is in conflict with predestination	A virtue to correct wrong doing	A virtue to maximize growth and enhances responsibility	An exercise of reasons and knowledge	Essential to deal with unexpected events	Essential to prevent chaos and authoritarian tendency

importance of future commitment and orientations. Imam Ali (AD. 598-661) states "Do not fill your heart with past sorrow; for this prevents you from making preparation for the future."

The above discussion evidences that change in Islamic culture is not only possible, but is also a virtue. The change, however, should focus on maintaining a balance between the individual and the community needs. It should ensure the continuity and welfare of the community.

To have a better understanding of the nature of change in Islam, it is necessary to identify the basic assumptions upon which change is based. Marshak (1993) identifies the basic assumptions of the Lewinian-based model (linear, progressive, destination-oriented, create disequilibrium planned and managed by people, and unusual) and Confucian (cyclical, processional, journey-oriented, maintain equilibrium, observed and followed by people, and usual) models underlying OD. Thus, an attempt is made here to highlight the nature of change in Islamic culture by contrasting the key features with elements used by Marshak. A word of caution is in order here. That is, the following model is not based on the current mind-sets of many Islamic people who are not familiar with Islamic tenets, but has been drawn from the ideas and thoughts contained in the Quran and Islamic traditions. In the Islamic culture change is:

1. Neither cyclical nor linear; rather change flows in a zig-zag pattern. During the Prophet Mohammed's time, change was a continuous process that often entailed going back to the initial stage of change all over again. He started with the emphasis on qualities from the pre-Islamic Arab culture (sensitize) and incorporated these in his teaching. In a second stage (*transitional*), he refined some instructions, gave the good and bad aspects of some qualities, forgave faults, but always reminded the Arabs of their pre-Islamic situation. In the third phase, he sought to establish a *desired state*. He was precise in his instruction clarifying what is "halal" right and what is "mahram" prohibited. However, change was frozen at certain points when he faced formidable resistance. In addition, there were many segments in Arabian society that initially subscribed to Islamic teaching, but had doubts about some of its aspects. Mohammed relied on re-intervention through reinforcement and group teaching methods. When sermons, admonitions, and reasoning failed, he resorted, as a last attempt, to forceful methods. Just after his death, many Arabs renounced Islam, thus his first successor had to start intervention to reinstate Islamic principles again. The case of possible regression was depicted in the Quran (3:144). It warned the people of Arabia that Mohamed was no more than a Messenger like many before him, "If he died or were slain,

will ye then turn back on your heels? Those who turn back on their heels, not the least harm will they do to God."

The progression-regression-progression aspects of change in Islamic culture have its roots in Islamic motivation. In the Islamic world, motivation, unlike Western and especially the American motivation system, human needs are not hierarchically arranged. For example, the spiritual need, an essential need in the Islamic motivation system, represents a cushion that helps to absorb frustration, crisis, failure, and so on. Theoretically, it is supposed to provide a balance among existing needs. There are four levels of the human psyche that are specified in the Quran (12:53, 12:18, 75:2, 89:27-30). First, Sawala (a passion for temptations): here a person soul's prompts him/her to follow only allurements and his/her desires, and to shy away from enlightenment. Second, Ammara (the prone-to-evil psyche): this is a primitive stage where a person inclines intentionally and, contrary to self-interest, to engage in wrongdoing. Third, Lawama (self-reproaching): in this stage, man is conscious of evil. There is a struggle between good and evil and man seeks to repent to achieve salvation. Fourth, Mutamainna (the righteous): the mind is perfectly in tune with good deeds and the individual realizes complete satisfaction and self-actualization. The domination by a particular psyche determines human needs and behavior. The four levels of psyche, however, are in a state of flux. The fourth level of the psyche is descriptive of personal values and lifestyles. At the first level, a person is motivated by the urge to engage in temptation for the sake of personal enjoyment. Consequences are not thought about and the aim is to maximize personal pleasure. The change strategy at this level should focus on self-awareness and sensitivity to others. At the second level (Ammara) a person is motivated by the urge to do things regardless of the consequences or harm that might be inflicted on others. Here a person is motivated by only maximizing self-interests. That is: spiritual needs are not internalized. Thus, a reorientation strategy is essential to focus attention on the benefits of change for self and others. At the third level (Lawama), a person is clear about the advantages of change but is influenced by selfish desire. Thus, the benefits of good deeds must be reinforced by persistent reminders and examples. The fourth level (Mutamainna) represents perfection and happiness in doing one's job and realizing one's goals. It is the ideal level, where change that maximizes societal welfare and organizational goals is undertaken.

2.   Processional. One moves from one state to another. In the process, however, a balance must be restored; otherwise disharmony prevails.

Mental states, however, are not mutually exclusive; rather there is a mix of states with a tendency to lean toward one or another until equilibrium is reached. Al-Sadr (1982) argues that "A Muslim's preoccupation with spirituality may sometimes create in him a negative attitude in regard to the worldly affairs and may lead him to renunciation, contentment or lethargy." The Quran urges a balance between the concerns of the spiritual and the material (20:77) stating, "But seek, with the wealth which God has bestowed on you, the home of the hereafter, nor forget thy portion in this world: but do thou good."

3. Goal-oriented and is a continuous or an open-ended process. Al-Sadr (1982) indicates that in the West, wealth and property have played a big role in "stirring up his potential to organize developmental activity in a particular manner." There is an ever increasing urge to exploit and accumulate wealth. In Islam, however, a balance must be achieved between the material and spiritual quests. In life a man has the capacity to pursue various enjoyments. It is in the hereafter, however, that unlimited enjoyment will be bestowed upon him. Quran states, "And verily the end is better for thee than the beginning."

4. Aimed at maintaining equilibrium. In the Islamic faith Man is a two-dimensional creature. Thus man needs religion to protect him from swinging from either asceticism or worldliness (Shariati, 1981). The Prophet Mohammed says that "The believers in their mutual love, sympathy and cooperation, are like the [interacting] parts of the human body: when one part complains, the other parts call each other to hasten to its rescue, each sharing its pain and sleeplessness."

5. Planned and managed by people. The Quran not only gave the responsibility for change to human beings, but also appointed Man as His deputy on earth (Quran 2:31). The Quran (2:29) declares, "It is He who created everything on earth for you [man]." Thus man has to master the universe and to have a purpose in life. According to the Quran (2:148), "Everyone pursues his goal. Compete with each other in performing good deeds."

6. Normal. In the Islamic religion change is a natural process. There are various forces that induce change and once conditions are ripe for change it is time for Man to act. Man, however, is, not a passive actor; rather Man is proactive in directing change in a way that serves his/her and the community interests. Salvation comes from within through knowledge and good deeds. Regression in life is a possibility. Nevertheless, it is an exception not the norm. The Quran (2:170) considers resistance to change a manifestation of rigidity and lack of enlightenment. It states that "When it [was] said to them follow what God hath revealed: they say 'nay! We

shall follow the ways of our fathers,' even though their fathers were void of wisdom and guidance."

The presumptions outlined above appear to share similarities with both Lewin (e.g., change is managed by people) and Confucius (change is a continuous process, maintain equilibrium) Models of change (see Table 11.2). In addition, the Islamic assumptions about change share similarities with the Western OD model. That is, both seek to make the organization more competitive and to make it more human. They differ with them, however, in many aspects (neither cyclical nor linear, normal process). This suggests that in the Islamic world different change approaches may be needed. It is necessary to note that some Western OD practitioners have reported successful change in selected states in the Islamic World (Ali, 1988). These practitioners were able to observe non-Western phenomena and react to it in a responsive way. Nevertheless, caution is in order. First, Muslim individuals, who are influenced by the teachings of the Quran and the Prophet Mohamed, are infatuated with ideal forms. Thus, there might be a tendency to inflate any feedback (especially survey feedback). For example, Ali (1989) compared the results of the same survey on work ethic conducted in the United States and Scotland to that in the Arab world and noticed that Arab managers scored higher than Western managers (American and Scottish) on work ethic. However, this does not mean that Arab managers are more productive than Western managers. Endorsement of a work ethic by Arab managers may not mirror that of the society as a whole. In addition, Islam innately views hard work positively, so the endorsement of the work ethic reflects a commitment to principles rather than a practice. Second, the outlined assumptions in the preceding paragraphs are based on Islamic principles and early Islamic practices. The majority of the population, however, is not aware of the tenets of their culture due to cultural discontinuity (Ali and Camp, 1995; Barakat, 1976; Jasim, 1978; Khadra, 1990). For example, issues of equity and justice, consultation and fairness, hard work and disciplines, honesty and faithfulness, cleanness and prohibition of briberies are detailed in the scriptures. A large segment of Islamic population is not familiar with these principles and often tends to violate them in practice.

Indeed, there are many segments in the Islamic world that come to treat foreign practices and rituals as their own. That is, illusion is confused with reality (Ali, 1992; Amara, 1984). Despite this fact, there are some cultural qualities that Muslims have been able to preserve generation after generation. These cultural qualities have been identified in the literature (Ali, 1992; Ali, 1989; Berger, 1964; Ali and Camp, 1995; Barakat, 1976; Jasim, 1978; Khadra,

1990; Amara, 1984). These qualities range from infatuation with ideal forms and willingness to change to strong social solidarity. Table 11.3 specifies some of these qualities and their implications for organizational change. Familiarity with cultural qualities often prevents cultural blunders, accentuates cultural peculiarities, and improves OD practitioners' judgments about the feasibility of some OD approaches. But most importantly, identifying cultural qualities facilitates a productive interaction and involvement between OD practitioners and Muslim participants.

4.   RELEVANCY OF OD INTERVENTIONS

Huse (1980) grouped OD interventions into ten basic classifications: individual consultation activities, unstructured group training activities, structured group training, process consultation, survey-guided development efforts, job redesign, personnel system methods, management information and financial control systems, organizational design, and integrated approaches. Many of these methods have been used in the Islamic world. In fact, personnel system methods, management information and financial control systems, and survey-guided development efforts have been used intensively by public and private organizations.   Unstructured group training approaches along with process and individual consultations may not be that adequate in achieving serious planned changes. One method that appears to be useful is "structured group training." Under this approach, various types of intervention are possible. The most common are: lectures, group exercises, group problem solving, story telling, and cases. Table 11.4 provides a comparison of these intervention methods across specific criteria. It is important to note that methods of intervention are useful, especially if trainers avoid the trap of "playing the expert" and strive to motivate participants and clients to tackle organizational issues in an environment of trust. Since Muslims rely often on common sense and trust, trainers should focus their attention on building trust by dealing with issues patiently, competently, and confidentially. This implies that the trainers should avoid condemnation, confrontation, but utilize dialogue in conducting intervention methods.   Furthermore, trainers should utilize traditional methods in facilitating changes under the above types of intervention. Three traditional methods stand out. The first is "Mudarasa" or "Munakash" (spirited debate). It is a means to stimulate discussion, generating better ideas, and develop new perspective. The role of leader is to identify specific issues for discussion, direct the meeting, and provides various options to tackle the problem.   The second is "Muthakrha" or specific goal-oriented assignments that will be the subject of intensive mudarasa. The third is "Murajah" in which competing ideas are introduced by designated or volunteer individuals. Informal groups also commonly use this in poetry sessions "Mudardha" during their leisure time. The fourth is "Munatharah," a theory building session where an individual introduces his/her theory and others comment on its strengths and deficiencies. All methods have been used in traditional Islamic culture and have helped, to some extent, in maintaining cultural transition. Their utility to OD should not be underestimated. They may call attention, however, to the need for a different set of facilitators.

5. GUIDELINES FOR OD PRACTITIONERS

The positive view of change and OD in Islam should be a motivating factor for OD practitioners and consultants. OD techniques and intervention methods, however, should be modified to be in harmony with cultural norms and expectations. As indicated before, the macro environment and colonial legacy appear to adversely affect the tendency for changes in the workplace (e.g., the rank and file discuss problems informally but are reluctant to formally voice solutions). Skillful OD practitioners can easily overcome this. The OD practitioner/consultant should identify carefully the initial "agents" for change; individuals who are receptive for change and able to influence the rank and file. Once such individuals agree on change targets, the rest are expected to follow. Nevertheless, the OD practitioner/consultant should maintain focus on the change direction and targets while showing sensitivity to a possible conformity of the rank and file to suggestions made by such "agents."

OD practitioners should be aware and sensitive to Islamic culture. In today's Islamic world, a large segment of the population is attempting to return to Islamic principles, and many of them are suspicious of Western methods. To achieve planned goals, the practitioner/consultant must not be aggressive in his/her approach and needs to play a low profile role outside the organization and be a facilitator/team player in any group setting. Furthermore, the practitioner/consultant should focus on the positive side of any organizational story while integrating it to Islamic history. While many OD changes in the United States were undertaken without having a specific purpose (Strauss, 1976), in the Islamic world, change must have a meaningful purpose for the organization and its members. Otherwise, the practitioner/consultant will be discredited. The reason is this; in the United States, socialization is pursued as a goal in almost all OD sessions. However, in Islamic societies, people often socialize intensively after work hours. Since members of organizations or communities develop close personal ties and come to know each other well away from the workplace, training or OD sessions in the Islamic world should concentrate on content and improving knowledge. Socialization during these sessions should be secondary.

Table 11.2   Assumptions about change

Lewinian/OD* change is:	Confucian/East Asian* change is:	Arab/Islamic change is:
1. Linear	Cyclical	Flows in a zig-zag pattern
2. Progression	Processional	Processional
3. Destination-oriented	Journey-oriented	Goal-oriented and is continuous
4. Based on creating disequilibrium	Based on restoring/maintaining equilibrium	Aimed at maintaining equilibrium
5. Planned and managed by people who exist separate from and act on things to achieve their goals	Observed and followed by people who are at one with everything and must act correctly to maintain harmony in the universe	Planned and managed by people who must act according to specific goals
6. Unusual, because everything is normally in a quasi-stationary or static state	Usual because everything is normally in a continually changing dynamic state	Normal because everything is subject to change and Man is proactive in directing change in a way that serves his/her and the community's interests.

* Marshak (1993).

Table 11.3   Societal qualities and their implication for organizational development

Qualities	OD Implications/ Strategies
Displaying flexibility in incorporating the new into traditional	Highlight the advantage of new methods in facilitating growth and achieving goals
Adapting to ever changing environment	Facilitate adaptation of new techniques
Infatuation with ideal forms	Relate intended changes to the experience of idealized Arab leaders; emphasize that these leaders were gifted and were agents of change
Love of normative and philosophical arguments	Discuss the philosophical dimensions of the new approaches/techniques
Politeness and enthusiasm	Encourage participants to be involved in the change process and identify possible avenues for productive conduct
Hopefulness	Identify the benefits of changes in the long term. Encourage participation and involvement in designing program after a short period of orientation
Belief in self-development Consultative	Encourage participation in the change process after a feeling of trust is established Consult with subordinates and participants after a feeling of trust is established
Identifying with the hero image	Consult/practitioner should display the image of protector who has courage in making decisions and is firm and responsible
Deep sense of family and primary group loyalty	Foster social relationships among groups, meet group interest, and emphasize that commitment to organization goals benefit everyone
Self and social censorship	Highlight the importance of involvement in organizational analysis by identifying weakness, and recognizing outstanding performance; place emphasis on the family aspects of the group and that involvement in the process of change fosters professional growth and development

Qualities	OD Implications/ Strategies
Respect for personal dignity	Emphasize personal relationship and the value of identifying with others in need of help and assistance
Avoidance of public conflict	Encourage intensive discussion of the problems to be solved and highlight that importance of an open agreement; disagreement and that the goal is to realize group cohesiveness
Problem solving best achieved through the immediate and integrated	Commit urgent attention to the problems at hand and provide a comprehensive solution on a timely basis
Respect for medication	Play the role of a mediator who is interested in avoiding/reducing conflict and in ensuring smooth operations
Intellectual superiority	Highlight that curiosity helps advance personal and professional growth and that seeking knowledge is a virtue that was accentuated in the Quran and in Prophet Mohammed's practice
Contempt for rigid rules and strict orders	Highlight the need to reduce rules and organizational constraints encourage openness and seek input from participants
Focus on equity and social Justice	Keep open channel of communications; show kindness and identify with participants' need
Focus on intentions	Clarify goals in advance and the benefits of new approaches to organization and the community
Focus on results	Clarify goals and identify the expected benefits for participants and organizations

In addition, OD programs should take advantage of the current trend for Islamic revivalism or "back to basics" that induces many people to search for alternatives to current business practices. This may be appropriate/beneficial because it forces people to reflect on their situation and broaden their horizons. Thus, it may be important for the practitioner/consultant to play a major role in sensitizing people to the difference between aspirations and reality, between principles and common but unethical practices. Likewise, OD practitioners should be familiar with possible flaws in certain intervention methods. For example, the result of "survey feedback" may not be reliable. The results of the survey may reflect "felt" attitudes and value or a "mere" infatuation with idealism. Again, there is almost always a tendency among some Muslims, because of their religious teaching and upbringing, to identify with the ideal form. For example, Kuroda and Suzik (1994) find that, relative to American and Japanese students, Arabs view organizations as a place where everything should be handled rationally without establishing primary group relations among its members. Thus, the authors concluded that favoritism, "give-and-take", paternalism and the like have no place in the Arab workplace. The reality of Arab organizations, however, indicates this is not the case. That is favoritism and paternalism are common in Arab organizations. International researchers should be cautious in making hasty generalizations.

Similarly, sensitivity training and conflict-oriented approaches may lead to sub-optimal results if not a collapse of OD. Muslims are inclined toward self-censorship and avoidance of open criticism. The Quran instructs Muslims (49:10-12) "Believers, let not a group of you mock another. . . . Let not one of you find faults in another nor let anyone of you defame another. . . . Stay away from suspicion, for suspicion in some cases is a sin." Self-criticism, however, is possible but is often done in an indirect way. This means that the OD practitioner should have the social skill to indirectly coach participants to be open. He/she can use story-telling methods to stimulate participation and build trust.

More importantly, OD practitioners should be aware of two issues that significantly differentiate Western-based OD from that in an Islamic culture. The first is the purpose of OD and the second is OD approach to problem solving. Islamic principles and ethics place more emphasis on the intention than on the results. That is, the value of any action is derived from the accompanying intention, rather than its results. Prophet Mohamed stated, "Actions are recorded according to intention, and a person will be rewarded or punished accordingly." Unlawful work such as gambling, drug trafficking, deceiving, extortion, hoarding, and monopolizing that results in accumulation of wealth or career success is condemned and those who engage in it are viewed with contempt. Thus, the OD practitioner or consultant should articulate change goals and ensure that no personal interests are pursued at the expense of the group or community.

In terms of approaching problem solving, in the West, a solution comes only through critical consideration of the mediate and compartmented, for adherent Muslims, of the immediate and undivided (Berque, 1978). The OD practitioner or consultant should address issues at hand and provide a clear blueprint on how the whole problem will be solved. That is, sub-organizational problems have to be addressed simultaneously and comprehensively. Compartmentalization of organizational problems eventually leads to mistrust, lack of enthusiasm and loss faith in OD process.

Table 11.4 A comparison of various intervention methods across specific criteria

Criteria	Method				
	Lecture	Group	Group Problem solving	Cases	Story telling
Acceptability	Medium to high	Fairly High	Fairly high	High	Very high
Feasibility	Very high	High	High	Very high	Very feasible
Ability to motivate using this method	It depends on the content and personality of the OD practitioner/ consultant	If status differences are avoided and the physical setting arranged carefully, it could stimulate and motivate participants to achieve a higher goal	Selecting a problem that relates to organization and competitors could produce a desired effect	Cases that are new and challenging could produce a desired impact	Story telling can be highly motivating especially if focus is on real foreign and domestic issues, and if stories with meaning are provided
Consistency with cultural norms	Very high	Medium to high	Medium to high	High to very high	Highly consistent
Achieving the desired change	Possibly high if the presenter manages to keep participants emotionally involved and sensitizes them to common problems	Possibly medium role playing tends to have immediate but not long impact on an individual's orientations, unless it is reinforced for a longer period and a variety of situations are covered	Possibly medium to high to meet the desired goal, practical and challenging problems must be provided	Possibly high as Arab participants prefer to identify with practical issues	Possibly very high-if stories are connected to organizational life and explained in the context of societal culture

6. CONCLUSION

This chapter sought to identify cultural assumptions in the Islamic world and their OD implications. In addition, the chapter reviewed major Islamic schools of thought and the application of OD under each school. General Islamic views and orientations were highlighted and the possibility of organizational change was addressed. The chapter concluded that cultural/Islamic values, if correctly identified and understood, would facilitate organizational change and development.

The issue of OD in the Islamic culture has seldom been addressed adequately in the literature. In this chapter several questions were raised and attempts were made to specify cultural assumptions and to identify societal qualities required for OD change. Future research should focus on the development of OD models that are relevant to Islamic culture. In particular, the chapter suggests issues of which OD consultants should be aware. Furthermore, the chapter raised the question, should OD consultants, in their process and work, advocate ideal principles in spite of the current prevalence of un-Islamic practices? This question needs to be answered by future research. There is a need to challenge the traditional role of OD consultants and to call for them to broaden their societal role, instead of confining it to the boundaries of organizations and to the limits set by their clients. This is especially true as more and more OD consultants engage in international or cross-cultural assignments. In addition, the chapter advocates that the role of the prophetic "Great Man" person in Islamic culture needs to be examined in the context of the OD process and organizational change

Bibliography

Abdel Hadi, H. (1990), *The Islamic Management Though*, Dar Al-fikr Al-Araby, Cairo.

Abdel-Halim, A. and A. Ashour (1995) 'Early Employment and Mobility Behaviors of Business Graduates in the Arab Gulf Region: Implications for Multinational Corporations', *International Studies of Management and Organization*, 25(3), pp. 67-86.

Abdel-Rahman, A. (1989), 'The Nature and Development of the Islamic State', *Arab Studies*, 26(91), pp. 3-24.

Abdul-Rauf, M. (1984), *A Muslim's Reflections on Democratic Capitalism*, American Enterprise Institute for Public Policy Research, Washington, DC.

Abu Dawod, E. (1996), *The Directory of Inquirers*, Jedha, Saudi Arabia.

Abu-Doleh, J. D. and B. M. Ayoun (2000), 'Human Resource Management; An Islamic Perspective', Unpublished paper, University of Yarmuk, Irbid, Jordan.

Abu-Doleh, J. and B. Ayoun (2001), 'Human Resource Management: An Islamic Perspective', (working paper) University of Yarmouk, Jordan, Irbid.

Adler, N. (1983), 'A Typology of Management Studies Involving Culture', *Journal of International Business Studies*, Fall, pp. 29-48.

Afanasev, V. (1979), 'Controlling Individual Development and Behavior', *The Soviet Review*, xx(3), pp. 15-37.

Ahmad, E. (1984), 'Islam and Politics', in Y. Haddam, B. Haines and E. Findley (eds.), *The Islamic Impact*, Syracuse University Press, New York, pp. 7-26.

Ahmad, K. (1976), *Islam: Its Meaning and Message*, Islamic Council of Europe, London.

Alaki, M. (1979), *Idart Al-Amal Fi Be'a Alsaudia* [Business Administration in Saudi Environment], Dar Al Shoroug, Jedda, Saudi Arabia.

Al-Barai, A. and A. Abdeen (1987), *Management in Islamic Culture*, Modern Service Library, Jeda, Saudia Arabia.

Al-Denoury, A. M. (1997), *Imamate and Politics*, Dar al-Kuotob al-ilmiyah, Beirut.

Al-Jafary, A. and A. Hollingsworth (1983), 'An Exploratory Study of Managerial Practices in the Arabian Gulf Region', *Journal of International Business Studies*, Fall, pp. 142-152.

Al-Jasmani, A. A. (1996), *The Psychology of Quran*, Arab Scientific Publishers, Beirut.

Al-Kubaisy, A. (1985), 'A Model in the Administrative Development of Arab Gulf Countries', *The Arab Gulf*, 17(2), pp. 29-48.

Al-Mahamy, S. (1987), *Monitoring Management Affairs under Islamic and Man Made Laws*, Dar Al-Faker Al-Araby, Cairo.

Al-Maqrizi, A. A. (1994), *Mamluk Economics*, University of Utah Press (a study and translation by Adel Allouche), Salt Lake City, Utah.

Al-Masudi, A. A. (n.d.), *Muroj Al-thahib Prairies of Gold*, Vol. 5(2-3), Dar-Almarifa, Beirut.

Al-Mawardi, Abu Al-Hasan Ali (1979), *Laws of Cabinet and the Statecraft*, [Commentary and Editing by Razown Al-Syed], Al-Talea Publisher, Beirut.

Al-Nimir, S. and M. Palmer (1982), 'Bureaucracy and Development in Saudi Arabia', *Public Administration and Development*, 21, pp. 93-102.

Al-Rasheed, A. (2001) 'features of Traditional Arab Management and Organization in the Jordan Business Environment', *Journal of Transnational Management Development*, 6 (1/2), pp. 27-54.

Al-Rasheed, A. (2002), 'Structure of Jordanian Business Organizations: Managers' Attitudes Towards Formalization and Centralization and Factors Affecting Them', *Dirast, Administrative Sciences*, 30(1), pp. 217-235.

Al-Rasheed, A. (2003), 'Institutionalism and Jordanian Business Organizations and Institutions', *Al-Yarmouk Research*, 19(91), pp. 229-276.

Al-Sadr, B. (1982), *Islam and Schools of Economics*, Islamic Seminary, New York.

Al-Sadr, B. (1983), *Bahouth Islama* [Islamic Subjects], Dar al-Zahra, Beirut.

Ali, A. (1982), 'An Empirical Investigation of Managerial Value Systems in Iraq', Unpublished Ph.D. Dissertation, West Virginia University, Morgantown.

Ali, A. (1986), 'Labor Immigration in the Arab Gulf States: Patterns, Trends and Problems', *International Migration*, 24(3), pp. 675-684.

Ali, A. (1986/87), 'The Arab Executives: A Study of Values and Work Orientations', *American-Arab Affairs*, 19, pp. 94-100.

Ali, A. (1987), 'Scaling an Islamic Work Ethic', *Journal of Social Psychology*, 128(5), pp. 575-583.

Ali, A. (1988), 'A Cross-National Perspective on Managerial Work Value Systems', *Advances in International Comparative Management*, 3, pp. 151-169.

Ali, A. (1989), 'Decision Style and Work Satisfaction of Arab Executives', *International Studies of Management and Organization*, 19(2), pp. 22-37.

Ali, A. (1990), 'Management Theory in a Transitional Society', *International Studies of Management and Organization*, 20(3), pp. 7-35.

Ali, A. (1992), 'Management Research Themes and Teaching in the Arab World', *International Journal of Educational Management*, 6(4), pp. 11-17.

Ali, A. (1993), 'Decision Making Style, Individualism, and Attitudes Toward Risk of Arab Executives', *International Studies of Management and Organization*, 23(3), pp. 53-74.

Ali, A. (1995), 'Cultural Discontinuity and Arab Management Thought', *International Studies of Management and Organization*, 25(3), pp. 7-30.

Ali, A., A. Al-Aali and R. Camp (1992), 'Cross-National Perspective on Strategic Behavior and Environment', *International Journal of Management*, 9(2), pp. 208-214.

Ali, A. and Ahmed Azim (1999), 'Islamic Work Ethic and Organizational Development', *Chinmaya Management Review*, 3(2), pp. 36-46.

Ali, A. and A. Al-Kazemi (2002), 'Islamic Work Ethic in Kuwait', paper presented at the American Society for Competitiveness Conference, Washington, DC, October 10-12.

Ali, A. and D. Schaupp (1992), 'Value Systems as Predictors of Managerial Decision Styles of Arab Executives', *International Journal of Manpower*, 13(3), pp. 19-26.

Ali, A. and M. Al-Shakis (1985), 'Administrators' Attitudes and Practices in Saudi Arabia', paper presented at the annual meeting of the Midwest Academy of International Business, Chicago, March 27-29.

Ali, A. and M. Amirshahi (2002), 'The Iranian Manager: Work Values and Orientations', *Journal of Business Ethics*, 40, pp. 133-143.

Ali, A. and P. Swiercz (1986), 'The Relationship Between Managerial Decision Styles and Work Satisfaction in Saudi Arabia', in E. Kaynak (ed.), *International Business in the Middle East*, Walter de Gruyter, New York, pp. 137-150.

Ali, A. and R. Camp (1995), 'Teaching Management in the Arab World: Confronting Illusions', *International Journal of Educational Management,* 9(6), pp. 10-17.

Ali, A., A. Taqi and K. Krishnan (1997), 'Expatriate and Indigenous Managers' Work Loyalty and Attitude Toward Risk', *Journal of Psychology,* 131(3), pp. 260-270.

Ali, A. and H. Sabri (2001), 'Organizational Culture and Job Satisfaction in Jordan', *Journal of Transnational Management Development,* 6(1/2), pp. 105-118.

Ali, A. and R. Wahabi (1995), 'Managerial Value System in Morocco', *International Studies of Management and Organization,* 25 (93), pp. 87-96.

Ali, A. (1961), *Short History of the Saracens,* Macmillan & Co., London.

Ali, I. (1989) *Nahjul Balagah* (translated and edited by F. Ebeid), Dar Alkitab Al-Lubnani, Beirut, Lebanon.

Ali, M. M. (1977), *A Manual of Hadith,* Olive Branch Press, New York.

Ali, S. A. (1964), *The Spirit of Islam,* Chatto & Windus, London.

Almaney, A. (1981), 'Cultural Traits of the Arabs', *Management International Review,* 21(3), pp.10-18.

Alowaihan, A. (2004), 'Gender and Business Performance of Kuwaiti Small Firms: A Comparative Approach' , *International Journal of Commerce and Management.* 14(3/4), pp. 34-42.

Amara, M. (1984), *Al-Arab Yastiquzoon* [Arab Awakening], Dar Alwahda Publishers, Beirut.

Amara, M. (1988), *Mutazilas and the Problem of Human Freedom,* The Arab Institute for Publishing and Studies, Beirut.

Amirshahi, M. (1997), 'Empirical Study of Managerial Value Systems and Decision Making Styles Among the Managers in Iran', Unpublished PhD. dissertation, Curtin University of Technology, Perth, Australia.

Amnesty International (2000), 'Saudi Arabia: Asian workers continue to suffer behind closed doors', Amnesty International, www.amnestyusa.org, May 1.

Arab Human Development Report 2002 (2002), United Nations Development Programme, New York.

Arkoun, M. (1986), *The Historical Base of Arabic-Islamic Thought,* Center for National Growth, Beirut.

Armstrong, K. (1992), *Muhammad: A Biography of the Prophet,* Harper Collins Publishers, New York.

Armstrong, K. (2002), An *Interview with Frontline, Muhammad: legacy of a prophet,* www.pbs.org , September 25.

Asaf, M. (1987), *The Islamic Way in Business Administration*, Ayen Shamis Library, Cairo, Egypt.

Ashmawy, M. (1992), *Islamic Caliphate*, Siena Publisher, Cairo.

Atiyyah, H. (1993), 'Roots of Organization and Management Problems in Arab Countries', *Arab Management Conference Proceedings*, July, pp. 223-247.

Azzaman (2003), 'Sale of Cement at Discount Price for Political Reason-Complaints for Giving Kurdish Higher Salary Relatives to the Rest of Iraqi Citizens', *Azzaman Newspaper*, issue 1680.

Baali, F. and A. Wardi (1981), *Ibn Khaldun and Islamic Thought Style*, Haland, Boston, MA.

Badawy, M. (1980), 'Styles of Mideastern Managers', *California Management Revie,* 22(2), pp. 51-58.

Banani, A. (1977), 'Conversion and Conformity in a Self-Conscious Elite', in Amin Banani and Speros Vryons (eds.), *Individualism and Conformity in Classical Islam*, Wiesbaden, Germany, pp. 19-31.

Barakat, H. (1976), 'Socioeconomic, Cultural and Personality Forces Determining Development in Arab Society', Social Praxis, 2, pp. 179-204.

Bass, B. and E. Valenzi (1974), 'Contingent Aspects of Effective Management Styles', in J. Hunt and L. Larson (eds.), *Contingency Approaches to Leadership*, Southern Illinois University Press, Carbondale, pp. 130-152.

Bate, P., R. Khan and A. Pye (2000), 'Towards a Culturally Sensitive Approach to Organization Structuring', *Organization Science*, 11(2), pp. 197-212.

Beenis, W. (1965), 'Beyond Bureaucracy', *Transaction*, 2(5), p. 31.

Bennis, W. (1969), *Organization Development*, Addison-Wesley, Reading, MA.

Berger, M. (1964), *The Arab World Today,* Anchor Books, Garden City, New York.

Berque, J. (1978), *Cultural Expression in Arab Society Today*, The University of Texas Press, Austin, TX.

Bhagat, B. and S. McQuaid (1982), 'The Role of Subjective Culture in Organization: A Review and Direction for Future Research', *Journal of Applied Psychology*, 67, pp. 653-685.

Bill, J. and C. Leiden (1984), *Politics in the Middle East*, Little, Brown & Company, Boston, MA.

Blyton, P. (1984), 'Some Old and New Problems in Employee Participation in Decision Making', *International Social Science Journal*, 37(2), pp. 217-231.

Boase, A. W. (1985), 'The Economic System in Islam: A Model for all Men', *Islamic Quarterly*, 29(3), pp. 129-147.

Bosworth, C. (1982), *Medieval Arabic Culture and Administration*, Variorum Reprints, London, UK.

Branine, M. (2001), 'Human Resource Management in Algeria', in Pawan Budhwar and Yaw A. Debrah (eds.), *Human Resource Management in Developing Countries*, Routledge, New York, pp. 156-173.

Bravmann, M. M. (1972), *The Spiritual Background of Early Islam*, E. J. Brill, Leiden.

Burke, W. (1982), *Organization and Development*, Little, Brown & Company, Boston, MA.

Bush, G. (2002), 'U.S., Russia Continue Joint Efforts to Fight Terrorism', *The White House*, Press Release June 27.

Carmi, T. (1981), *The Penguin Book of Hebrew Verse*, Penguin Books Ltd., New York.

Chandler, A. (1962), *Strategy and Structure*, The MIT Press, Cambridge, MA.

Child, J. (1976), 'Participation, Organization, and Social Cohesion', *Human Relations*, 29(5), pp. 429-451.

Chow, C., M. Schields and Y. Chan (1991), 'The Effects of Management Controls and National Culture on Manufacturing Performance', *Accounting, Organizations and Society*, 16(3), pp. 209-226.

Collier, A. (1971), 'Business Leadership and Creative Society', *Harvard Business Review*, Part II, 15-23.

Conaty, J. H. Mahmoudi and G. Miller (1983), 'Social Structure and Bureaucracy: A Comparison of Organizations in the United States and Prerevolutionary Iran', *Organization Studies*, 4(2), pp. 106-128.

Congleton, R. (1991), 'The Economic Role of a Work Ethic', *Journal of Economic Behavior and Organization*, 15(3), pp. 365-385.

Cooper, M. (1979), 'Ethics, Values and Systems', *Journal of System Management*, September, pp. 6-12.

Cummings, L. and C. Berger (1976), 'Organization Structure: How Does it Influence Attitudes and Performance?', *Organizational Dynamics*, 5 (2), pp. 34-49.

Davies, F. (2003), 'Many Misinformed About Iraq, September 11 Attacks', *Knight Ridder News Service*, www.krtdirect.com, June 13.

Davila, G. and G. Sampler (1994), 'Innovative Management and Organizational Development in Latin America', *The International Executive*, 36(6), pp. 671-688.

De Kervasdoue, J. and J. Kimberly (1979), 'Are Organization Structures Culture-Free? The Case of Hospital Innovation in the U.S. and France', in G. England, A. Negandhi and B. Wilpert (eds.), *Organizational Functioning in a Cross-Cultural Perspective*, Kent State University Press, Kent, OH, pp. 191-210.

Delo, B. (1985), *Mushama Fe Eadit Katabit Al-Taryk Al-Arabi* [A Contribution in Rewriting Arab-Islamic History], Dar Al-Farabi, Beirut.

Dessler, G. (1986), *Organization Theory*, Prentice-Hall, Englewood, Cliffs, NJ.

Duncan, R. (1979), 'What is the Right Organization Structure?', *Organizational Dynamics*, 7(3), pp. 59-80.

Elkholy, A. (1984), 'Socioeconomic Institutions and the Quran: Cultural Sequential Approach to Human Society', *Hamdard Islamicus*, 7(3), pp. 3-19.

El-Tayeb, H. (1986), 'Administrative Reform in the Arab Countries', in N. Al-Saigh (ed.), *Administrative Reform in the Arab World*, Arab Organization of Administrative Sciences, Amman, Jordan, pp. 116-165.

Enayat, H. (1982), *Modern Islamic Political Thought*, University of Texas Press, Austin, TX.

Erikson, E. (1964), *Chidhood and Society*, Norton, New York

Faridi, F. R. (1985), 'Islamic Concept of Ideal Society', *The Muslim World League Journal*, 12(4), pp. 5-9.

Flowers, V. S., C. L. Hughes and S. Myers (1975), *Managerial Values for Working, an AMA Survey Report*, AMACOM, New York.

Flowers, V. S. and C. L. Hughes (1978), 'Choosing a Leadership Style', *Personnel*, January - February, pp. 48-59.

Fredrickson, J. (1986), 'The Strategic Decision Process and Organization Structure', *Academy of Management Review*, 11(2), pp. 280-297.

French, J. and B. Raven (1959), 'The Bases of Social Power', in D. Cartwright (ed.), *Studies in Social Power*, University of Michigan, Ann Arbor, MI, pp. 150-167.

French, W., C. Bell and R. Zawacki (1983), *Organizational Development*, Business Publications, Plano, TX.

Freud, S. (1960), *Psychopathology of Everyday Life*, Vol 6, in The Standard Edition of the Complete Psychological Works of Sigmund Freud (Transulated by, J. Strachey), Hogarth Press, London, UK.

Friedman, H. H. (2001), 'The Impact of Jewish Values on Marketing and Business Practices', *Journal of Macromarketing*, 21(1), pp. 74-80.

Gibb, H. (1962), *Studies on Civilization of Islam*, Princeton University Press, Princeton, NJ.

Gibson, J., J. Ivancevich and J. Donnelly (1988), *Organizations*, Business Publications, Plano, TX.

Glaachi, M. (2000), *Studies in Islamic Economy*, Dar An-Nafaes, Kuwait.

Goitein. S. (1967), *A Mediterranean Society*, University of California Press, Berkeley and Los Angeles, US.

Goitein, S. (1968), *Studies in Islamic History and Institutions*, E. J. Brill, Leiden, The Netherlands.

Golembiewski, R. (1993), 'Organizational Development in the Third World: Values Closeness of Fit and Culture-Boundedness', *International Journal of Public Administration*, 11(11), pp. 1667-1691.

Graves, C. W. (1966), 'Deterioration of Work Standards', *Harvard Business Review*, September-October, pp. 117-126.

Graves, C. W (1970), 'Levels of Existence: An Open System Theory of Values', *Journal of Humanistic Psychology*, X(2), pp. 131-154.

Green, R. (1997,) 'Guiding Principles of Jewish Business Ethics', *Business Ethics Quarterly*, 7 (1), pp. 21-30.

Guth, W. D. and R. Tagiuri (1965), 'Personal Values and Corporate Strategies', *Harvard Business Review*, September-October, pp. 123-132.

Hanson, M. J. (1999), 'Indulging Anxiety: Human Enhancement from a Protestant Perspective', *Christian Bioethics*, 5(2), pp. 121-138.

Hawi, S. (1982), *Fisoul Fi Alamrh Wa Alamer* [Lectures on Leadership and Leader], Al-Sharq, Amman, Jordan.

Heller, F. (1971), *Managerial Decision Making*, Tavistock, London, UK.

Hickson, D., C. Hinings, C. McMillan and J. Schwitter (1974), 'The Culture-Free Context of Organization Structure: A Tri-National Comparison', *Sociology*, 8, pp. 1-14.

Hitti, P. K. (1959), *The World of Islam*, Macmillan, London, UK.

Hitti, P. (1964), *History of the Arabs*, Macmillan, London, UK.

Hofstede, G. (1976), 'Nationality and Espoused Values of Managers', *Journal of Applied Psychology*, 61(2), pp. 148-155.

Hofstede, G. (1980), *Culture' Consequences: International Differences in Work-Related Values*, SAGE Publications, Beverly Hills, CA.

Hofstede, G. (1981), 'Culture and Organization', *International Studies of Management and Organization,* 11(4), pp. 15-41.

Hofstede, G. (1983), 'The Cultural Relativity of Organizational Practices and Theories', *Journal of International Business Studies*, Fall, pp. 75-89.

Hofstede, G. (1993), 'Cultural Constraints in Management Theories', *The Executive*, 7(1), pp. 81-94.

Hofstede, G. (1999), 'Problems Remain, but Theories Will Change: The Universal and the Specific in 21st-Century Global Management', *Organizational Dynamics*, 28(1), pp. 34-43.

Hollander, E. (1978), *Leadership Dynamics*, The Free Press, New York.

Holy Bible (1977), *King James Version*, Thomas Nelson, New York.

Hourani, A. (1991), *A History of the Arab Peoples*, The Belknap Press, Cambridge, MA.

Hourani, G. (1985), *Reason and Traditions in Islamic Ethics*, Cambridge University Press.

Hudson, M. (1977), *Arab Politics*, Yale University Press, New York.

Hughes, C. and V. Flowers (1978), *Values Systems Analysis: Theory and Management Application*, Center for Values Research, Inc., Dallas, TX.

Hurgronje, C. (1957), *Selected Work of C. Snouck Hurgronje*, edited in English and in French by G.-H. Bousquet and J. Schacht, E. J. Brill, Leiden, The Netherlands.

Huse, E. (1980), *Organization Development and Change*, West Publisher, St. Paul, Minn.

Hussein, T. (1999), *The Great Internal Strife: Othman*, Dar Al-Maraf, Cairo.

Ibn Abed Raba Al-andelesy, Ahmed (1996), *Al-Agid Al-Fared*, Vol 1Dar Iyha Al-Tarth al-Araby, Beriut.

Ibn Abed Raba Al-andelesy, Ahmed (1996), *Al-Agid Al-Fared*, Vol. 5, Dar Iyha Al-Tarth al-Araby, Beriut.

Ibn Khaldun, Abd al-Rahman (1989), *The Maqaddimah*, (trns. By Franz Rosenthal & edited by N.J. Dawood), Princeton University Press, Princeton.

IbnTaimiya, Ahmed (2002), *A Lawful Policy in Reforming the Leader and Followers*, Dar Al-Faker Publishing, Beirut.

Ikhwan-us-Safa (1999a), *Letters of Ikhwan-us-Safa*, Vol. 1, Dar Sader, Beirut.

Ikhwan-us-Safa (1999b), *Letters of Ikhwan-us-Safa*, Vol. 3, Dar Sader, Beirut.

Inzerilli, G. and A. Laurent (1983), 'Managerial Views of Organization Structure in France and the USA', *International Studies of Management and Organization*, XIII(1-2), pp. 97-118.

Issawi, C. (1970), Economics and Social Foundations of Democracy in the Middle East', in A. Lutfiyya and C. Churchhill (eds.), *Reading in the Arab Middle Eastern Societies and Culture*, Mouton, the Hague.

Izeddin, N. (1953), *The Arab World*, Henry Regnery, Chicago, IL.

Jaeger, A. (1986), 'Organizational Development and National Culture: Where's the Fit?', *The Academy of Management Review*, 11(1), pp. 178-190.

Jasim, A. (1987), *Mhammad: Al-Hagigaha Al-Kubra* [Mohammed: the Greatest Truth], Dar al-Andalus, Beirut, Lebanon.

Jones, M. L. and P. Blunt (1993), 'Organizational Development and Change in Africa', *International Journal of Public Administration*, 16(11), pp. 1735-1765.

Kalleberg, A. (1977), 'Work Values and Job Rewards: A Therapy of Job Satisfaction', *American Sociological Review*, 42(February), pp. 124-143.

Keller, Bill (202) 'The Sunshine Warrior', *New York Times*, www. Nytimes.com, September 22.

Khadra, B. (1990), 'The Prophetic-Caliphal Model of Leadership: An Empirical Study', *International Studies of Management and Organization*, 20(3), pp. 37-51.

Kipnis, D. (1983), 'The Use of Power', in R. Allen and L. Porter (eds), *Organizational Influences Processes*, Glenview, IL, Scott, Foresman and Company, pp. 17-32.

Koontz, H., C. O'Donnell and H. Weihrich (1980), *Management*, McGraw-Hill, New York.

Kurd Ali, M. (1934), *Islamic Management in the Golden Age of the Arabs*, Egypt Press, Cairo.

Kuroda, Y. and T. Suzik (1994), 'A Comparative Analysis of Arab Culture: Arabic, English and Japanese Languages and Values', in A. Temimi (ed.), *The State of Arts of Middle East Studies*, Ceromdi, Tunisa, Zaghouan, pp. 85-102.

Kushner, H. S. (2001), *Living a Life That Matters: Resolving the Conflict Between Conscience and Success*, Alfred A. Knopf, New York.

Lapidus, I. M. (1988), *A History of Islamic Societies*, Cambridge University Press, New York.

LaPiere, R. (1959), *The Freudian Ethic*, George Allen & Unwin Ltd., London.

Laurent, A. (1981), 'Matrix Organizations and Latin Cultures', *International Studies of Management and Organization*, XIII(1-2), pp. 101-114.

Lawrence, P. and J. Lorsch (1969), *Organization and Environment*, Richard Irwin, Homewood, IL

Lewis, B. (1966), *The Arab in History*, Harper, New York.

Lewis, B. (1993), *Islam in History*, Open Court, Chicago, IL.

Likert, R. (1967), *The Human Organization*, McGraw-Hill, New York.

Lowry, R. (1998), 'The Dark Side of the Soul: Human Nature and the Problem of Evil in Jewish and Christian Traditions', *Journal of Ecumenical Studies*, 35(1), p. 88.

Machiavelli, N. (1980), *The Prince*, Penguin Books, New York.

Marshak, R. (1993), 'Lewin Meets Confucius: A Re-View of the OD Model of Change', *Journal of Applied Behavioral Science*, 29(4), pp. 393-415.

Maslow, A. (1959), 'Psychological Data and Value Theory', in A. Maslow (ed.), *New Knowledge in Human Values*, Harper, New York, pp. 119-136.

McClelland, D. (1961), *The Achieving Society*, The Free Press, New York.

Mellahi, K. and G. Wood (2001), 'Human Resource Management in Saudi Arabia', in Pawan Budhwar and Yaw A. Debrah (eds.), *Human Resource Management in Developing Countries*, Routledge, New York, pp. 136-15.

Milbank, D. (2003, March 9), 'For Bush, War Defines Presidency', *Washington Post*, www.washintgtonpost.com, March 9.

Miles, R. (1997), *Leading Corporate Transformation*, Jossey Bass, San Francisco, CA.

Miller, E. (1984), 'Comparative Management Conceptualization: An Assessment', in R. Farmer (ed.), *Advances in International Comparative Management*, JAI Press, Greenwich, CT, pp. 69-82.

Mindell, M. and W. G. (1981), *Employee Values in a Changing Society*, AMA Management Briefing, New York.

Miskawayh, A. (n.d.), *Tajarub Al-umam*, Dar Al-Kitab Al-Islami, Cairo.

Moore, C. (1970), *Politics in North Africa*, Little, Brown & Co., Boston, MA.

Mottahedeh, R. (1981), 'Bureaucracy and the Patrimonial State in Early Islamic Iran and Iraq', *Al-Abhath*, XXIX, 25-36.

Muna, F. (1980), *The Arab Executive*, St. Martin's Press, New York.

Nabi, M. (1982), 'Islam and Arab Traditional Concepts', *The Muslim World League Journal*, 9(3), pp. 6-12.

Nagvi, S. N. (1981), *Ethics and Economics*, Islamic Foundation, London.

Nasr, S. H. (1981), *Islamic Life and Thought*, State University of New York Press, Albany, NY.

Nasr, S. (1984),'Islamic Work Ethics', *Hamdard Islamicus*, 7(4), pp. 25-35.

Nawawawi, Mehi Al-Dean (2001), *The Garden of Righteousness from the Sayings of Prophet Mohamed*, Ibna Sherif Al-Ansary Publisher, Beruit, Lebanon.

Niebuhr, R. (1964), *The Nature and Destiny of Man: A Christian Interpretation, Volume II: Human Destiny*, Westminster John Knox Press, Louisville, KY.

Nunnally, J. (1967), *Psychometric Theory,* McGraw-Hill, New York.

Nusair, N. (1983), 'Human Nature and Motivation in Islam', *Islamic Quarterly*, 29(3), pp. 148-164.

Olan, Levi (1964), 'The Nature of Man', in Abraham E. Millgram (ed.), *Great Jewish Ideas*, B'nai B'rith Department of Adult Jewish Education, Washington, D.C, pp. 165-181.

Osborn, R. D. (1876), *Islam Under the Arabs*, Longman, London.

Patai, R. (1983), *The Arab Mind*, Charles Scribner's Sons, New York.

Pateman, C. (1970), *Participation and Democratic Theory*, Harvard University Press, Cambridge, MA.

Peng, M. and P. Heath (1996), 'The Growth of the Firm in Planned Economies in Transition: Institutions, Organizations, and Strategic Choice', *Academy of Management Review*, 21(2), pp. 492-528.

Qur-an (1981), *Arabic Text and English Translation* [Sarwari Translation], Islamic Seminary, Elmhurst, New York.

Qur-an (1988) *English Translation of the Arabic Text and Commentary* [transulated by Mir Ahmed Ali] Tahrike Tarsile Qur'an, Inc., Elmhurst.

Qur-an (1989), *English Translation of the Meanings and Commentary, King Fahd* Holy Qur-an Printing Complex, Al-Madinah Al-unawarah.

Raban, J. (2003),'The Greatest Gulf', *The Guardian*, www.guardian.co.uk, April 19

Rahman, F. (1966), *Islam*, Holt, Rinehart and Winston, New York.

Riggs, F. (1969), *Administration in Developing Countries*, Houghton-Mifflin, Boston, MA.

Rodinson, M. (1974), *Islam and Capitalism*, Allen Lane, London.

Rodinson, M. (1981), *Marxism and the Muslim World*, Monthly Review Press, New York.

Rokeach, M. (1973), *The Nature of Human Values*, The Free Press, New York.

Rosen, L. (2002), *The Culture of Islam*, The University of Chicago Press, Chicago, ILL.

Roy, C. (1977), 'Management Education and Training in the Arab World', *International Review of Administrative Sciences*, 43(3), pp. 221-228.

Rowe, A. and J. Boulgarides, 'Decision-Styles: A Perspective', *Leadership and Organizational Development Journal*, 4(4), pp. 3-9.

Sabri, H. (1997), 'The Impact of the National Culture on Organizational Structure and Culture', Unpublished doctorate dissertation, University of Leeds, Leeds, UK.

Saraj, M. (1986), *Pearls and Valuables from the Legacy of the Forefathers* (*Part I*), Ministry of Information, Damascus, Syria.

Schein, E. (1980), *Organizational Psychology*, Prentice - Hall, Englewood Cliffs.

Sekaran, U. (1983), 'Methodological and Theoretical Issues and Advancement in Cross-Cultural Research', *Journal of International Business*, Fall, 14, pp. 61-74.

Shariati, A. (1979), *On the Sociology of Islam*, Mizan Press, Berkeley, CA.

Shariati, A. (1980), *Man and Islam,* Free Islamic LIT, Houston, TX.

Shariati, A (1981), *Man and Islam*, Filing, Houston.

Sherif, C. (1979), 'Social Values, Attitudes, and the Involvement of Self', in Monte Page (ed.), *Nebraska Symposium on Motivation*, University of Nebraska, Lincoln, pp. 1-64.

Siddiqui, M. (1987), *Organization of Government Under the Prophet*, Idarah-i Adabiyat-i Delli, Delhi, India.

Simon, Smithburg and Thompson (1982), 'Authority: Its Nature and Motives', in D. Hampton, C. Summer and R. Webber (eds.), *Organizational Behavior and the Practice of Management*, Glenview, ILL, Scott, Foresman and Company, pp. 154-156.

Simpson, J. (1991), 'Globalization and Religion', in R. Robertson and W. Garrett (eds.), *Religion in Global Order*, Paragon House Publishers, New York, pp. 1-17.

Singh, J. (1986), 'Performance, Slack, and Risk-Taking in Organizational Decision Making', *Academy of Management Journal*, 29(3), pp. 562-585.

Srinivas, K. (1992), 'Organizational Development: Maya or Moksha', in R. Kanungo (Ed.), *Work Motivation: Models for Developing Societies*, SAGE, New Delhi, CA, pp. 248-282.

Strauss, G. (1976), *Organization in Development*, University of California, Institute of Industrial Relations, Berkeley, CA.

Szilagyi, A. (1988), *Management and Performance*, Scott, Foresman, Glenview, ILL.

Tamari, M. (1987), *"With All Your Possessions": Jewish Ethics and Economic Life*, The Free Press, New York.

Tannenbaum, A. and R. Cooke (1974), 'Control and Participation', *Journal of Contemporary Business*, Autumn, pp. 35-46.

Tayeb, M. (1988), *Organizations and National Culture*, SAGE, Publications Inc., Beverly Hills, CA.

Time (1996), '*Time*'s 25 most influential American', June 17, pp. 53-79.

Tomer, J. F. (2001), 'Economic Man vs. Heterodox Men: The Concepts of Human Nature in Schools of Economic Thought', *Journal of Socio-Economics*, 30(4), pp. 281-294.

Turner, B. (1981), *Weber on Islam,* Rountledge & Kegan Paul, London.

Udovitch, A. (1977), 'Formalism and Informalism in the Social and Economic Institutions of the Medieval Islamic World', in Amin Banani and Speros Vryons (eds.), *Individualism and Conformity in Classical Islam*, Wiesbaden, Germany, pp. 60-81.

Useem, J. (2002), 'Tyrants, Statesmen, and Destroyers', *Fortune*, November 18, pp. 82-90.

Vickers, G. (1973), *Making Institutions Work*, Wiley, New York.

Vroom, V. and P. Yetton (1973), *Leadership and Decision Making*, University of Pittsburgh Press, Pittsburgh.

Vroom, V. (1984), 'Decision Making and the Leadership Process', *Journal of General Management*, 9(3), pp. 18-36.

Watt, W. M. (1961), *Islam and Integration of Society*, Northwestern University Press, Evanston.

Weber, M. (1958), *The Protestant Work Ethic and the Spirit of Capitalism*, Charles Scribner's Sons, New York.

Wilber, K. (1998), *The Marriage of Sense and Soul*, Random House, New York.

Wilber, K. (1999), *The Collected Works of Ken Wilber*, Shambhala, Boston & London.

Wilson, Charles (1993),'Training for Quality (UAE Context)', Proceedings: Arab Management Group, University of Bradford, UK, pp. 624-632.

Witt, L. (2003), 'A Nation of Scared Sheep', *Salon*, www. Salon.com, July 9.

Woodward, J. (1965), *Industrial Organization: Theory and Practice*, Oxford University Press, London.

Wrightsman, L. S. (1992), *Assumptions About Human Nature: Implications for Researchers and Practitioners*, SAGE Publications Inc., Newbury Park, CA.

Yahfoyfi, S. (1982), *Elzhman Alijtimai Fi Al-Islam* [Social Welfare in Islam], International, Beirut.

Yucelt, U. (1986), 'Managerial Practices in the Middle East', in E. Kaynak (ed.), *International Business in the Middle East*, De Gruyter, New York, pp.113-126.

Yukl, U. (1981), *Leadership in Organizations*, Prentice-Hall, Englewood Cliffs, NJ.

Zaleznik, A. (1971), 'Power and Politics in Organizational Life', *Harvard Business Review, Leadership Part II*, pp. 1-14.

Index